Kesheng Wang   Ove Rustung Hjelmervik   Bernt Bremdal

Introduction to Knowledge Management
Principles and Practice

Kesheng Wang   Ove Rustung Hjelmervik   Bernt Bremdal

Introduction to Knowledge Management
Principles and Practice

Akademisk Forlag

© Tapir Academic Press, Trondheim 2001

ISBN 82-519-1660-7

This publication may not be reproduced, stored in a retrieval system or transmitted in any form or by any means; electronic, electrostatic, magnetic tape, mechanical, photo-copying, recording or otherwise, without permission.

Layout: The Authors
Cover design by: Tapir Academic Press
Printed by Tapir
Binding: Grafisk Produksjonsservice AS

Tapir Academic Press
N–7005 TRONDHEIM

Tel.: + 47 73 59 32 10
Fax: + 47 73 59 32 04
E-mail: forlag@tapir.no
http://www.tapir.no/forlag

PREFACE

In the quest for a sustainable competitive advantage, companies have finally come to realize that technology alone is not enough. What sustains is the knowledge that is in people's minds, processes and experience in your company.

If your organization is confused by vendor buzz and consultant's pitches about how they and their products can solve all your knowledge problems, be forewarned: it is not that easy, knowledge management (KM) is only about 20-30 % technology. The technology is the easy part, it is the people and processes part that is hard.

Knowledge management is a hybrid discipline, containing elements from the social sciences, technology and business. Its origin can be discussed, but a KM system has been associated with the Artificial Intelligent community. Some point to two American writers, Tom Davenport and Larry Prusak who raised the issue of how to manage knowledge. Others point to Xerox Parc and its director and chief scientist, John Seely Brown, who in the early 1980s built up one of the most advanced science parks, first established on the grounds of Stanford University at Palo Alto. Brown was one of the initiators of the Institute for Research on Learning, where Dr Etienne Wenger developed the concept of Communities of Practice. In all this one must not forget the authors of "The Knowledge-creating Company", Ikujiro Nanaka et al., who wrote the trend-setting book on creating explicit knowledge from tacit knowledge. We should also include Peter Senge from MIT who wrote: "The Fifth Discipline", concerning organizational learning. Finally, we have Jim Botkin et al. who wrote: "A Monster under the Bed", which raised the whole issue of life-long learning.

The sum of all this academic input and initiatives has landed us a new hybrid discipline: Knowledge management, with its core focus on creating and sharing knowledge. The discipline is a holistic system for the management of intellectual capital, organizational change, knowledge creation and sharing for continuous improvement and innovation. This adds up to a learning organization, resulting in increased value creation, and improved bottom-line results. This symbiosis of disciplines takes place within the organization's vision, purpose and strategy, and will provide your organization with an advanced business system.

This book, "Introduction to Knowledge Management" will give you a strategic roadmap for knowledge management and teach you how to implement KM in your company, step by step.

The material is organized in nine chapters. In Chapter 1, a general picture of knowledge management starts off with a brief introduction of the definition of knowledge and knowledge management and describes how, why, where and when it functions. Chapter 2 presents an information value chain from data and information to knowledge and wisdom, which explains why knowledge discovery and management is so important in a modern organization for competitive advantages. How to use information, communication and artificial intelligence techniques for building the infrastructure of your knowledge management system is presented in Chapter 3. Chapter 4 explains the relationship between communication and knowledge so you can learn how to share and extract knowledge effectively. Chapter 5 illustrates the structure and dynamics of the knowledge management system. It proposes a genetic and holistic model that may be of use when planning and designing knowledge management systems for all types of enterprises. The practice of developing a knowledge management system - Faros in Chapter 6 enables you learn more about how the concepts, models and infrastructure of a knowledge management system can be implemented in your organization. Chapter 7 describes the principle and methodology of measuring intellectual capital. More experience from practical life is presented in Chapter 8, which will help you avoid going in the wrong direction when working on your knowledge management system. The last chapter describes the future of the organization, which is related to organizational structure and the assets required for operating in the knowledge economy, including customer and people in a virtual organization.

The book meets the needs of several groups of readers and can thus be:

- A course for senior undergraduate and graduate students in engineering and management.
- A concise introduction to knowledge management that is accessible to a broad range of people in different engineering and management fields. The book also is ideally suited as material for individual study.
- A fully updated, practical and comprehensive reference book on knowledge management that can be of interest to any practitioner or researcher, who is already active in one of the following: Knowledge Management, Business Intelligence and e-commence.

This book has been used for a senior undergraduate and graduate course and a continuing education course at the Norwegian University of Science and Technology (NTNU) in Trondheim. We expect that it will help you and your organization or enterprise to solve all your knowledge problems.

We would like to thank Hirpa L. Gelgele and Yi Wang for careful editing assistance and Stewart Clark for his English language editing. We also would like to thank the editor Lasse Postmyr for his interest in our book and patience. We also give our thanks to John Seely Brown, Jim Botkin, Larry Prusak, Tor G. Syvertsen and Rolf Lenschow for the challenging discussions over the past few years.

Finally, we would like to thank our wives and children for their understanding and encouragement.

Kesheng Wang
Ove Rustung Hjelmervik
Bernt Bremdal

October 2001
Trondheim, Norway

TABLE OF CONTENTS

PREFACE III

CHAPTER 1 PRINCIPLES OF KNOWLEDGE MANAGEMENT 1
  1.1. Introduction 1
  1.2. What is knowledge management? 2
      1.2.1. Knowledge 5
      1.2.2. Management 6
      1.2.3. A working definition 6
  1.3. Why is KM being widely adopted now? 7
  1.4. What is the purpose of knowledge management? 9
      1.4.1. The main purpose of the knowledge management system .. 10
      1.4.2. The purpose of knowledge in business applications 11
      1.4.2.1. Delivering customer value 12
      1.4.2.2. Product innovation and delivery 12
      1.4.2.3. Improved organizational effectiveness 13
  1.5. Who is knowledge management for? 14
  1.6. What does knowledge management consist of? 14
      1.6.1. Knowledge desktop - an interface to corporate knowledge 16
      1.6.2. Knowledge services - from content to collaboration 17
      1.6.3. System - a platform for knowledge management 17
  1.7. Why does knowledge management work? 18
      1.7.1. The Internet and Web technology 18
      1.7.2. Database technology, data warehouse 19
      1.7.3. Multimedia technology 19
      1.7.4. Communication technology 19
      1.7.5. Software technology 20
  1.8. What is the logic of a knowledge management system? 20
      1.8.1. The data layer 21
      1.8.2. The knowledge logical layer 21
      1.8.3. The presentation layer 22
  1.9. Who should be using knowledge management? 22

1.10. Cultural aspects 23
1.11. What knowledge management is not about 25
1.12. Ten strategies for knowledge management 26
    1.12.1. Establish a knowledge management methodology 26
    1.12.2. Designate a point-person 28
    1.12.3. Empower knowledge workers 28
    1.12.4. Manage customer-centric knowledge 29
    1.12.5. Manage core competencies 30
    1.12.6. Foster collaboration and innovation 31
    1.12.7. Learning from best practice 31
    1.12.8. Extend knowledge sourcing 31
    1.12.9. Interconnect communities of expertise 32
    1.12.10. Report the measured value of the knowledge asset 32
1.13. Conclusions 32
1.14. Lessons learned 33

REFERENCES 35

CHAPTER 2 DATA, INFORMATION, KNOWLEDGE AND WISDOM 37
2.1. Introduction 37
2.2. Information value chain 38
    2.2.1. Data is not information 38
    2.2.2. Information is the beginning of meaning 39
    2.2.3. Knowledge 40
    2.2.4. Wisdom 43
2.3. Classifying knowledge 44
    2.3.1. Categories of knowledge 45
    2.3.2. Types of knowledge 46
    2.3.3. Key components of knowledge 47
2.4. The three fundamental steps 49
    2.4.1. Knowledge acquisition 49
    2.4.2. Knowledge sharing 49
    2.4.3. Knowledge utilization 49
2.5. Business and knowledge 49
2.6. Content management and information extraction 50
    2.6.1. CORPORUM and MIMIR 52
    2.6.2. Virtues and shortcomings of CORPORUM technology 64

2.7. Conclusions 64
2.8. Lessons learned 65

REFERENCES 67

CHAPTER 3 BUILDING THE TECHNICAL INFRASTRUCTURE OF KNOWLEDGE MANAGEMENT 69
3.1. Introduction 69
3.2. The computer network as a knowledge conversion enabler 73
3.3. Basic consideration for a KM system 75

3.3.1. A life-cycle of knowledge 75
3.3.2. Selecting technology 76
3.3.3. Connecting professionals and information sources 77

3.4. The vital integrator: The World Wide Web 79

3.4.1. Client software 80
3.4.2. Server software 80
3.4.3. Server hardware 80
3.4.4. Gateways 81
3.4.5. GroupWare versus Web-client interface 81

3.5. Technology components of the Web-based KM architecture 82
3.6. The interface layer 83

3.6.1. Selection criteria for the collaborative platform 83
3.6.2. Steps to get you there 84

3.7. Access layer 84

3.7.1. Why is this important? 84
3.7.2. Things to consider 85
3.7.3. Steps to get you there 85

3.8. Collaborative intelligence and filtering layer 86

3.8.1. Information feeds 87
3.8.2. Infrastructural elements of collaborative intelligence 88
3.8.3. Level of knowledge granularity in objects 109
3.8.4. Infrastructural elements for searching, indexing and retrieval 110
3.8.5. Tagging knowledge elements with attributes 114
3.8.6. Push/pull revisited 117
3.8.7. A short summary 118

3.9. Applications layer 118

    3.10. Transport layer 119
        3.10.1. Why is this layer important? 119
        3.10.2. Relevant items 119
    3.11. Repository Layer 120
        3.11.1. Things to consider 121
        3.11.2. Steps to get you there 121
    3.12. Conclusions 121
    3.13. Lessons learned 122

REFERENCES 123

CHAPTER 4 INFORMATION, KNOWLEDGE AND MEANING – *SOME THEORETICAL ASPECTS ABOUT WHAT CREATES REAL COMMUNICATION*. 125
    4.1. Introduction 125
    4.2. Goal 127
    4.3. What governs communication and knowledge sharing? 128
    4.4. Language and concepts 130
    4.5. Understanding concepts depends on what they do and how they are applied 131
    4.6. Language meaning depends on how we use it 132
    4.7. Relativism in art and science – a modern virtue in the Western world 133
    4.8. Elements of the Japanese world order 136
    4.9. Implications of communication and knowledge sharing 137
    4.10. Principles to be observed 139
        4.10.1. Context 139
        4.10.2. Expectation- driven understanding 139
        4.10.3. Subjectivity 139
        4.10.4. Syntax versus semantics 140
        4.10.5. Discretization 140
    4.11. Conclusions 141
    4.12. Lessons learned 142

REFERENCES 144

CHAPTER 5 MODEL - *THE STRUCTURE AND DYNAMICS OF A KNOWLEDGE MANAGEMENT SYSTEM* 145

   5.1. Introduction 145

   5.2. Background 147

   5.3. Ideas and structure of a holistic KM system 150

   5.4. The holistic knowledge management model 152

      5.4.1. The structure of knowledge management 153
      5.4.2. The process model 156
      5.4.3. The dynamic model 157

   5.5. The Faros concept 158

      5.5.1. Integrating the user 159
      5.5.2. Roles for managing work processes 162
      5.5.3. Availability and focus 162
      5.5.4. Redundancy and learning 164
      5.5.5. The organization's value chain 165
      5.5.6. The feedback function 172
      5.5.7. The Community of Practice matrix 174

   5.6. The setting 176

   5.7. The Knowledge Navigator 179

   5.8. Cultural aspects 181

   5.9. The learning effect 182

   5.10. Innovation 182

   5.11. Conclusions 182

   5.12. Lessons learned 183

REFERENCES 186

CHAPTER 6   PRACTICE: THE FAROS CASE STUDY 187

   6.1. Introduction 187

   6.2. Creating a knowledge management system 189

      6.2.1. The Faros concept in Statoil 190
      6.2.2. Organizing information 192
      6.2.3. Structured information 193
      6.2.4. Unstructured information 194

   6.3. Building the Faros knowledge management system ... 195

    6.3.1. The Faros Knowledge Room *195*
    6.3.2. The Work Process Navigator *196*
    6.3.3. Information elements linked to the Faros Knowledge Room *202*
    6.3.4. Use of information technology *206*
 6.4. Faros goes live 208
    6.4.1. Implementing Faros *208*
    6.4.2. Evaluating Faros: customer satisfaction *210*
    6.4.3. The Faros system tools *211*
 6.5. The learning effect 211
    6.5.1. Knowledge vs. Information Management System *213*
    6.5.2. Innovation through a KMS *214*
    6.5.3. Information overload *215*
    6.5.4. Collaborative systems *216*
    6.5.5. The life-long learning organization *217*
    6.5.6. Tacit to explicit knowledge *219*
    6.5.7. Towards system thinking *219*
    6.5.8. Information Technology and user threshold *220*
    6.5.9. Infrastructures and costs *221*
    6.5.10. Benefits *221*
    6.5.11. Qualitative advantages *221*
    6.5.12. Quantitative advantages *222*
 6.6. Conclusions 224
    6.6.1. Summary *224*
    6.6.2. Further work *228*
 6.7. Lessons learned 228

REFERENCES **230**

CHAPTER 7 EXPERIENCE **231**
 7.1. Introduction 231
 7.2. The customer 232
 7.3. Developmental issues 234
    7.3.1. The purpose of Faros *234*
    7.3.2. One pilot *235*
    7.3.3. One original document *236*
    7.3.4. Intranet *237*
    7.3.5. Redundancy *238*

  7.3.6. Facilitation 238
  7.3.7. Two clicks to the information 239
  7.3.8. The Knowledge Room 239
  7.3.9. Improvement and innovation 240
 7.4. Implementation 242
  7.4.1. Service Unit 243
  7.4.2. Business Unit 245
  7.4.3. The holistic model approach 248
  7.4.4. Redundancy for JIT-JE information retrieval 249
  7.4.5. Communities of Practice 250
  7.4.6. The practice of improvement, innovation and learning 250
  7.4.7. Developing Good Practice 252
 7.5. Industrializing Faros 253
  7.5.1. Roles 253
  7.5.2. Organizational structures 256
  7.5.3. Standard products, applications and business modules ... 256
  7.5.4. The business case 257
 7.6. The engaged user - key to success 257
 7.7. Verification of Faros 258
 7.8. Conclusions 258
 7.9. Lessons learned 259

REFERENCES 260

CHAPTER 8 MONITORING AND MEASUREMENT IN KNOWLEDGE MANAGEMENT 261
 8.1. Introduction 261
 8.2. Scientific management vs. knowledge management 262
 8.3. The need to measure results 265
 8.4. What today's measurement systems measure 267
 8.5. Criteria for a KM monitoring and measurement system 270
  8.5.1. The aim and objective of monitoring KM 271
  8.5.2. What to measure 271
  8.5.3. How to apply the result 274
 8.6. Case study 274
 8.7. Conclusions 276

    8.8. Lessons learned 276

REFERENCES 277

CHAPTER 9 STRATEGY AND STRUCTURE: *SCENARIO 2010* 279
    9.1. Introduction 279
    9.2. Historical reflections 282
    9.3. Moving from our ancestors to modern market economics 284
        9.3.1. Conditions that brought us forward 284
        9.3.2. Dateline 2010 – New societal demands 286
        9.3.3. Scenario: Health 287
        9.3.4. Scenario: Knowledge 287
        9.3.5. Scenario: Life style 289
    9.4. The change agents that brought us to 2010 291
        9.4.1. Leading technology 291
        9.4.2. Other change agents 292
    9.5. Structure follows strategy 292
        9.5.1. The company's social profile 292
        9.5.2. IT/IS industry 293
        9.5.3. The petroleum industry 294
        9.5.4. Network 295
    9.6. The knowledge-based society 296
        9.6.1. The organization of resources for economic gain 297
        9.6.2. Strategy followed by structure 311
    9.7. A new order of things 315
        9.7.1. The networks and the virtual organization 315
        9.7.2. What implications will these future perspectives have on organizations? 316
    9.8. Conclusions 317
    9.9. Lessons learned 318

REFERENCES 320

CHAPTER 1

PRINCIPLES OF KNOWLEDGE MANAGEMENT

> **Objectives**
>
> - Define knowledge management.
> - Understand why knowledge management is widely adopted now and what is behind it.
> - Evaluate the purpose of knowledge management.
> - Understand why and how it functions.
> - Understand whether your company is ready for knowledge management.
> - Define what knowledge management is not.
> - Understand ten strategies of knowledge management.

1.1. Introduction

Over the past 50 years, the world's economies have evolved from a pure production-based value system to an intellectual and skills-based one. Today, what organizations know is becoming much more important than the traditional sources of economic power - capital, land and labour. This knowledge is also the key to business success in the knowledge-based economy. Knowledge creation is the central theme of the knowledge-based economy. However, innovation will be an increasingly important capability in the knowledge-based economy, where *intellectual capital* (IC) is the principal asset in company survival and value creation. Today's knowledge-based economy requires new rules in a new game.

The game is knowledge creation and sharing, and the structure of productive resources is skewed towards neural networks with their customer focus. In order to win the game in the knowledge era, you need to apply the principles of knowledge management in every learning organization.

Every organization has valuable knowledge, which is locked away in people's minds, on paper, or in electronic form. Knowledge management (KM) delivers this powerful knowledge into the hands of the individual user who makes the day-to-day decisions that ultimately determine the success or failure of a business.

What KM can do is straightforward: create powerful, easy and familiar ways to empower users with fast and easy access to the right knowledge for a particular task. The primary goal of knowledge management is delivering the intellectual capacity in the organization to the individual knowledge workers who make the day-to-day decisions that in aggregate determine the success or failure of a business. The key to business success is exploiting organizational knowledge by providing the culture, processes and technology to facilitate the sharing of information.

This chapter presents a broad view of the principles of knowledge management and attempts to integrate or relate the various aspects, including a working definition, history, purposes and values of knowledge management; to explain how and why it functions in an organization. The chapter also points out which kinds of companies are ready for knowledge management.

1.2. What is knowledge management?

One has to first acknowledge that KM is non-technical. Theorists like Drucker [1988] and Davenport [1998] see computers and electronic networks as tools that are there to serve KM, not the basis for realizing KM. In a sense, they take it for granted – just like the telephone. The real issue is to get people to share and build bases of knowledge and experience, which they believe can be done in a variety of ways as long as we use our wits. Computers and computer networks are just part of that picture.

KM is the management of the cognitive production factors (resources) accommodated in a business or government organization. The whole idea is that we recognize that the competitive edge no longer lies in what computers and machinery you have, where you are located or what government you work under. In a global society anyone can access the same assets as everyone else. A business can move its operation to whatever low-cost land it fancies. The real competitive edge is in the organization's ability to absorb the information flow and make a coordinated effort to respond to it.

After trying *expert systems, core competencies, best practice, learning organizations* and *corporate memory*, more businesses have finally come to the realization that the only sustainable source of competitive advantage is their knowledge. This realization is not the result of a vision, but harsh, real experience that has led many organizations to the brink of catastrophe or oblivion. The management fads so far explain much of the rationale for why theorists have focused on KM. We have had a series of what some have unkindly called 'flavours of the month' that include:

- Downsizing and rightsizing,
- The focus on cross-functional teams,
- The outsourcing race,
- The move-the-production-to-a-low-cost-country effort and
- Business-process re-engineering.

All have contributed to condition managers all over the world to take a critical look at what assets they have and need. Spurred by real threats on their own home front, consultancy services like Accenture, E&Y (Ernst and Young) and PWC (PricewaterhouseCoopers) have felt an inherent threat close to their own back yard. They have had to face up to the fact that some of the real assets in their company move into a new business on their own two feet. There are plenty of references to companies that have felt this.

Take Nycomed that was the king of the contrast liquid twenty years ago. This was a money earner that started to falter when the competition caught up. Nycomed tried desperately to create a new success story in their labs. They simply could not produce knowledge fast enough to stall their fall in market position and revenues in the early 1990s. Failed synergies in the hundreds speak their own tales of management's former ignorance of the knowledge factor when they are only eager to restructure whole industries. The tremendous restructuring of the European defence industry since the fall of the Berlin Wall are such examples. Other examples are the current restructuring of the Norwegian oil industry and, most recently, the rise and fall of the "dot.com" companies. Very often we see energetic managers making cuts here and there but failing to create a common culture that shares values and initiates broad communication across old company boundaries.

According to Mintzberg [Mitzberg, 1998], changing operations driven from top management and their consultants hurts more than it cures. Employees see executives come and go, while they all try out their personal recipe of change leading to what has become known as *change fatigue*. Mergers are other cases in such a situation. Too often big mergers shake the confidence of the employees and the best ones are quick to leave, very often creating small independent business units of their own that cultivate a core competency or technology that paves the way for new investment and growth and sometimes a new industry. The superman behind the merger finds soon enough that he manages a dinosaur where both movement and intelligence are slow. The "saver" often leaves after 3 – 6 years when the grim result of his killer therapy becomes apparent to the shareholders.

Sometimes the manager conceals the faith for a while by butchering what is left or another strategy – continuing with mergers. As we all know, there is little value creation in all this. Gradually board members, shareholders and since 1995 a few management schools have seen this. It drives them into thinking knowledge management, but unfortunately with the load of the past. KM in its true sense is a revolution. It yields the power of *decision-making* to the players. The manager is an onlooker that coaches and helps from his sideline position and whenever somebody calls time-out. True KM rules out the top executive as being the major player on the business scene. Few management schools dare tell their students that. Any dean would see that it would be a bullet in the leg for the educational institution. The renowned professor of McGill University, Henry Mintzberg has acidly expressed the following, "The notion that changes come from the top is a fallacy driven by ego, the cult of heroic management, and the peculiarly American overemphasis on taking action. It is like nothing, but a John Wayne type of approach can save the future". Mintzberg continues by saying "If companies are, in fact, dependent on dramatic and top-down change, few would survive. Instead, most organizations succeed because of the small change efforts that begin at the middle or bottom of the company and are only belatedly recognized as successful by senior management".

Knowledge management became one of the hottest topics in business consulting because of the efforts of much of corporate life to meet the challenges of competition in the modern *knowledge economy*. It also provides a powerful way of looking at the way society organizes itself and uses its *intellectual resources* and promises a means of humanizing our approach to modern technology, putting the understanding of human intellect and motivation at the centre. Successful managers have always known that their company's key asset was not its buildings, facilities and equipment, its products and services, or its market share, but its people, their knowledge and skills. Let us first define the two key words: one is knowledge and other is management. Then it will be easy to establish a working definition of knowledge management.

1.2.1. Knowledge

The definition of *knowledge* is complex and controversial, and can be interpreted in many different ways. Much of the knowledge management literature sees knowledge in very broad terms, covering basically all the "software" of an organization. This involves the structured data, patents, software and procedures, as well as the more intangible knowledge and capabilities of the staff. It can also include the way that organizations function, communicate, analyse situations, come up with novel solutions to problems and develop new ways of doing business. We may call this the *cognitive capacity* of the organization. It can also involve issues of culture, custom, values and skills as well as its relationships with its suppliers and customers. But first and foremost, knowledge resides in people's minds, from where it is turned into information as printed or electronic documentation, or made into artefacts such as tools, equipment or processes. Once knowledge has been converted into information, it can be used as the basis for creating new knowledge. It is this process of a swinging pendulum at constantly higher levels that is the process for invention, innovation and change.

Let us look at the formal definition of knowledge given by Webster's dictionary:

Knowledge:
1. Applies to facts or ideas acquired by study, investigation, observation or experience
2. Rich in knowledge of human nature
3. Learning applies to knowledge acquired especially through formal, often advanced, schooling,
4. A book that demonstrates vast learning. The definition implies that knowledge extends beyond information. It has something to do with facts, options, ideas, theories, principles and models that have been acquired mostly through experience and includes formal and informal learning.

Knowledge can be classified into two types: *explicit knowledge* (sometimes referred to as formal knowledge) and *tacit knowledge* (also termed personal informal knowledge). Explicit knowledge is the knowledge that can be articulated in language and transmitted among individuals, while tacit knowledge is the knowledge people have that is rooted in the experience of individuals and involves people's beliefs, perspectives and values. In traditional perceptions of the role of knowledge in business organizations, tacit knowledge is often viewed as the real key to getting things done and creating new value, not explicit knowledge. Thus we often encounter an emphasis on the "learning organization" and other approaches that stress the internalization of information (through experience and action) and the generation of new knowledge through managed interaction.

1.2.2. Management

Management's prime objective is to create values for its stakeholders, such as owners, employees, customers and society. Management's two principal tasks are to secure appropriate and sufficient innovation within an organization and to market their organization's output.

Management includes all the ways in which a particular asset or process is handled, including, but going well beyond the work of the manager. As an analogy, *financial management* includes the work of management, some specialists such as accountants, and often the work carried out by people throughout the organization. Together these people manage the financial resources based on particular processes, structures and supporting technology. In the same way, knowledge management is a process that involves people throughout the organization, as well as management and possibly some key professionals such as *knowledge officers*.

1.2.3. A working definition

In our option, the definitions in the meaning of knowledge are not very important. It does not matter whether a written procedure or an expert provides a solution to a particular problem, as long as a positive result is achieved. Irrespective of whether knowledge is acquired explicitly or tacitly, the acid test is how we can apply it in order to achieve a positive result that meets business requirements. That is a very important issue in knowledge management.

Today, most people agree that *knowledge management* (KM) is concerned with effectively connecting those who know with those who need to know and, furthermore, being able to convert *personal knowledge* into *organizational knowledge*. There also seems to be agreement that managing knowledge requires collaborative understanding. Managing collaboration requires special skills, with less emphasis on individual achievement and more on teamwork. KM, therefore, is the discipline required to achieve organizational learning, that is, an organization's ability to utilize its *intellectual capital* for the capture, creation, delivery and use of knowledge.

Another way to define KM is that *knowledge management* is the conceptualizing of an organization as an integrated knowledge system, and the management of the organization for the effective use of that knowledge. Here, knowledge refers to *human cognitive* and innovative processes and the artefacts that support them.

This definition emphasizes the conceptual integration of the different types of knowledge, in other words, the management of the organization, not of the knowledge directly. This avoids the problems in the direct management (and measurement) of knowledge. The definition of knowledge focuses on the human element yet includes explicit knowledge, which is only seen as a support for human thought. Knowledge management, therefore, relates to the individual employee's ability to manage his/her own knowledge and all the information necessary to fulfil his/her obligations that are relevant to being a *knowledgeable employee*.

1.3. Why is KM being widely adopted now?

While the concepts of knowledge and management have been known for a long time, it is only quite recently that they have been put together. This is probably because management has been seen to be principally about clearly definable objects and processes such as production, finances, *project management* and *corporate strategy*. Those elements that did not appear on the financial returns often escaped specific attention. Even the task of managing people (human resource management) has only recently been established and often still has had difficulty in gaining recognition. Thus, despite its obvious importance for many industries, the roles of the various types of knowledge have seldom been specifically addressed in management theory and practice. Accountants normally covered it under terms such as intangibles and goodwill. The recent attractiveness of the term knowledge management appears to have been prompted by four major forces:

- Knowledge has been recognized as a basis for organizational effectiveness.
- It is difficult to use models to represent the dynamics and adaptability of organizational activities.
- Information technology by itself is not able to achieve substantial savings, significant improvements in human performance and competitive benefits for organizations.
- The application of knowledge for enhanced value creation has, in our knowledge-based economy, a speed, impact and extent, which is without parallel in the history of mankind.

The concept has developed over nearly two decades and Figure 1.1 shows the manager's tools as they evolved from the 1950s to 2000s. Notably, one consistent thread runs through all of these – about leveraging knowledge, experience, intellectual assets and their management. This consistent thread has led business to what we now call knowledge management.

Toffler [1990] explains things well without mentioning KM by name. This is the management perspective, typically promoted by publications like HBR (Harvard Business Review). Yet there is another movement: that of the information technology. The University of Compiegne in France was running conferences on KM long before Harvard started to take it seriously. The forces in *technology management*, typically stemming from French, German and Dutch industry, led this movement. Their motivation was seeking new ways to deal with mergers and pan-European projects such as Airbus. Company names include Peugeot, Aerospatiale, Citroen, Unilever. We should also highlight on BPR (Business Process Re-engineering), championed by Hammer and Champy [1993]. BPR paved the way for knowledge management in a sense, although unconsciously. Several of the cases that Hammer and Champy used as archetypes of BPR thinking used IT as the backbone for how to deal with processes. Many of these cases highlighted increased knowledge sharing, distributed decision making and peer-to-peer networking as essential for the value increase caused by BPR.

Chapter 1 Principles of Knowledge Management

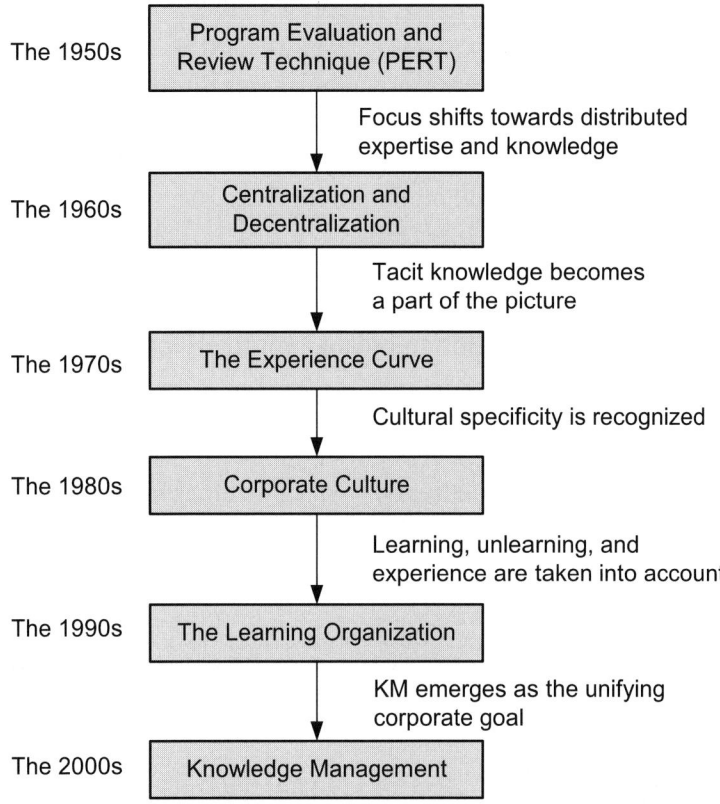

Figure 1.1: Developments in knowledge management since the 1950s

1.4. What is the purpose of knowledge management?

Knowledge management seeks to optimize the value of an organization by helping its people to innovate and adapt in the face of change. Some significant forces are pushing organizations to use knowledge management to manage their experiential and intellectual capabilities more systematically. The reason is obvious. Today, in the global and *Darwinist market economy*, the survival of the fittest implies more smartness than shear brute force. Things change so rapidly that swift and acute adaptability is required in order to endure. This calls for an organization that operates as one harmonic body of knowledge that can turn attention to the critical issues, perceive and learn rapidly as well as decide and act without hesitation.

1.4.1. The main purpose of the knowledge management system

The *knowledge management system* (KMS) is the instrument required for creating dynamic learning organizations, resulting in:

- Rapid response to a changing business environment
- Continuous improvement and innovation
- Improved bottom-line results.

Information and communication technology (ICT) is just an enabler that will help an organization to create a more effective KMS.

Through the knowledge management system, we can:

- Simply and expediently, store valuable data, information and knowledge in the knowledge management system. We have four types of knowledge:

    (1) The first is in people's minds, such as experience, insight, thought, value (personal knowledge).
    (2) The second is on paper, such as in books, newspapers, and magazines.
    (3) The third is in electronic form, such as text documents, electronic reports and electronic files.
    (4) The fourth is in artefacts such as tools and equipment.

    All of them can be stored in the knowledge management system.
    In storing process, we must solve two issues:
    (1) The first is that we must choose what is the useful and valuable data, information and knowledge to store.
    (2) The second is that we must store this data, information and knowledge according to defined format.
- Get the useful and valuable data, information and knowledge directly from the knowledge management system. This system offers us the knowledge we need simply and directly. We call this the *Just in time – Just enough information* concept.
- Share the knowledge and information across time and distance. The knowledge management system enables the knowledge to be spread and shared.
- Get collaborating and comprehensive knowledge efficiently.

- Using the knowledge management system, some data, information or knowledge will be processed and analysed to get more comprehensive and higher level data, information or knowledge.
- Increasing the value of knowledge through the intelligence decision-making in knowledge management.

We can now see that the purpose of knowledge management is to concentrate the collaborating and sharing of knowledge in order to promote intelligent decision-making, which affects the knowledge value of an organization, increasing the company's *intellectual capital* (IC).

We have defined knowledge management; let us now consider intellectual capital. Intellectual capital consists of three elements:

- *Personal*: that equals the knowledge stored in employees' minds.
- *Organizational*: all company documentation, Good Practice, external relations, technology, etc.
- *Structural*: the company's bricks and mortar, inventory tools and equipment, computer infrastructure, etc.

1.4.2. The purpose of knowledge in business applications

In business, there are three key areas where exploiting knowledge can create significant value for a business:

- ***Delivering and making transparent customer value***
  Using information and knowledge to identify and react to customer needs is vital. Staff that handle customers need accurate information to deliver first class service and process the needs and interests of all stockholders in a company i.e., authorities, shareholders, employees, media, suppliers, local and global communities as well as general public opinion.
- ***Producing innovative products and services***
  Promoting innovation in the product development process, analysing shifting trends in the market and adjusting development processes accordingly depends on integrating expertise within the company.
- ***Increasing organizational effectiveness***
  Improving the responsiveness of the business through organizational learning, faster planning and decision making.

1.4.2.1. Delivering customer value

Being able to access and manage knowledge about your customers is central to anticipating and satisfying their needs. An organization that can identify a set of consistent customer profiles can use this data to better understand customer needs, behaviour and value.

Analysing customer purchasing habits can identify patterns that lead to new market opportunities or help to develop existing customer accounts. Customer service can be improved through immediate access to the right customer information as well as the issues that need to be resolved quickly.

Focus can be placed on key customers where the revenue opportunities are greatest. Armed with the right background information on a customer profile, and knowledge on specific historical changes in the market, staffs can cross-sell new products and services, generating new streams of revenues and servicing the needs and interests of all stakeholders. In a world where everything else is equal, knowledge and branding make the difference. Branding is a promise fulfilled, also in terms of know-how. A brand signals the collective values, the ethics, the competencies and the future of the company. A brand may appeal to the social conscience of the public and attract the attention of the investors. Examples from the fashion and the perfume industries show that global business is more and more about brand making. This trend is evident, even for traditional industries. A brand transmits the understanding or failure to understand the need of any stakeholder. An oil spill may hurt the whole image of a global company and thus its bottom line, despite only local damage. Similarly when the Marathon champion crosses the finishing line with a company logo displayed on his singlet and this is framed by the TV cameras, the whole world focus on the brand for some decisive seconds: here comes a winner. The brand of the future will be a token of the know-how: the know-how that distinguishes a winner from a loser.

1.4.2.2. Product innovation and delivery

In any industry, the creation of the best possible products and services for its customers, and the delivery of those products ahead of the competition, determines success in the marketplace. Collaborating across groups of multiple disciplines is critical to ensure that products and services are designed to meet customer needs.

This means capturing input from sales, marketing, engineering, design and other groups, as well as sharing ideas and adopting good practice in design and development. It also means integrating your partners, suppliers and customers in product design and development process regardless of their location.

For example in the financial services industry, failure to deliver the right product could result in customer dissatisfaction. Indeed in many industries today, whether oil, car manufacturing, personal finance, banking or retail, a customer's allegiance to a brand is vital for the success of the company. It is all too easy for customers to switch brands if their requirements are not being satisfied.

1.4.2.3. Improved organizational effectiveness

Organizational effectiveness involves improving the organization's responsiveness and the efficiency of business processes by enabling employees to make faster, more informed decisions. It also means continually improving the skills, knowledge and capability of its most important asset - its staff.

- ***Organizational learning*** - In the knowledge-based economy, the company's single most valuable asset is its workforce. Using effective management systems, the skills and competencies of staff can be tracked. Performance reviews can be made easier with clear processes. Training can be provided, benefits can be managed and company information can be shared to improve morale and knowledge. Good practice can also be shared to improve individual performance. With an appropriate infrastructure in place, managers can share the information of high performing divisions regardless of time and location.
- ***Successful planning and decision-making*** - Where "change is a constant", businesses are challenged to constantly revise strategies within every area of the company, from the supply room to the executive suite. Companies are embracing the idea that information must be shared across levels. They are acknowledging that decision-making authority needs to be distributed widely through systematic access to business data, competitive information and market demographics that support the decision-making process.

1.5. Who is knowledge management for?

Knowledge management can be used for businesses, education and research; it also can be used for government bodies and many organizations. The variety in *management objectives* means that there are different requirements in knowledge management.

In its practical implication, knowledge management is often an integral aspect of IT improvements in the following critical areas:

- **E-commerce** - Practical, fast-to-market, flexible channels to connect to customers and partners online.
- **Industries/Line of Business** - A practical, open and flexible way to get the right solution for running a business.
- **Infrastructure** - A long-term, end-to-end platform to manage and ensure the return on the next generation of information technology investments.
- **Education and research** - A practical, open and flexible way to obtain and exchange information or knowledge with academic or scientific partner organizations.

1.6. What does knowledge management consist of?

Knowledge management's basic elements are:

- Capture knowledge
- Create knowledge
- Deliver knowledge
- Disseminate knowledge and
- Use knowledge

The main process of creating knowledge can be illustrated as in Figure 1.2).

Chapter 1 Principles of Knowledge Management   15

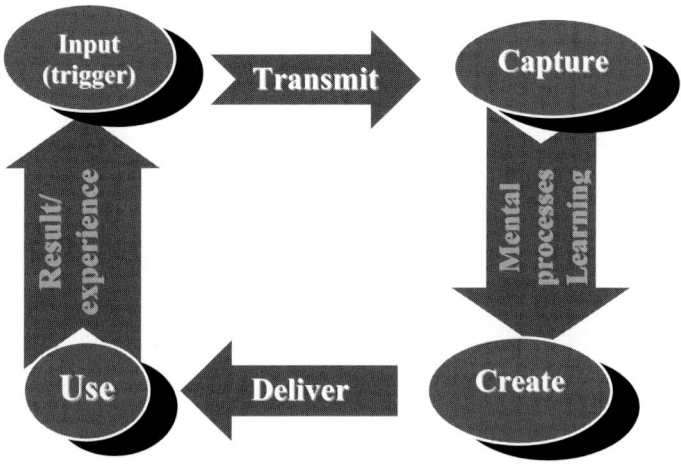

Figure 1.2: The main process to create knowledge

A lifecycle of comprehensive knowledge management includes the following processes:

- Knowledge conversion
- Knowledge store
- Knowledge organization and creation
- Knowledge acquisition

Knowledge management is tightly linked with modern science and technology, especially information technology including research in business, strategy and operations. In some ways it is tightly coupled with TQM (*Total Quality Management*). It is Web technology that facilitates knowledge management and makes the sharing of knowledge possible across the time and space.

The technical imperative for knowledge management came from the technology itself. The ability to capture data information and knowledge has far outstripped people's ability to absorb and analyse this information in a focused way.

As indicated, the various users have different management content and patterns in knowledge management. In business, the main content includes customers, partners, production, business information and data. Though there are many differences in content and patterns between the users from the perspective of technology, they have the same knowledge management framework and technology and application platform. The framework of knowledge management is shown in Figure 1.3.

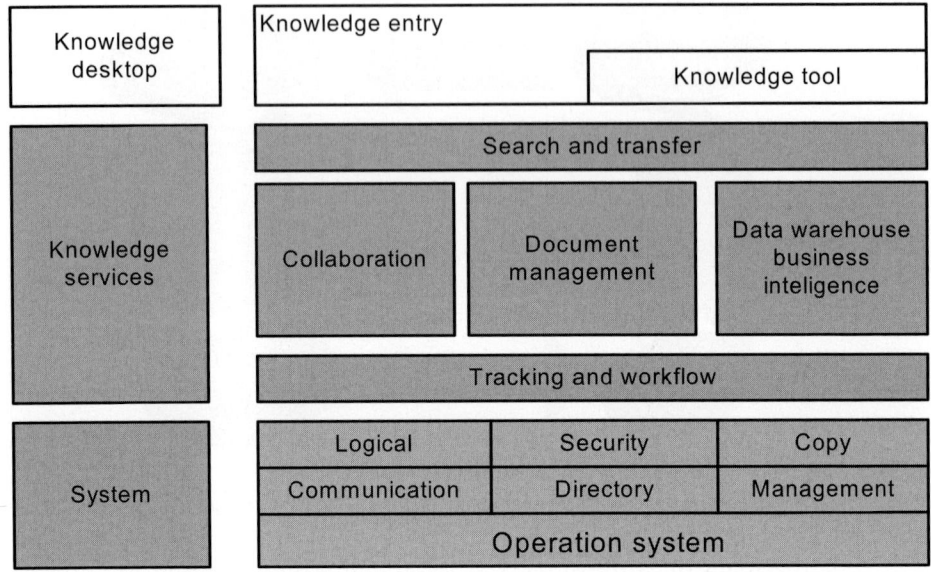

Figure 1.3: The knowledge management architecture

1.6.1. Knowledge desktop - an interface to corporate knowledge

Desktop interfaces are the means by which employees access the organization's knowledge, and enable them to capture and manage ideas. It is a familiar environment and is easily integrated with the Internet environment to allow the sharing of ideas across Intranets or secure Extranets.

Desktop consolidates personal, team, corporate and external information with single-click access to analytical and collaborative tools. A desktop interface is responsible for knowledge conversion and knowledge acquisition. In the knowledge desktop, the knowledge tool is used for acquiring and creating new knowledge. It is the first step in the knowledge management lifecycle. These knowledge tools are dedicated tools just like Word and Outlook on our PCs. They are for a special purpose - for knowledge.

Knowledge entry is an interface where we can share knowledge from knowledge management. It is responsible for linking the user and knowledge management. Through it, the user can enter the knowledge system and get the knowledge service, such as collaboration, content management, analysis, tracking and workflow.

1.6.2. Knowledge services - from content to collaboration

Knowledge services is responsible for the organization of knowledge and its creation. Knowledge services is built on a single, integrated platform, providing centralized management of the core knowledge assets of a user, as well as supporting the seamless delivery and tracking of those assets. It can be enabled by:

- *Collaboration* - Sharing tacit knowledge across time and space.
  The integrated collaborative capabilities allow users to innovate together using their familiar productivity tools. Capabilities such as shared calendars and tasks; threaded discussions, folder home pages and conferencing software allow users not only to communicate, but also to work together on knowledge assets as they collaborate.
- *Content Management* - Capture, search and delivery - bringing knowledge to teams and communities. Content management technologies allow people to capture, codify and organize experiences and ideas in central repositories and deliver personalized information to either community portals or directly to users' desktops, *CORPORUM* and Autonomy are two examples. Microsoft Site Server, Exchange and Office integrate to provide the ability to manage documents and content as well as searches across databases, public folders, web sites and file sharing.
- *Analysis* - Turning valuable data into knowledge. Being able to quickly spot trends in some data allows decision makers to plan better strategies. The data warehousing and business intelligence features enable knowledge workers at all levels of a corporation to better understand their markets. They bring together information from many aspects and process systems to present a transparent view of an entire organization and allow users to easily analyse vast amounts of data. Its main effect is increasing knowledge value.
- *Tracking and workflow* - Capture and enforce best practice. Tracking services allow companies to identify best practice by measuring successes, while workflow tools enable the creation of process-based applications to ensure that the practice is followed and measured.

1.6.3. System - a platform for knowledge management

Knowledge management must be supported by system software. The system is responsible for the basic functions, such as security management, communication management, directory management and system management. The system plays an essential role in knowledge management by providing a scalable set of services that manage all core elements in any solution. Knowledge management is built on the system. Normally, the operation system, some application servers play the system roles, such as Windows NT and Exchange server.

1.7. Why does knowledge management work?

Knowledge management includes many functions. We can list some knowledge functions in the lifecycle of knowledge.

- Knowledge conversion and transformation of data and information into knowledge
- Identify and verify knowledge, knowledge store
- Knowledge acquisition and capture
- Knowledge combination and interaction
- Creation of knowledge
- Distributing and selling knowledge

In order to effectually implement any function, knowledge management must rely on the following technology and is implemented based on these technologies.

- The Internet and Web technology
- Database technology, data warehouse
- Multimedia technology
- Communication technology
- Software technology

1.7.1. The Internet and Web technology

It is Internet and Web technology that makes knowledge management feasible. It makes knowledge sharing, exchange and transformation possible with a quick, high-efficiency and low-cost method. Thanks to Web technology, it can generate information, share and exchange it all over the world. Today, the Internet has spread everywhere and the information on the Internet also increases rapidly. As a section of Internet technology, Web technology makes it possible to simply and efficiently get and retrieve knowledge. The world has become much smaller because of it. As the Internet and Web technology are suitable for knowledge management, almost all knowledge management is established on the Internet platform and supported by Web technology.

1.7.2. Database technology, data warehouse

The knowledge management process is not only a knowledge storing process; it also involves knowledge organization and combination. In all knowledge management processes, the knowledge store is imperative. Original data, information and knowledge must be saved on a database. At the same time, in a knowledge management process, much process information, such as new knowledge and information also must be saved on the database. Because of the many types of knowledge in stored format, a comprehensive data warehouse platform is very important. Today, database technology and application platforms offer overall solutions for data storage. These can save all types data regardless of the data format and type. At any one time, the database platform also provides data management and analytic ability. For all different, but correlative data, this data warehouse possesses the comprehensive solution. The database is very effective for saving all data. It is database technology and the data warehouse platform that make knowledge management possible.

1.7.3. Multimedia technology

Multimedia technology offers overall solutions for knowledge conversion, transfer and exchange. In everyday life, knowledge has many different forms of representation such as books, videos and audio recordings and electronic documents. We acquire knowledge through reading, watching, listening and thinking. But, in knowledge management, all information must be saved on the database. In transforming different forms of knowledge into this database, multimedia technology has a key role for us. It records and converts this knowledge to a format suitable for storage and transfer. It is multimedia technology that makes it possible to deal with different forms of knowledge for knowledge management.

1.7.4. Communication technology

With the development of communication technology, it has become easier to acquire knowledge. Today, the PC is no longer a unique tool for knowledge management entry. The PDA, mobile, some mobile devices and embedded devices have become our important desktop tools for getting knowledge. Communication technology also enhances the capability of knowledge transfer and exchange.

1.7.5. Software technology

Knowledge management also relies on software technology. From knowledge desktop to knowledge services, all stages are implemented by software technology. The software is the carrier of the knowledge management. Today, in software technology, Web technology, database technology and distribution components are applications of technology that improve the knowledge management and make it possible.

1.8. What is the logic of a knowledge management system?

We can now turn to the technological aspects required in a knowledge management system. From the perspective of the technology used to implement the knowledge management system, we can divide the infrastructure of the knowledge management system into three layers according to the logical relationship. Namely: data layer, knowledge logical layer and presentation layer, as is shown in Figure 1.4.

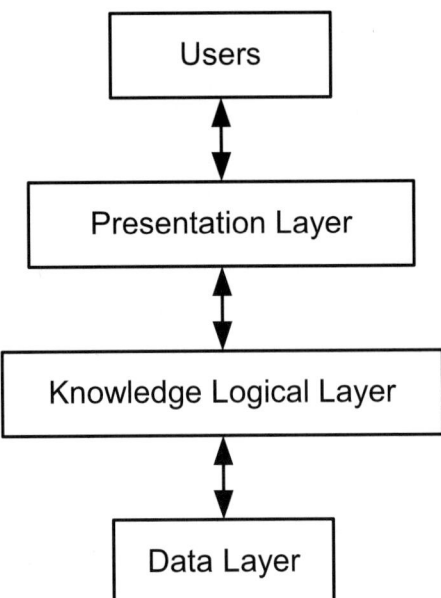

Figure 1.4: The main three layers in the KM infrastructure

Each logical layer corresponds to some function in the knowledge management system and is linked with a relevant technology platform. We will now discuss the function and technology platform for each layer.

1.8.1. The data layer

The data layer is responsible for the storage of all data, information and knowledge. It is supported by a database on a technology platform. All data, information and knowledge are saved into the database or data warehouse. In physical terms, the database platform gives all data, information and knowledge, space to be saved in the database servers. There are two data types in such a warehouse, one is structured data, like customer lists and production lists; another is the unstructured data, like texts, documents and e-mails. Though there are many formats, such as data, words, figures, images, voices and videos, we can store them according to whether they are structured or unstructured data. In order to save the two types of data, there are two different database platforms. We can save the structured data on a structured database like the Microsoft SQL Server, Access database and IBM's DB2, Oracle database, and save the unstructured data on an unstructured database, like Microsoft Exchange and IBM's Lotus.

1.8.2. The knowledge logical layer

This layer is responsible for processing and analysing the information and knowledge. It organizes and generates new knowledge from the original information and knowledge according to the different requirements of knowledge management. It picks up the data, information and knowledge from the knowledge store and then processes it. At the same time, the middle-layer is also responsible for capturing, organizing and creating knowledge. So, it is a vital section in knowledge management.

The middle layer organizes knowledge based on the user's request and the requirements of knowledge management. It accepts the user's request for a presentation, and then responds to the request according to the requirements of the knowledge management. For example, we can search content, which is valuable for us on the Internet through Web technology. This is a typical application of knowledge management. Here, the middle layer offers the search engine and organizes the new knowledge information dynamically. From the logical view, the middle layer can function on the special software server. But in physical terms, the software server is perhaps in an independent hardware server, or in another hardware platform, such as the database server or the client PC. Today, with the development of Web technology and distribution application technology, more and more knowledge management is based on Web applications. Middle layer applications for knowledge management will become more and more important and be the core of knowledge management.

1.8.3. The presentation layer

This layer is the entry and interface of the knowledge management system. It is also the interface between the system and the user. Its main function is not only a bridge between the system and the user, but it is responsible for knowledge input and output. On the one hand, the presentation layer is responsible for transforming new data, information and knowledge into the knowledge management system. For example, we add new business data, we create new documents that will be saved and transformed into the knowledge through the presentation layer. On the other hand, we ultimately get and receive new knowledge from the knowledge management system through the presentation layer. It offers the interface to manipulate and manage knowledge for the user. Storing, searching and capturing knowledge are very important functions.

1.9. Who should be using knowledge management?

Two prime types of companies should be using knowledge management. The first type has realized the need to keep up with its competitors and remain a legitimate player through the process of maintaining core knowledge in its line of business. The second type already has the core knowledge necessary. This company realizes that what is innovative knowledge today will be commonplace, core knowledge tomorrow. Such companies are struggling with their ability to keep ahead, not just compete viably. In addition, as mentioned, we have all types of public or private organizations that want to operate in a more effective manner, securing higher quality in the products or services they deliver to their customers.

Knowledge workers have mobility unlike that ever seen before. Since your company's capability is between the ears of such knowledge workers, your key competencies can walk out, lured into your competitor's corner office. We can all cite examples of this. The productivity of your company's knowledge workers, and in effect the productivity of their knowledge, determines the productivity of your company. Effective knowledge management will allow you to unleash that productivity. Knowledge management can deliver equally astounding results in small and as well as large companies.

Knowledge management has been taken up in a big way by many of the major management consultants, and by a lot of smaller specialized ones too. They use it in two ways:

- As a means of leveraging their own collective expertise
- To enable them to perform far more effectively

The concept of *knowledge management* sounds uncomfortable for many people. This is partly because business has seen a plethora of fads, which have come and gone that are often poorly understood, naively implemented and sometimes just based on bad principles. It is easy to see knowledge management as just another one of those. Also some find a lack of harmony in management, which is about planning and controlling, and knowledge, which is difficult to plan and control.

These concerns are valid, and need to be taken seriously. KM can easily fall into traps like the preceding ideas have done and be reduced to a series of mechanisms and tools and used in ways that will destroy its essence.

1.10. Cultural aspects

Companies and organizations have identified cultural issues as being the greatest barrier to the successful implementation of knowledge management (Figure 1.5). These cultural barriers are in two areas:

Knowledge sharing
People spend a great deal of time and energy developing their own professional knowledge as a way of differentiating themselves in an organization. This naturally breeds an attitude of *knowledge is power*. By rewarding those with greatest knowledge, managers reinforce this attitude and foster an environment of distrust.

Fear of innovation
Dealing with shifting markets in the entrepreneurial economy requires innovative thinking and action. However, innovation is often considered to be a risk venture. People tend to gravitate towards the tested and tried, which often results in a missed market opportunity.

Overcoming these cultural barriers requires an organization that creates an atmosphere where sharing knowledge and innovating are valued and rewarded. If people feel alone or unrewarded when changing their behaviour, they will not participate in the practice of knowledge management.

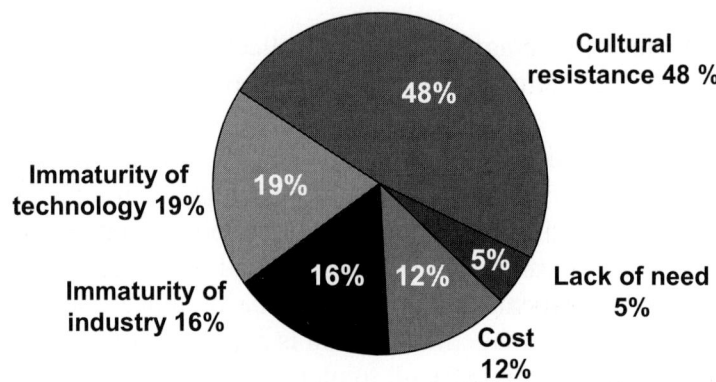

Figure 1.5: Barriers to knowledge management implementation

For an organization that lives by the knowledge created by its employees, collaboration becomes a central theme in the utilization of its human capital. In organizations that are ruled by strong hierarchies, where dictates are followed by threats of disciplinary action if there is non-compliance, collaboration will not blossom and thus KM will not succeed. As collaboration is built on trust, one has to turn to the issue of corporate cultural values if KM is to succeed as a value-creating instrument within an organization. Respect for fellow colleagues, goodwill, and the ability to make a difference to the common good are values to be instilled in the organization in order to secure a positive cultural environment for collaboration. This is the basis for securing successful implementation of KM. It was the realization of this fact, which resulted in the following vision for Faros: (see Chapter 6)

- Make our colleagues' workdays simpler and give them a better overview and
- Make the value creating work processes more qualitative and more secure.

In order to succeed with such a vision, you have to create an environment within the organization that is capable of strengthening the culture of serving the needs of its human capital. The virtue of the organization, therefore, becomes one of doing its employees good, and its purpose is to strengthen the employees' capability in:

- Implementing collaborative work practice, including creating and sharing knowledge, delivering and using information
- Establishing methods for experience transfer
- Developing systems for creating innovative and good practice
- Securing a *Just-in-time/just-enough* (JIT/JE) information retrieval and redundancy method, and with burden of proof on the owner of the information.
- Developing good practice
- Developing new products/processes
- Using benchmarking (e.g. Balanced Score Card) for improved productivity
- Securing lifelong learning.

1.11. What knowledge management is not about

Knowledge management is not solely a technology issue; it is mainly a matter of management. Only by aligning both of them can you build knowledge management systems that will enable effective knowledge management. To make it clear, let us clarify what knowledge management is not:

- Knowledge management is not *knowledge engineering*. Knowledge engineering is a methodology to be used as an instrument and is related to KM in developing a knowledge system to be used in KM. Knowledge management is the management of an organization's knowledge resources and for many organizations that means people with skills, competence and experience as well as documentation in non-electronic form. KM needs to integrate information systems and people in ways that knowledge engineering has never been able to do.
- Knowledge management is also about processes, not just digital networks. The management of knowledge has to encompass and improve business processes. Digital networks are the greatest enablers of effective knowledge management if used correctly. A digital

system will never be used effectively if the people who are supposed to use it are not in the equation right from the start.
- Knowledge management is not about building a *"smart"* Intranet. A KM system can use your company's Intranet as its front end, but do not say that your Intranet is your knowledge management system. The Intranet is just a part of a knowledge management system.
- Knowledge management is not a one-time investment. Knowledge management like any other future-oriented investment requires consistent attention over a substantial period even after it begins to deliver results.
- Knowledge management is not about enterprise-wide *infobanks*. While enterprise integration helps in creating, getting, importing and delivering knowledge, the primary focus of KM is most importantly helping the right people apply the right knowledge at the right time. Knowledge management solutions must reflect the way individuals and organizations have managed and shared information.
- Knowledge management is not *document management*. Document management systems lack context, experience and insight and they still have a marginal place in knowledge management technology. Knowledge cannot be captured.

1.12. Ten strategies for knowledge management

Ten strategies for KM that can be used to guide firms or organizations, which want to develop and implement pragmatic strategies for KM. The early adopters of KM have successfully employed these strategies. Each strategy focuses on a different aspect of KM, yet they are related [Huang, 1999].

1.12.1. Establish a knowledge management methodology

Managing the knowledge assets requires a common process and a common language. The roles and responsibilities involved in knowledge management must be well understood by all participants. As part of creating and sharing a common language in KM, IBM has developed the intellectual capital management (ICM) methodology, as shown in Figure 1.6.

Chapter 1 Principles of Knowledge Management

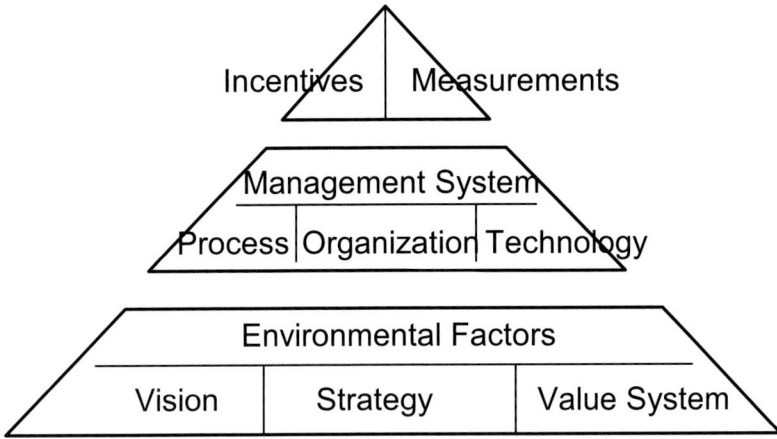

Figure 1.6: IBM's intellectual capital management methodology

The ICM methodology incorporates the following key components:

- A vision that values sharing and reusing knowledge.
- Processes for efficiently gathering, evaluating, structuring, and distributing intellectual capital.
- A competency community consisting of knowledge workers in a core competency area.
- Technologies that enable company-wide knowledge sharing.
- Incentives to encourage intellectual capital contribution and reuse.

This methodology is developed at IBM to feed the knowledge obtained from a project back to its competency community. This reduces the cycle time in transferring knowledge gained from specific projects. Because of the temporal nature of projects such as consulting engagements, it is critical that the knowledge gained from these projects is harvested, hardened and reused.

Since 1994, IBM Global Services has employed ICM methodology to support intellectual capital and asset reuse for their engagement teams. The purpose of using ICM is to institutionalize the knowledge management process throughout IBM Global Services and Global Industries.

1.12.2. Designate a point-person

Many early adopters of knowledge management have created a focal point for accountability. The most common focal point is the *Chief Knowledge Officer* (CKO), whose responsibility is to oversee knowledge management for the firm. Regardless of the aliases used for the CKO, firms need a person to be in charge of promoting and managing the activities of knowledge management in their company. Appointing a CKO clearly signals that the company is committed to knowledge management. The CKO is responsible for overseeing the harvesting and shaping of organizational knowledge from knowledge workers representing different disciplinary areas, project teams and geographic locations. The CKO is an administrator, a planner and a marketer of the firm's knowledge assets. As an administrator, the CKO seeks to maximize the value of the company's knowledge asserts. As a planner, the CKO provides the key leadership in designing and implementing knowledge management strategies to guide the process of managing the knowledge asserts. As a marketer, the CKO directs the campaign to market knowledge assets internally and externally.

In large organizations, the CKO often delegates the management responsibilities to local department managers who are responsible for domain-specific knowledge. As the re-engineering of the organization progresses and the organizational structure becomes more process oriented, as opposed to domain specific, the CKO assigns the responsibility for knowledge management of a specific process to the process managers. The CKO then oversees the firm's knowledge assets across its domains and processes.

1.12.3. Empower knowledge workers

Knowledge workers are the source of knowledge and its derivatives. A key to successful knowledge management is to empower and leverage knowledge workers by making them an essential component of a knowledge management system. Empowering the workforce must be a fundamental commitment by the firm not just a line in the mission statement. A better-trained workforce strengthens the firm's core competency. Management must understand that the empowerment of the knowledge worker establishes communities of competent agents for the firm.

There are other reasons to institute empowerment policies in firms. Companies are increasingly experiencing the effects of disintermediation and globalization. The changing environment demands increased decision-making at the lower levels of the firm. It requires that more organizational knowledge is available. All levels of decision makers, therefore, need to acquire new competencies necessary to operate in the market. In addition, an increased trend towards group work and virtual teaming demands more management and technical support for knowledge exchange. The knowledge that is harvested and shaped in the knowledge management system should be made available to all members of an organization.

To create, share, and transfer organizational knowledge, all participants must play their roles in identifying their explicit and tacit knowledge. To achieve this end, the management team, the organizational culture and the incentive structure must create a conductive environment. Management must carefully identify and eliminate inhibitors that prevent the creation and sharing of knowledge within and across departments. A company's value, incentive and reward system must work coherently with its empowerment policy.

When implementing an empowerment policy, two levels of programmes must be launched. The first level involves skill management programmes based on the domain knowledge of knowledge workers. The second level involves integrating the knowledge of the workforce with the business process and information systems.

1.12.4. Manage customer-centric knowledge

Customer-centric knowledge management is a management approach that focuses on knowledge about the customer. Externally, it aims at improving customer satisfaction, which in turn strengthens the firm's competitive position in its market. Internally, it aims at the transformation of the firm's operation into an agile operation based on the knowledge of and the feedback from customers, which in this case strengthens the firm's internal performance. Practising agile operation means rapidly reconfiguring business operations and delivering products and services that fit the changing needs of customers. It requires that the firm transforms the information collected on customer behaviour into knowledge that can be reused to gain market shares.

In order to achieve customer-centric knowledge management, firms must improve two key areas. First, they must streamline the business processes based on information and knowledge gained from customers. Second, firms must restructure their information. They need to adopt the view that information flows from customers to firms, not the other way around. Customer-centric systems capture this view of customer information flow.

Within the knowledge management process, firms require a model that specifically structures how information collected from customers will be used in business operations for customer care management. Figure 1.7 illustrates the process of customer knowledge management.

Figure 1.7: The customer-centric knowledge management process

This process begins with the customer information collected from various business operations and stored in an information warehouse. This information is further improved, extracted and analysed. The results are harvested and hardened knowledge that is reused in developing customer relationship strategies encompassing customer value management, customer portfolio management, customer care management and customer marketing programmes.

Projects involving data mining and data warehousing are common responses to retrieving and restructuring customer-centric knowledge. Companies also streamline their business processes to improve the relationship with their customers.

1.12.5. Manage core competencies

To successfully compete in the future a company must be capable of enlarging its opportunity horizon. This requires top management to view the company as a portfolio of core competencies rather than a portfolio of individual business units. Business units are typically defined in terms of a specific product-market focus, whereas core competencies connote a broad class of customer benefits such as "user friendliness" at Apple, "pocket-ability" at Sony, and "untethered communications" at Motorola.

Managing knowledge assets is necessary to produce a firm's core competencies. A core competency is the end product of combining human capital, processes, intellectual and intangible assets with technologies to enable a company to provide a unique benefit to customers. It represents the sum of learning in the areas spanning individuals, business units and product/services.

A core competency does not belong to individuals, but organizational capability, which has been created by combining knowledge assets, business processes, and supporting technology. Firms must manage knowledge assets and the derivations of applied knowledge. Examples of knowledge assets include methodologies, tools, techniques, analysis, intellectual property, priced knowledge derivatives, packaged solutions and customer knowledge. In particular, the firm's knowledge assets that are part of the core competency must be identified, recorded, shared and protected. To effectively manage competency, three major processes are needed: (1) develop and identify competency, (2) formulate and deploy competency, and (3) protect, extend and reconfigure competency.

1.12.6. Foster collaboration and innovation

Continuous innovation must be at the centre of knowledge management. This is because the optimum value of knowledge is realized when ideas are turned into innovative solutions. Companies are constantly searching for ways to effectively manage people and processes without the bureaucracy that stifles creativity and innovation.

1.12.7. Learning from best practice

Successful firms learn from best practice that is produced either internally or externally. Best practice can come from other industries as well. Companies must provide a networked environment for recording and sharing best practice.

Some companies focus on sharing best practice as a way of knowledge transfer and innovation. They have established the office of best practice. The best practice office provides a facilitator network in the form of a professional help desk and coordinates the recording and reuse of best practice. Their key message is *do not reinvent what has already been discovered.* Companies also learn from best practice developed by others. Conferences and seminars provide a forum for learning about best practice.

1.12.8. Extend knowledge sourcing

Knowledge sourcing refers to a method of retrieving information from multiple sources and delivering value-added knowledge to customers to solve business problems. The media for retrieval and delivery of the knowledge product include Intranets, the Internet and Extranets. Knowledge sourcing is provided in the context of a domain of knowledge, a business discipline or a competency within a firm. This is the electronic equivalent of conducting a library search or requesting a research study to gain knowledge and solve business problems.

1.12.9. Interconnect communities of expertise

Firms interconnect internal and external communities of expertise. The internal experts have the primary responsibility for problem solving. The external experts constitute the network of experts who are loosely connected to the senior management of the firm. Firms interconnect their internal communities of experts by using electronic libraries, often called "knowledge banks" or "white pages". They establish electronic corporate white pages to share documents and information.

1.12.10. Report the measured value of the knowledge asset

A clear measure that quantifies how knowledge management contributes to the business is needed. Skandia, a Stockholm-based insurance company has established a methodology for recording knowledge assets in their financial report. Skandia links the value of intellectual capital to their balance sheet. It supplements its annual financial report with an emphasis on the qualitative and quantitative value of their intellectual capital. Extension of traditional measures for customers, processes and competence are some of the ways Skandia reports to its shareholders.

1.13. Conclusions

Knowledge management fundamentally changes how a company conducts business. KM is a new way of leveraging the value derived from the collective knowledge of customers, expertise, processes, and product and services. Companies are leveraging their knowledge assets for competitive advantage in the market. Effectively managing knowledge as a strategic asset will enable companies to adapt to new ways of thinking, to respond to change quickly and easily, and to adapt a broader view when defining products and services.

A successful knowledge management effort requires a leadership with vision, commitment, reward and an organizational culture that facilitates collaboration. The process of managing knowledge involves designing and implementing policies and procedures that utilize technology, measures performance and provides rewards for collaboration and innovation. As companies continue to explore ways to strengthen their competitive advantages, they need to manage their intellectual assets prudently. In this age of information explosion, knowledge will be the most valuable assets of the company and the "innovative organization" is the way of the future.

In this chapter, the concept of knowledge management has been introduced together with the purpose of knowledge management applications. We have presented the benefits of knowledge management and why it is important and imperative today. Finally, we have introduced the process of knowledge management from the perspective of technology and the application framework of knowledge management.

1.14. Lessons learned

We have now considered knowledge management and to understand some of the concepts and the infrastructure in knowledge management, six of the main points presented are listed below.

- **What is the *working definition*?**
  After defining the concepts of knowledge and management, knowledge management was described: *Knowledge management* conceptualizes the organization as an integrated knowledge system and the management of the organization for the effective use of that knowledge. Here *knowledge* refers to human cognitive and innovative processes and the artefacts that support them.

- **What is its purpose?**
  Knowledge management has numerous applications, the sharing, exchanging, collaborating and intelligent decision-making are its main purposes.

- **Who is it for?**
  Today, the knowledge creator, the knowledge user and organization involved in information management will benefit from knowledge management. In addition to serving the needs of employees that are capturing, creating, delivering and using knowledge, knowledge

management is the foundation of E-commerce. Knowledge management will benefit many business organizations.

- **How does it function?**
  The *knowledge management framework* consists of three sections, namely, the desktop and tools for knowledge management, the service for the knowledge management and the system. The desktop is the interface between the user and the knowledge management system. The service of knowledge management offers various functions for sharing, collaborating and increasing the value of knowledge. The system offers a platform for knowledge management and ensures that the knowledge management system is available.

- **Why does it function?**
  A number of technologies make knowledge management possible. These are network technologies, communication technologies, computer technologies, software technologies. Finally multimedia technology ensures that the knowledge is available and efficient.

- **Where does it function?**
  From the view of technology we have described a three-layer structure in knowledge management. The structure defines where all the functions are implemented. The presentation layer corresponds to the knowledge management desktop and is responsible for exchanging information between the user and the knowledge management system. The middle layer is related to the function of the knowledge management service and is responsible for managing knowledge flow and creation. The data layer is responsible for storing knowledge and harvesting and retrieving it.

REFERENCES

1. Champy, J. and Hammer, M., (1993), *Reengineering the Corporation: A Manifesto for Business Revolution*, Harper Business, New York.

2. Daveprot, T. and Prusak, L., (1998), *Working Knowledge: how organizations manage what they know*, Harvard Business School Press, Boston.

3. Drucker, P.K. (1988), *The Coming of the New Organization*, Harvard Business Review.

4. Huang, K., Lee, Y. W. and Wang, R. Y., (1999), *Quality Information and Knowledge*, Prentice Hall PTR, New Jersey.

5. Mintzberg, H., Aulstand, B. and Lampe, J. (1998), *Strategy Safari: A Guided Tour through the Wilds of Strategic Management*, Free Press.

6. Tiwana, A., (2000), *The Knowledge Management Toolkit: Practical Techniques for Building a Knowledge Management System*, Prentice Hall, Inc.

7. Toffler, A. (1990), *Powershift – Knowledge Wealth and Violence at the Age of 21st Century*, Bantam Books.

CHAPTER 2

DATA, INFORMATION, KNOWLEDGE AND WISDOM

Objectives

- Understand the four layers in the information value chain.
- Differentiate between data, information, knowledge and wisdom.
- Understand the importance of knowledge in an organization.
- Understand knowledge categories, components and flows in an enterprise.
- Understand explicit and tacit knowledge.
- Know the processes underling the information to knowledge transformation.
- What is the relationship between knowledge and innovation?
- What is the relationship between knowledge and business?
- Understand the concept of content management.
- How to capture and extract knowledge from text documents.

2.1. Introduction

A general definition of knowledge was presented in Chapter 1, but the real meaning of knowledge is explained or expressed differently by people with a variety of backgrounds. This chapter will attempt to build upon a general understanding of knowledge, which is commonly accepted by many enterprises and people. But before we discuss what knowledge means, it is important for us to pin down the meaning of data and information.

2.2. Information value chain

What is relationship between *information management* and *knowledge management*? In order to answer the question clearly, we have to understand the difference between the meaning of the terms: "information" and "knowledge". Information is really data that is transformed into something more valuable by building a context around it so that it becomes understandable. One of the first things we can learn about understanding is that there is a continuum from data, a somewhat raw ingredient, to wisdom, an ultimate achievement. In the information value chain, there are four layers: data, information, knowledge and wisdom (Figure 2.1). Along this spectrum is an ever-increasing value chain of understanding, which is derived from an increasing level of context and meaning that becomes more personal and more sophisticated as it approaches wisdom.

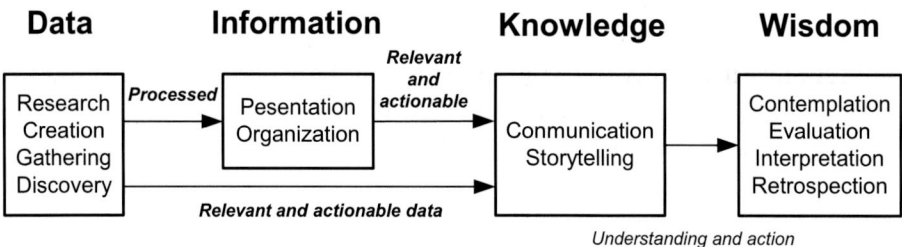

Figure 2.1: Four layers in information value chain

2.2.1. Data is not information

In general, data is a set of independent, isolated facts, measurements, characters, numerical characters and symbols. Data is raw and often overabundant. While it may have meaning to experts, it is, for the most part, only the building blocks on which relevance is built. Also it should never be produced for delivery in its raw form to an audience. Until it is transformed into information, its meaning is of little value and only contributes to the anxiety we feel dealing with so much information in our lives.

Let us take a look at the words: weight, material, teeth, 10 kilogram, steel, 26. Such figures, in themselves, do not say anything meaningful. What is 10 kg? What is steel used for? And what does 26 mean?

From the perspective of a firm, data is particular and objective facts about an event or simply the structured record of transaction. The event might be the purchase of your favourite beer at the grocery store or a change in the stock price of the stock you might be betting your life's savings on. A transaction at a grocery store does not tell whether the brand of beer you bought is selling more than on other days – in this store or nationwide – and whether it did so yesterday. In a similar fashion, stock prices do not tell you whether the company is doing better than it was doing yesterday, or whether you would have reaped a windfall had you sold your stock that morning. Such meaning comes to these raw facts and figures once they are converted into some form of information. Though raw data has its purpose, it might have little or no relevance.

The raw data is very important for the survival of some firms and organizations. Thus there is focus on the effectiveness and efficiency in handling and keeping this raw data. When we talk about managing data, our judgement is mostly quantitative. How much data can be processed in an hour, how much it costs to capture a transaction, how much capacity we have, and so on.

As business grows, the amount of data that has been gathered may become so overwhelming that they might end up in an insurmountable data glut. Many companies have turned to the interesting field of data mining, which helps them find things that are valuable in a huge amount of raw data. These valuable things are called knowledge.

2.2.2. *Information is the beginning of meaning*

Although it is important for firms, data has little use by itself unless it is converted into information. What then is information? Information is data put into context with thought given to its organization and presentation. But even so, it is only the lowest form of meaning as the context involved in creating and presenting data is usually basically generalized. However, at least there is a context, unlike data.

We can use the example above to illustration what information means. The weight of a gear is 10 kg. The material of the gear is steel. The number of teeth of the gear is 26. Now we get meaningful information about the gear and a clear picture of the gear appears.

Because information is so basic, it tends to be formal and rather impersonal. Also, most of us have such poor information skills – that is, the skills necessary for reorganizing, analysing, synthesizing and presenting data – that information tends to be even less sophisticated when it finally comes into being.

Like data, information can be captured and frozen in time. It can be printed in books or be inherent in natural phenomena. However, it is only of value if we know how to decode it and if we can speak the language with which it has been encoded. This also assumes that the information has not been obscured by other phenomena.

Information is the result that people obtain after the process of gathering, organizing, adjusting and analysing the raw data. The purpose of the information process is to make raw data become a structured, ordered and related product.

Information has its root in inform, which means something that changes or shapes the person who gets it. It is the recipient of this information who decides whether it is truly information or purely noise. Information can help a manager run a business better, make effective decisions and change things in the right direction.

2.2.3. Knowledge

2.2.3.1. Knowledge – what is it?

The difference between information and knowledge is a difficult one to explain. Knowledge is not just a more complex version of information – its use is different as well. Knowledge is a kind of meta-information that must be understood in a more general way. In fact, a definition of knowledge could be "sufficiently generalized solutions gained though experience". This means that knowledge is something that is necessarily accessible in many varied contexts and situations and not merely descriptive of details in particular ones. As we know, a successful firm should make the right decisions, use them well and then learn from experience in order to do better next time. To make a correct decision, one needs more than data and information about the specific problem, but also an understanding of the problem. In other words, one needs a set of principles, models, templates or other abstractions. These abstractions are then re-usable for making new decisions with different information. Knowledge is re-usable – unlike data and information, which relates to specific problem. We may say that knowledge is a sct of re-usable abstractions that assist understanding and provide meaning to decision-making. Data and information are about specific instances and is the raw material of particular decisions. Having established this, it is easy for us to differentiate knowledge from information and many of us will have an intuitive feeling about what knowledge means.

We can still use the example of a mechanical engineering business context that designs a gear to explain how we understand knowledge in the business. The knowledge of the engineer resides in his/her understanding of how to design gears, how to select materials, how to use surface treatment, how to handle cost and time etc. It is obvious that these skills or knowledge are re-usable. As we discussed before, data and information about the gear design business are about specific gears, materials, and budgets etc., which are essentially transitory.

Of course, if one knows how to design gears, but has no data and information about a particular gear that needs designing, one is not going to be in business for long. Conversely, one has a lot of data and information about a particular gear but no understanding of how to design a gear; one will soon be out of business. It needs the combination of knowledge about gears-design and data and information on gears.

Knowledge is the full utilization of information and data, coupled with the potential of people's skills, competencies, ideas, intuitions, commitments and motivations.

In today's economy, knowledge is people, money, leverage, learning, flexibility, power and *competitive advantage*. Knowledge is more relevant to sustainable business than capital, labour or land. Nevertheless, it remains the most neglected asset. It is more than justified true belief and is essential for action, performance and adaptation. Knowledge provides the ability to respond to novel situations.

A holistic view considers knowledge to be present in ideas, judgements, talents, root causes, relationships, perspectives and concepts. Knowledge is stored in the individual brain or encoded in organizational processes, documents, products, services, facilities and systems.

Knowledge is the basis for, and the driver of, our post-industrial economy. Knowledge is the result of learning, which provides the only sustainable competitive advantage. Knowledge is the next paradigm shift in computing following data processing from 1945 to 1965 and information management from 1966 to 1995. Knowledge is action, focused innovation, pooled expertise, special relationships and alliances. Knowledge is value-added behaviour and activities. For knowledge to be of value it must be focused, corrected, tested and shared.

2.2.3.2. Knowledge and information – a vital difference

How often have you heard boards of directors defer a difficult decision and ask for more information? In many cases, the reason is that they inadequately understand the key decision drivers and know they impact decisions. They seek comfort in asking for more information. Managers often mistakenly seek more and more information instead of better knowledge or understanding.

Better understanding enables the identification of what information is relevant. Consequently, less information is required because the irrelevant can be ignored.

Better understanding, at the conventional best practice level, can be the springboard to innovation. Could Einstein have developed the theory of relativity without an understanding of standard best practice, i.e. Newton's Laws of Motion? It would have been much more difficult.

The challenge is to encourage the capturing and understanding of business best practice at the strategic level to improve performance and provide the platform for dramatic innovation. Figure 2.2 shows the difference between information and knowledge.

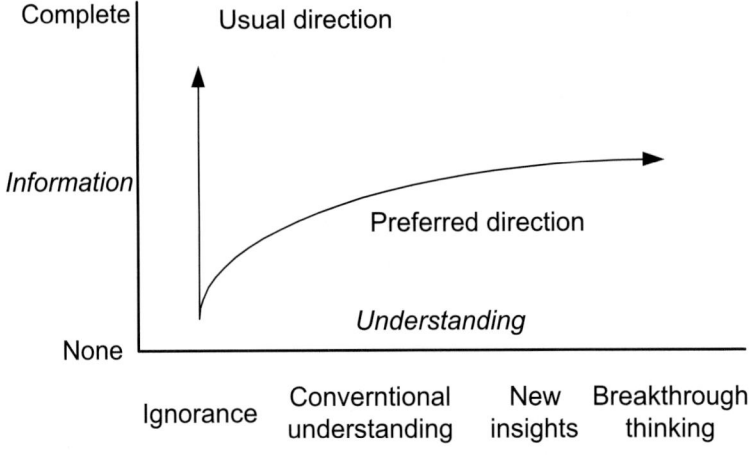

Figure 2.2: The difference between information and knowledge

2.2.3.3. Knowledge and innovation

There is a cycle to the creation and use of knowledge. Figure 2.3 shows the knowledge cycle and innovation. We have already mentioned how increased understanding of current best practice in strategic thinking can lead to innovative breakthroughs.

Chapter 2 Data, Information, Knowledge and Wisdom

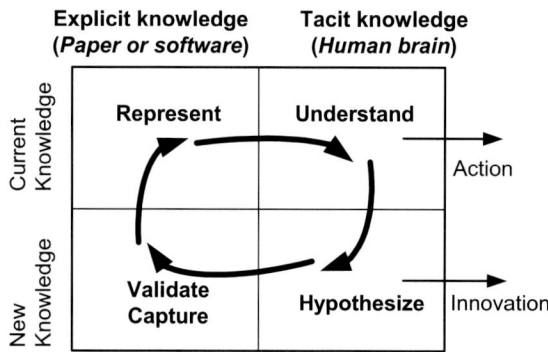

Figure 2.3: The knowledge cycle and innovation

Current knowledge is explicitly represented and processed by human brains (together with information about the specific issue at hand) leading to understanding, decisions and action.

New ideas or hypotheses sometimes accompany this. If supported, the new ideas lead to innovative actions, and also to new knowledge that is added to the explicit representation of current knowledge

2.2.4. Wisdom

Wisdom is even more difficult to explain than knowledge since the levels of context become even more personal, and thus the higher-level nature of wisdom renders it more obscure than knowledge. While knowledge is mainly sufficiently generalized solutions, wisdom is best thought of as sufficiently generalized approaches and values that can be applied in numerous and varied situations.

Wisdom cannot be created like data and information, and it cannot be shared with others like knowledge. Because the context is so personal, it becomes almost exclusive to our own minds and incompatible with the minds of others without extensive transaction. This transaction requires not only a base of knowledge and opportunities for experiences that help create wisdom, but also the processes of introspection, retrospection, interpretation and contemplation.

We can value wisdom in others but we can only create it for ourselves. Because of this it does not come naturally or accidentally; it is for the most part created deliberately. Exposing people, especially children, to wisdom and the concept of wisdom is critical in opening the door to becoming wise or having common sense. However, others cannot do the work for us. We can only do it ourselves and this requires an intimate understanding and relationship with ourselves.

It is quite possible that the path to wisdom is not even open until we approach understanding with an openness and tolerance for ambiguity. Fear and rigid tenets often create barriers to understanding experiences and situations and creating wisdom from them. This does not mean that we must be without principles, but we must be constantly willing and open to challenging our principles and modifying them – even abandoning them – in the face of new experiences that prove more reliable or illuminating. Since wisdom is so personal, a fear or lack of understanding about yourself becomes one of the most extreme roadblocks to becoming wise. Since we are always striving to understand ourselves better, this becomes a continuous process that requires that we constantly evaluate previous understanding of functions and ourselves.

When knowledge can be applied, acted upon, when and where it is needed, it can be brought to bear on present decision, and when these lead to better performance or results, knowledge qualifies as wisdom. When it flows freely throughout a company, is exchanged, grows, is validated, it transforms an information-based company into an *intelligent enterprise*.

2.3. Classifying knowledge

Knowledge may be about your customers, your company's own markets, its products and services, its competitors, its processes, its employer skills, regulatory environments, or methods, but in general it can be classified along four key dimensions, as shown in Figure 2.4 [Tiwana, 2000]. These four dimensions are:

- Complexity which includes categories and types, and specifies the context needed to give it meaning and make it useful
- Life span
- Dynamics
- Focus: operational or strategic.

Chapter 2 Data, Information, Knowledge and Wisdom

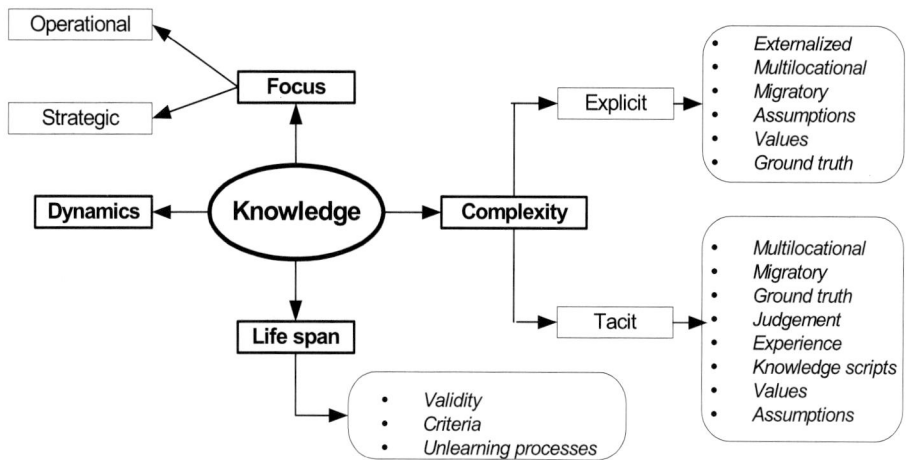

Figure 2.4: A chart of some key facets of knowledge

Let us consider one key sub-dimension of categories – complexity. We can deal with this as follows.

2.3.1. Categories of knowledge

Knowledge complexity can be divided into two categories: explicit and tacit. Polanyi [1958] first conceptualized and distinguished between an organization's explicit knowledge and tacit knowledge.

Explicit knowledge is that component of knowledge that can be codified and transmitted in a systematic and formal language: policies, procedural guides, white papers, reports, designs, products, documents, databases, webs, e-mails, charts and core competencies of the enterprise.

Tacit knowledge is the cumulative store of the experiences. This includes mental maps, insights, acumen, expertise, know-how, trade secrets, skills, understanding and learning that organization has, as well as the organizational culture that has embedded in it the past and present experiences of its people, processes and values. Tacit knowledge, also referred to as embedded knowledge [Badarcco, 1991; Madhaven and Grover, 1998], is usually localized either within the minds of people or embedded in the group's activities within a department or branch office. Tacit knowledge typically involves expertise or high-level skills. It is personal, context-specific, diffused, unstructured, without tangible form and therefore difficult to codify, formulize, record, or articulate. Polanyi [1966] suggests that it is difficult to put tacit knowledge into words. For example, procedures for making the process planning for a complex mechanical product would be difficult to document explicitly, thus they are tacit. The tacit component is mainly developed through a process of trial and error. Successful transfer or sharing of tacit knowledge usually takes place through associations, internships, apprenticeships, conversations, other means of social and interpersonal interaction, or even through simulations. Nonaka and Takeuchi [1995] claim that intangibles like insights, intuitions, hunches, gut feelings, values, images, metaphors and analogies are the often-overlooked assets of organizations. Harvesting this intangible asset can be critical for a firm's bottom line and its ability to meet its goals.

2.3.2. Types of knowledge

Explicit and tacit knowledge interact in these types:

- **Externalized knowledge**

Knowledge is complex and initially tacit; however, it can be externalized and embedded in a company's products and processes. One of the aspects of tacit knowledge is the cognitive dimension that comprises beliefs, ideals, values, schemata, and mental models that are deeply ingrained in participants, but are often taken for granted by the possessor. While this cognitive component, like any other aspect of tacit knowledge, is difficult to articulate, it shapes the perception of the participants. This cognitive component should be extracted to retain the context and fullness of the captured explicit knowledge.

- **Mulitilocational knowledge**

Knowledge might be resident both within the organization and outside it. Knowledge management encompasses activities surrounding the integration of this knowledge from different sources in various forms and maintaining it. Knowledge management creates value by actively leveraging the knowledge, experience and judgement resident within and outside a company. The initial key to knowledge creation lies in mobilization and conversion of this tacit knowledge into a form of explicit knowledge.

- **Migratory knowledge**

Migratory knowledge is knowledge that is independent of its owner or creator. As knowledge becomes more and more extensively codified, its capacity to move increases. Codification implies some kind of capture – in documents, databases, pictures, illustrations, spreadsheets on a disk, e-mails, videotapes, or on a Web page on a corporate Intranet. Codification however does not imply that capture has been electronic. It could be on paper, on tape or on film. Converting these to an electronic format that is more amenable to ease transfers is rarely a challenge these days. When we talk about the movement of knowledge, we are talking about our ability to transfer knowledge from one person or company to another without losing its context and meaning.

2.3.3. *Key components of knowledge*

A knowledge management system must support all of these components: *ground truth*, *judgement*, *Intuition*, *experience*, *values*, *assumptions*, *beliefs* and *intelligence* [Daveport and Prusak, 1998].

- **Ground truth**

Ground truths are the truth gained from experience, not theory; this is what works in practice. Decisions made in organizations are often based on a set of ground truths. These truths might be about markets, products and service, the business environment, competition etc. Discovering, recording, maintaining and sharing these truths is a critical component of a complete knowledge management system.

The problem, however, is that these truths are often deeply embedded in individuals from a specific domain. Getting employees to talk about these truths and record them is often very difficult. Engaging in a conversational mode of communication rather than in information transfer provides a partial solution to this problem. Consequently, emphasis on conversation, communication and discussion as an integral part of the knowledge management system is well placed.

- **Judgement**

Judgement puts knowledge into an actionable context. Knowledge evolves and may no longer apply to the situation that it originally did. Unlike data and information, knowledge has a component of judgement attached to it. Judgement allows knowledge to rise above and beyond an opinion when it re-examines itself and refines every time it is applied and acted upon. A number of tools including case-based reasoning, data mining and a machine-learning system can be used to make these kinds of judgements very accurately and in real time. But these come only when the business case has been evaluated and the preceding data-cleaning stages have been accomplished perfectly.

- **Heuristic knowledge (rule of thumb), intuition and experience**

Heuristics and intuition are guides to action, shortcuts and simplifications for problem solving. As we know, knowledge is largely derived from experience. Being able to transfer knowledge implies that a part of experiential knowledge also gets transferred to the recipient. Experience provides a historical perspective that helps better understand the present situation and predict future events. Experienced people are usually valued in an organization because they possess something that a typical newcomer will almost never have.

How do the experienced people solve a problem? When they see a new problem, they match it to compare patterns that they are aware of and make the correct decision. With experience - these scripts guide our thinking and help avoid mistakes and failures. Such rules of thumb or heuristics provide a single option out of a limited set of specific, often approximate, approaches to solving a problem or analysing a situation accurately, quickly, and efficiently. Many of these rules of thumb are in people's minds as tacit knowledge.

- **Values, assumptions, and beliefs**

Different people have a range of problem-solving frames. Very often, business processes are based on sets of values, assumption and beliefs. These are ingrained within the minds of different people who hold them and they find their way into most of the decisions that people make, but they are almost never expressed. For example, engineers assume that anything that is behaving strangely has to have an underlying rational. Managers might assume that their ordinate goal is to maximize their financial profits. Companies are often governed and shaped by the beliefs of a few key people working there.

Such values, assumptions and beliefs are integral components of knowledge and probably explain why different companies take varying actions when facing the same developments. These values, assumptions and beliefs differentiate a risk-competitor from a risk-averse one. And knowing, capturing and sharing this component of knowledge can make all the difference between complete knowledge and incomplete, unactionable information. Not all beliefs can be "captured" explicitly. This is still a challenge of ongoing research, and initial results show promise in terms of the mechanisms for capturing beliefs. Until more can be done about this area in a systematic manner, we must rely on who holds the critical beliefs that drive processes. Consequently, this is why you will see repeated emphasis put on providing systemic pointers to people with such integral components of knowledge.

2.4. The three fundamental steps

Three basic steps are involved in the knowledge and learning process. Nonaka has given us a better grasp of what types of information technology functionality will support them. The three fundamental steps are *knowledge acquisition, sharing and utilization*. The three stages do not need to be in a sequence and they are often run in parallel.

2.4.1. Knowledge acquisition

Knowledge acquisition is the process of development and creation of insight, skills and relationships. Information technology components, such as data-capture tools and electronic whiteboards, can support knowledge acquisition.

2.4.2. Knowledge sharing

Knowledge sharing is the next component. This stage comprises disseminating and making available what is already known.

2.4.3. Knowledge utilization

Knowledge utilization comes into the picture when learning is integrated into the organization. Whatever is broadly available throughout the company can be generalized and applied, at least in part, to new situations. Often in a company, sharing and utilization of knowledge take place simultaneously. Any computer-supported facilities to enhance these functions will have to keep these three broad concepts apart before successful implementation can begin.

2.5. Business and knowledge

Well-established firms that were probably doing well, innovating and leading their industries have gradually begun to fade. The diminishing competitive power of leading firms, global competitive demands, and ever-changing business scenarios have convinced many organizations facing a highly unpredictable business environment, about the survival instincts inherence in managing their primary, or only competitive asset – their knowledge and their ability to learn faster than their competitors.

While knowledge is thought of as the property of individuals, a great deal of knowledge is produced and held collectively. Such knowledge is produced when people in a company work together in tightly knit groups or communities of practice. Even though the employees and the knowledge they carry around in their heads are beginning to play a very significant part in successful companies, it is unfortunate that companies fail to recognize this early enough – before it is too late.

Managing an organization's collective and largely tacit knowledge has become the critical survival factor for companies that intend to maintain or improve performance based on their experience. Gaining new knowledge, managing it, and applying it have become as imperative as the ability to produce high quality goods and services.

2.6. Content management and information extraction

Content management and *information extraction* technology represent a group of techniques for managing and extracting information from documents, ultimately delivering a semantic "meaning" for decision makers or learners alike. This is a new type of computer application targeted at capturing and extracting the content of free-text documents.

With the entry of large document bases supported by systems such as Lotus Notes and the WWW, content management has really become an issue. Companies do not really know what they have. Effective sharing of carefully authored assets is very low in most companies and government agencies. Re-use of content is close to nil. The issue is being amplified by the fact that the threshold for publication is lowered every year. With the advent of new user interfaces that are voice-based, the number of publications that need to be managed will soar.

There are several tasks that fall within the scope of content management and information extraction:

1. **Abstracting and summarizing:** This task aims at delivering shorter, informative representations of larger (sets of) documents.
2. **Visualization:** Documents can often be visualized according to the concepts and relationships that play a role. Visualization can be either in an introspective manner, or using some reference model/view of a specific topic.
3. **Comparison and search:** This task finds semantically similar pieces of information. Comparisons can be based on knowledge about a text generated in one of the specific processing levels discussed above.

4. **Indexing and classification:** This considers (partial) texts, usually according to certain categories.
5. **Translation:** Context-driven translation of texts from one language into another. Language translation has proven to be highly context specific, even among closely related languages. Some kind of semantic representation of meaning is needed in order to be able to make good translations.
6. **Question formulation and query answering:** This is a task in human-computer interaction systems.
7. **Extraction of information:** The exact definition of the difference between information and knowledge varies among approaches. However, it is arguable that *information extraction* refers to the generation of all additional knowledge that is not explicit in the original text. This information can then be more or less elaborate. *Knowledge extraction* would then refer to the processes that follow the "syntactical level", i.e., those processes that aim at induction and deduction of semantic, discourse and commonsense reasoning.
8. **Induction/deduction of knowledge:** This is based on extracted information. Many approaches from the field of Machine Learning can play a role here.
9. **Task Definition:** This is also based on the extracted information. Scenarios: robots or electronic services that get their orders through some natural language interface. Goal definition, planning and task execution are then based upon the extracted information (which can be at all the levels of abstraction discussed).
10. **Knowledge base generation:** Information that is extracted, deduced or induced can be used in other scenarios as well. A *knowledge base* can be regarded as a typical "container" for the transfer or sharing of such knowledge across applications and time.

We have treated a group of general computational techniques that are typically used to alleviate the burden of these tasks. They include fuzzy technology, neural networks and expert systems. On a more application-oriented level there are several approaches that apply one or more of the general techniques. For an excellent overview and discussion of these, Engels and Bremdal [2000] have provided thorough documentation. The field is currently very dynamic and new advances are made continuously. Here, we will highlight one novel approach that we know well, namely the *CORPORUM* system and *MIMIR technology*.

2.6.1. CORPORUM and MIMIR

CORPORUM supports both personal and enterprise-wide document and information management - that is management by content. The CORPORUM system is based on CognIT's Mímír technology developed in Norwegian research labs. This technology focuses on meaningful content rather than odd data or standardized document parameters. CognIT's approach is to capture the content with respect to the interest of the individual rather than address the document itself. There are three essential aspects of this.

- CORPORUM interprets text in the sense that it builds ontologies. Ontologies describe concepts and relationships between them. Ontologies can be seen as the building blocks of knowledge. CORPORUM captures ontologies that reflect world concepts as the user of the system sees and expresses this. The ontology produced constitutes a model of a person's interest or concern.
- The interest model is applied as a knowledge base in order to determine contextual and thematic correspondence with documents presented before it.

The interest model and the text interpretation process drive an information search and extraction process that characterizes the hit in terms of both relevance and content. This information can be stored in a persistent database for future reference.

The CORPORUM software consists of a linguistic component, taking care of tasks such as lexical analysis and analysis at the syntactical level. At the semantic level CORPORUM performs word sense disambiguation by describing the context in which a particular word is being used. This is naturally closely related to knowledge representation issues. CORPORUM is able to augment "meaning" structures with concepts that are invented from the text. The core of the CORPORUM system (the MIMIR engine) is also able to extract the information most pertinent to a specific text for summary creation, extract the so-called Core Concept Area from a text and represent results according to ranking which is based on its interest for a specific contextual theme set by a user. On top of that, the CORPORUM system is able to generate explanations, which will allow a user to make an informed guess about which documents to look at and which to ignore. CORPORUM can point to exactly those parts of the targeted documents that are most pertinent to a specific user's interest.

2.6.1.1. Overall architecture

The overall architecture of the CORPORUM system is depicted in Figure 2.5. It consists of four basic software components. The MIMIR-based engine is the heart of the CORPORUM system. The various components can be configured in various ways to suit different applications. One example could be an ERP (Enterprise Resource Planning) system that needs contextual indexing of different types of documents. The user may have access to CORPORUM from any Web browser hooked up on the Internet or the Intranet. Access to CORPORUM is given through regular ASP (Active Server Pages) functionality that communicates with a Web Data Server. The Web Data Server handles the interface to the database. CORPORUM is matched to a standard relational database. However, any database can be applied. A change in this part will not have any effect on the main architecture since both the Web Data Server and the Data Server are designed according to a pure object-oriented standard.

All database calls from CORPORUM components are made on an abstract level. The servers interpret this to SQL-calls or similar of the type required for any given database. The Data Server feeds analysis results from the CORPORUM kernel so that it can be maintained in the database. The kernel consists of several lesser components. The most important of these are the ones that accommodate the MÍMÍR technology. This consists of several algorithms that drive the analysis and information extraction functions. Several of these algorithms apply linguistic rules and information contained in separate files. In order to handle multiple languages CORPORUM will contain several sets of these files. The MÍMÍR technology will now be described in more detail.

The CMWebHandler contains both crawler capabilities as well as document processing functions. CORPORUM can be equipped with a set of such handlers in order to treat different types of document formats beyond standard HTML. The CMWebHandler receives search instructions from the kernel component.

2.6. Content management and information extraction

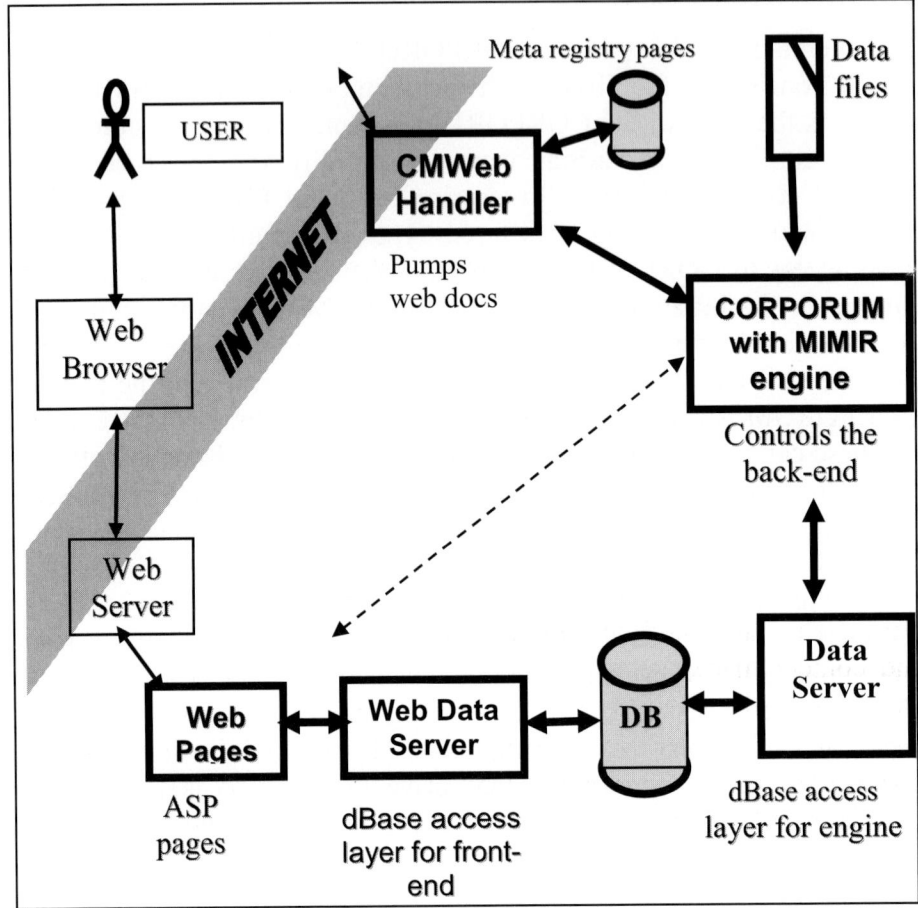

Figure 2.5: The overall CORPORUM architecture

2.6.1.2. Ontologies

CORPORUM applies ontologies in order to establish whether two entities communicate or not. In order to establish "real communication" both the speaker and the listener must share an ontology. If an author wants a reader to understand what he/she writes, the author must attempt to find terms that can serve two basic purposes:

- Express his/her ideas and
- Trigger understanding for the reader

Chapter 2 Data, Information, Knowledge and Wisdom

Only when this is achieved can the message get across. CORPORUM applies these principles in its treatment of the document text to be analysed.

2.6.1.3. The MÍMÍR approach

And Odin hungered for the wisdom that the well could yield. "Nay", said the giant, he stepped up against the mighty god himself. Odin[1] mustered the other, "You ask a high price". "Wisdom gives power. MÍMÍR has got what you want. An eye and you may drink". Odin ripped his eyeball out and bent over the rim in the shade of the huge tree. He filled his mouth and drank. The well of MÍMÍR was truly strange. As he devoured the liquid that tasted like water he sensed a new divine feeling. Even without his eye he could see so much further.
-- Free translation of Norwegian mythology

The CORPORUM products are powered by a technology that represents a fresh and unorthodox approach to computational linguistics and content management. It consists of two basic concepts, a concept extraction facility and a resonance algorithm. Concept extraction focuses on the semantics of a text. The approach is rooted in classic information theory dating back to the seminal work of Claude Shannon [Shannon, 1948]. However, MÍMÍR goes beyond the mere signal and looks at the concept behind the term. The concept extraction effort combines natural language processing and knowledge intensive methods.

The resonance algorithm enables comparison between the content of two texts. This implies that the conceptual structures of the two texts are analysed against each other. The resonance metaphor stems from the idea that the match process triggers violent reactions if the frequency of the emitted signal is close to the natural undamped frequency of the objects themselves. In other words, if there is a good match then there is high resonance with respect to the content of the text found. The difference in amplitude determines the degree of resonance. This is illustrated in Figure 2.6. The information model that represents the semantic content of the text that is being analysed will yield a broad, albeit a minor response if there is a form of resonance. Text B is an example where the whole of the model is stimulated rather than an

---

[1] **Odin** - The Norse god of wisdom, war, art, culture, and the dead. The supreme deity and creator of the cosmos and human beings.

isolated part. Two discrete bars represent mere lexical responses in Text A. Despite high amplitudes, they stand out as very isolated with no intermediate amplitudes. The set of amplitudes generated reflects the degree of match and determines the contextual and thematic aspects of a text.

An inherent feature of the resonance algorithm is that it applies a multiplier effect. This is a typical feature of many complex systems, both socio-economic and natural. Multipliers are immediate feedback mechanisms that enable complex structures to prosper despite the fact that they are often supported with very lean input that fuel their growth. MÍMÍR does the same thing with scarce data. It reapplies it in multiple ways almost simultaneously in order to build up understanding that can justify a conclusion.

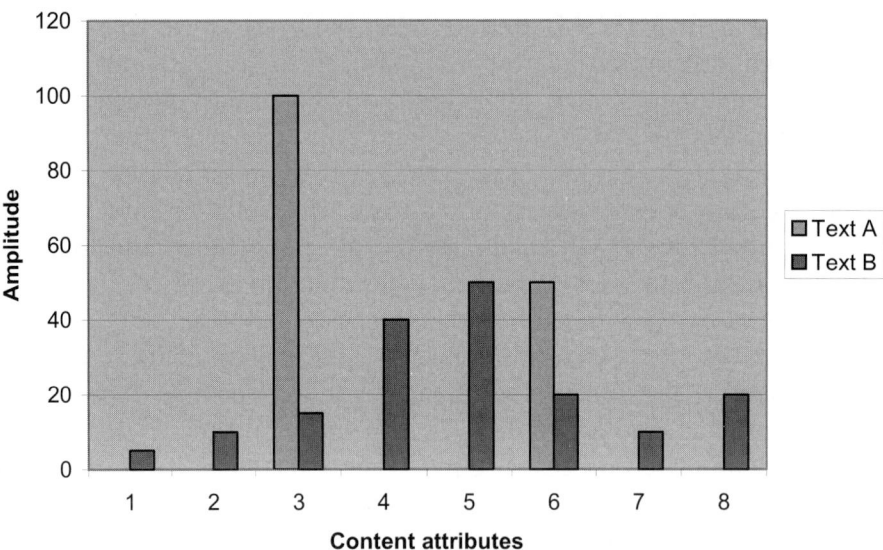

Figure 2.6: Illustration of resonance

In Figure 2.6, if the match process is unable to find any similarities between the content of two texts there will be no resonance. It may well be that there are few words that are common to both, but this alone may not yield sufficient response across the full context. Text A shows this type of match result. Text B shows a distributed response across the full

Chapter 2 Data, Information, Knowledge and Wisdom   57

text content, thus indicating resonance and a good match in terms of content.

2.6.1.4. Contextual interpretation

The basic text interpretation capability of MÍMÍR is contextual [Bremdal, 1999]. Framing the context inherent in a document is fundamental if you want to enable prudent indexing, grouping and extraction. In such a case, you let the content of the document rather than an ad hoc set of keywords determine the indexing. Once you have settled the context, it is possible to determine what the document is all about, how it overlaps with the content of other documents. Moreover, contextual homogeneity assures that quick lexically based searches return the desired results. The MÍMÍR technology also enables mapping the document content. Since the approach focuses on meaning, it is possible to visualize the knowledge inherent in a document. Linked with objective parameters such as name of author and creation date it is possible to build a "who knows what" directory and measure development in knowledge focus for both individuals and groups.

Example:

ASEAN signs deal to create free investment area

MANILA, Oct 7 - The Association of South East Asian Nations (ASEAN) signed a framework agreement on Wednesday to create an ASEAN Investment Area (AIA) to stimulate investment in the economically battered region. The agreement calls for the creation of a competitive ASEAN Investment Area with a more liberal and transparent investment environment among member states by 1 January 2010. Effective immediately, the agreement calls for all ASEAN members to give each other Most Favoured Nation status, effectively endowing preferential investment privileges upon all ASEAN states equally. The agreement also calls for ASEAN members to start gradually removing investment barriers to allow a much freer flow of capital and skilled labour by the 2010 deadline.

By that date, ASEAN has committed itself to treating all member citizens as national citizens for investment purposes. It has also agreed to open up all industries completely to ASEAN investment by the 2010 deadline, with a goal of opening up all industries to foreign investment by 2020.

An AIA Council made up of ministers responsible for investment will oversee the establishment of the AIA. ASEAN ministers signed the document into being at the 30th ASEAN Economic Ministers conference in Manila, but they refused to answer questions about the framework agreement until the closing news conference on Thursday. But throughout the meeting, ASEAN representatives have stressed the important role the AIA will play in opening up and stimulating investment in this region, which is now struggling with the aftershocks of the 1997 financial crisis. ASEAN groups Brunei, Indonesia, Laos, Malaysia, Myanmar, the Philippines, Singapore, Thailand and Vietnam.

Based on this, the system is able to establish the following conceptual relationships that together constitute the context:

Investment: Investment purpose
Investment: Investment barrier
Investment: ASEAN investment area
Investment: Framework agreement - ASEAN
Investment: Minister Conference, Asian minister
Asian group: Brunei, Philippines, Myanmar, Vietnam, Singapore, Thailand, Laos, Malaysia and Indonesia.
AIA: Investment, region

MÍMÍR technology would pin down the following names and check their relationships with other contextual elements such as Manila, ASEAN and AIA. Manila is associated with signing. ASEAN is connected with such information as conference opening and nations. AIA is closely related to "members".

2.6.1.5. Thematic interpretation

The MÍMÍR technology is also able to determine the governing theme of an article as the one shown in the previous paragraph. The news story from Manila would have been classified in terms of:

Framework agreement
ASEAN investment

Although always subjected to subjective judgement, it is not difficult to agree on the output given here.

2.6.1.6. *Information distribution*

Ontologies embedded in text will define its content. Central concepts constituting the core can be listed once the document is analysed. This summary function provides a simple, but important overview of the text found and can serve as a useful "super abstract". In the event that agents work on behalf of the user, it is important that the analysis and match operation is made transparent. It is important that the agent conveys his/her findings and the match results in a way that enables the user to make decisions based on that. Explanations are central in that respect. The shared ontology between the analysed document and the interest model defines the rationale for why a document is important to read. The indexing system is non-binary. In other words, it provides an analogue representation of the fit between interest and document. This has been exploited in order to show how the information is distributed across the document. A simple histogram will tell the user what part of the document is pertinent to the issues that he/she is interested in knowing more about (Figure 2.7). The histogram shows where the desired content in the document can be found, and to what degree it is pertinent. The top of the document is to the left, while the end of document is on the right hand side of the diagram. If a bar is selected and double-clicked, the system will launch the paragraph represented by the bar.

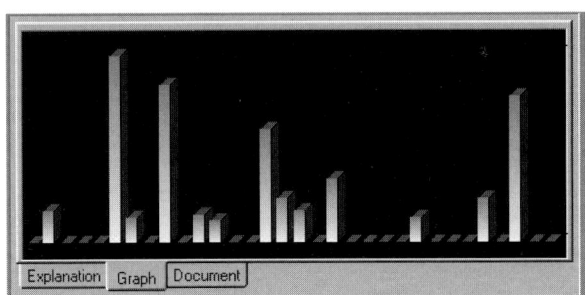

Figure 2.7: Histogram

2.6.1.7. *Simple summarization*

At the time of writing, the least developed part of MÍMÍR is the summarization function. However, it is possible for the system to quote the paragraph that most closely matches the general interpretation model defined in terms of MÍMÍR. The Manila story would thus read in the news summary:

"MANILA, Oct 7 - The Association of South East Asian Nations (ASEAN) signed a framework agreement on Wednesday to create an ASEAN Investment Area (AIA) to stimulate investment in the economically battered region"

2.6.1.8. Applications

CORPORUM may serve several purposes. It is typically useful for knowledge management purposes in order to use a corpus of documents as a knowledge base to support both problem solving and learning. Hence it should serve an important role within the Intranet. How this can done is described in detail in [Bremdal, 1999]. It should also be a candidate for E-business applications and serve various types of Internet services. Portal builders would certainly benefit from the use of CORPORUM, which we will briefly address. Also application of the various components may enhance the performance of classic document management systems as well as ERP applications.

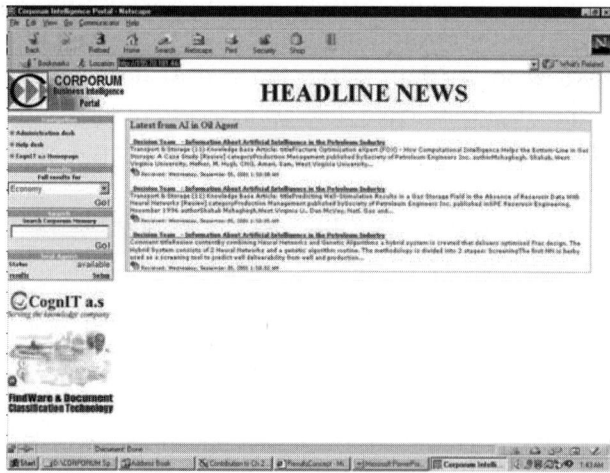

Figure 2.8: The interface for the system

2.6.1.9. Alleviating search on the Internet

Front end to search engines

In its simplest form, CORPORUM can be used as a front end to search engines. Given an interest model it is capable of feeding search engines with a set of keywords based on the thematic focus that resides in the interest model and post-process the results that these engines produce.

Knowing that search engines like Alta Vista and Lycos are prone to how you specify a query, this application can be very convenient. When constructing a query most search engines will be sensitive to the selection of both keywords and in which sequence you enter them. For any given query the probability that a very good hit will show up among the first 10 is close to 1. However, the likelihood that all the most relevant can be found among the first 10 (or say 100) is very small. CORPORUM can be set up to process a theme by pushing various combinations of the same query. Several hits can be analysed in parallel and ranked accordingly. This secures a very systematic approach and can be supported with no human intervention.

Portal building

Search is necessary when you do not have sufficient knowledge of what you are looking for or where interesting things may be located. A portal is a hub that brings links from several URLs together. A portal may take considerable effort to build, but once it is there URLs that belong to the same theme or have the same focus can be accessed by a simple click. Portals will provide a simple passageway to a specific domain or trade. A good portal can serve both news functions as well as e-commerce functions. However, a good portal needs to be maintained so that it does not point to dead links – URLs that no longer contain valid content. CORPORUM can be set up to create and maintain a portal. Agents may nominate new and interesting links. These links can be included directly or be handled manually through a best-link nomination facility.

2.6.1.10. News and personalized information feeds

By defining agents that focus on various subjects of interest, it is possible to build personalized newspaper functionality. Headline news can be fed in from several online media services from all over the world. Interest models could be set up for business, politics, sports, entertainment and similar. The user will be the editor in chief and the agents will be the journalists. Through agent training it is possible to customize focus so that events that are most important to you will be rated more important than others. An agent could be set up for sports while emphasizing news about the soccer team of your heart. An agent could monitor the Arab-Israeli conflict. It would automatically fill in news about the involvement of Yassir Arafat, but restrain any accounts on his social life. However it would most likely volunteer news about analogue conflicts if you wish to receive this. It can be used to monitor news stories, conflict areas and political events.

Figure 2.9: CORPORUM can be used to monitor news stories

2.6.1.11. Public information systems

The age of the Internet has generated a bias with respect to who will be updated and who will be not. Some groups in a population have access to the Internet while others do not. Some have the competence to surf out there while many others do not. This division is strongly related to age. Older people have rare encounters with the Internet while younger groups apply this as a routine means of information access. Although this may be a temporary problem, we have found that there exists a profound imbalance in terms of access as more and more governments and public services make public information available on the net. This can be alleviated through the use of CORPORUM. We have applied CORPORUM as a service for local government. Information pertinent to the local community has over the years become available on the net. This information embraces news feeds provided by the community itself. It includes calls for meetings supervized by the municipality and it includes updates on rules and regulations. By defining the interest profiles of demographic groups CORPORUM has successfully demonstrated news feed capability that is able to channel information about new information available on the net through e-mails and SMS messaging on the wireless telephone network.

2.6.1.12. Business intelligence

A particular version of CORPORUM is called the *CORPORUM Business Intelligence Portal*. This is an application that supports expert agents that will systematically collect information about a certain market and market opportunities. It may solicit notes referring to two parties meeting and rumours about upcoming events such as the signing of an agreement or publication of a new and competing patent. Applications of this include financial intelligence, systematically searching for investment opportunities posted on the WWW. Maritime intelligence is another case in point. Here CORPORUM tracks sales signals, such as when reports are posted about a ship owner having talks with the management of a yard. Thirdly, there are applications where CORPORUM is used in *military intelligence* where agents systematically gather open information and reports from newspapers and government agencies on arms trade.

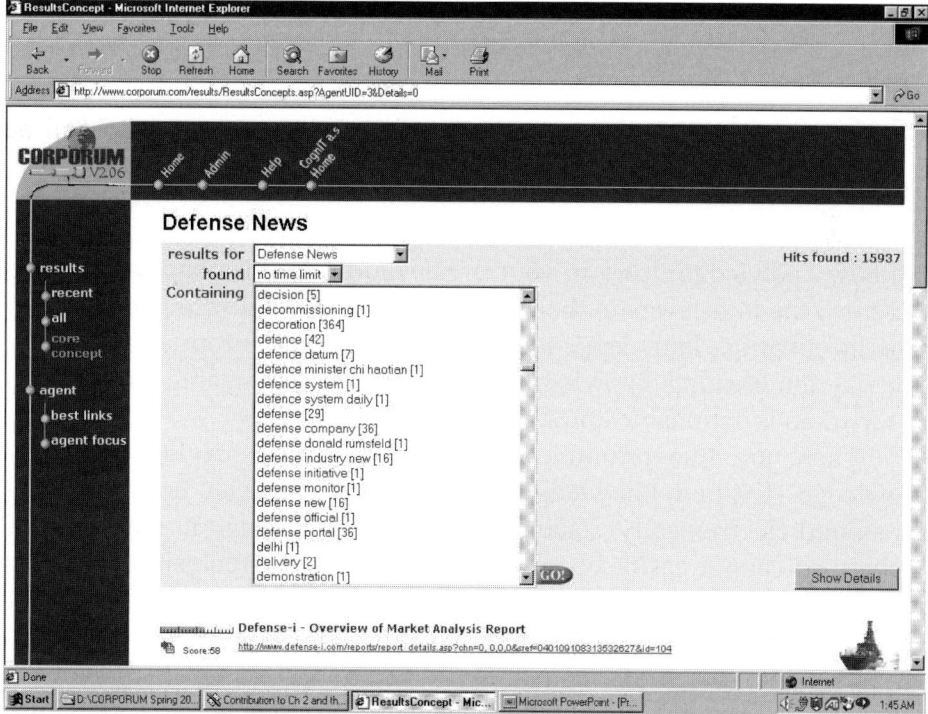

Figure 2.10: Business intelligence portal function of CORPORUM

2.6.2. Virtues and shortcomings of CORPORUM technology

CORPORUM, as currently available, shows a rather high functionality. It represents a type of new technology that is suitable for a whole range of applications within both business intelligence and content management, both are important within the scope of knowledge management. However, where the CORPORUM components are able to capture thematic contexts, there are cases in which intentional knowledge is asked for. CORPORUM is not capable of capturing such intentional knowledge. It cannot yet judge what the goal of the discourse is – only the context and theme. The main cause for this will presumably be the fact that no extensive world and discourse models are generated, on the contrary, CORPORUM aims at capturing contextual knowledge instead of performing deep semantic analysis according to (predefined) world models.

Currently there is much more knowledge and information available from analytic processes than the information that is communicated to the user.

2.7. Conclusions

Before you are able to develop a knowledge management system for your organization, you have to obtain the background about what knowledge is and how knowledge flows in your organization. In this chapter, we have presented the four layers in the information value chain, which consists of data, information, knowledge and wisdom. Data and information are raw material for creating knowledge. Knowledge is actionable information and wisdom is actionable knowledge.

There are two primitive types of knowledge: explicit and tacit knowledge. Explicit knowledge is knowledge that can be stored and transferred electronically. Tacit knowledge is knowledge in the minds of people and cannot easily be encoded or explicated. Acquisition, sharing and utilization of both explicit and tacit knowledge are the basic steps in the knowledge and learning process.

One of the most competitive assets for enterprises is their knowledge. Therefore, current knowledge should be explicitly represented and shared. A human brain that leads to understanding, decision and action processes this knowledge. This is sometimes accompanied by new ideas or hypotheses. If supported, the new ideas lead to innovative actions, and also new knowledge that is added to the explicit representation of current knowledge. Managing knowledge has become a survival factor for companies.

Content management and information extraction technology represent a group of techniques for managing and extracting information and knowledge from documents, ultimately delivering a semantic meaning for decision maker or learners alike. This is a new type of computer application that targets at capturing and extracting the content of free-text documents and plays a very important role in knowledge management.

2.8. Lessons learned

Knowledge is best defined as actionable information. Actionable implies that it is available when and where it is needed to make the correct decisions, and in the right context. Management of knowledge, not data or information, is therefore the primary driver of a firm's competitive advantage.

- **Four layers in the information valued chain**
  The information value chain has four layers: data, information, knowledge and wisdom (see Figure 2.1). Along this spectrum is an ever-increasing value chain of understanding, which is derived from an increasing level of context and meaning that becomes more personal and sophisticated as it approaches wisdom.

- **There are two primitive types of knowledge**
  Explicit knowledge is knowledge that can be stored and transferred electronically while tacit knowledge is knowledge in the minds of employees that cannot be easily codified or explicated (therefore it is hard to manage or support with technology. Using the process of externalization, subjective tacit knowledge based on experience can be converted into objective explicit knowledge. Explicit and tacit knowledge can further be organized as strategic and operational, migratory and situated at multi-locations and centralized. These include components such as ground truths, judgement, heuristics, experience, values, assumptions and beliefs.

- **Experience knowledge is stored as scripts**
  Knowledge is largely derived from experience. Being able to transfer knowledge implies that a port of experiential knowledge – scripts,

intuition, rules of thumb, heuristic and empirical methods – get transferred to the recipient as well.

- **Knowledge is essentially collaborative and falters with a data-holding mentality**
  New knowledge is created, in part, through the collaborative processes that employees pursue as part of their work. The threat to enabling such collaboration comes from the "more is better" data-hoarding mentality that is inherited from the data processing and data management eras.

- **Managing knowledge is essential**
  Knowledge management can help your company deal with market pressures; avoid the infinite, expensive loop of work duplication; prevent reinvention; and deal with the threat of job mobility of employees that possess critical parts of your firm's tacit knowledge.

- **Managing knowledge has become a survival factor for companies**
  Managing an organization's collective and largely tacit knowledge has become the critical survival factor for companies that intend to maintain or improve performance based on their experience. Gaining new knowledge, managing it, and applying it have become as imperative as the ability to produce high quality goods and services.

- **Capturing and extracting knowledge from free-text documents**
  Content management and information extraction technology represent a group of techniques for managing and extracting information and knowledge from documents, ultimately delivering a semantic meaning for the decision maker or learners alike. This is a new type of computer application that targets at capturing and extracting the content of free-text documents and plays a very important role in knowledge management.

REFERENCES

1. Badracoo, J. L., (1991), *The Knowledge Link*, Harvard Business School Press, Boston.
2. Bremdal, B.A. (1999), *Creating a Learning Organization Through Content Based Document Management*, CognIT report #2.
3. Davenport, T. H. and Prusak, L., (1998), *Working knowledge: how organizations manage what they know*, Harvard Business School Press, Boston.
4. Engels, R. and Bremdal, B. A., (2000), *Information Extraction: State-of-the-Art Report,* IST Project IST-1999-10132 On-To-Knowledge. Deliverable #5. European Commission, Brussels.
5. Madhaven, R. and Grover, R., (1998), From embedded knowledge to embodied knowledge: New product development as knowledge management, *Journal of Marketing*, Vol. 62, No. 4.
6. Nonaka, I. and Takeuchi, H., (1995), *The knowledge creating company: How Japanese companies create the dynamics of innovation*, Oxford University Press, New York.
7. Polanyi, M., (1958), *Personal knowledge*, University of Chicago Press, Chicago.
8. Polanyi, M., (1966), *The tacit dimension*, Routledge & Kegan Paul, London.
9. Shannon, C.E. (1948), The mathematical theory of communication. *The Bell Systems Technical Journal* (27), pp.379-423.
10. Tiwana, A., (2000), The knowledge management toolkit, Prentice Hall PTR, NJ.

REFERENCES

CHAPTER 3

BUILDING THE TECHNICAL INFRASTRUCTURE OF KNOWLEDGE MANAGEMENT

> **Objectives**
>
> - Define the role of information technology in KM systems
> - IT components for awareness, perception, knowledge and action.
> - The collaborative platform: Web or Notes?
> - Intelligent components in KM: Artificial intelligence, expert systems, case-based reasoning, data mining, artificial neural networks, Fuzzy logic systems, Genetic algorithms, etc.
> - Optimize knowledge object granularity.
> - The techniques for searching, indexing and retrieval.
> - Create knowledge tags and attributes.

3.1. Introduction

In his seminal book *Powershift*, Toffler [1991] spelled out the importance of knowledge and information in the emerging society. Knowledge will be the key to control and dominance. He claims that modern information technology and hyper-based systems will revolutionize the way we live and the way we work. "Hyper systems are like a web, making it possible to move easily from one piece of information to another contextually". He continues, "... the new systems, by permitting intuitive as well as systematic searching, open the door to precisely the serendipity needed for innovation".

In his famous article published in the Harvard Business Review, Drucker states that "large business 20 years hence is more likely to resemble a hospital or a symphony orchestra than a typical manufacturing company" [Drucker, 1988]. Businesses, especially large ones, have little choice to be information-based. Both future demographics and the need for continuous reinvention of the business will require a type of dynamics that has not been seen before. This requires fast decision-making and efficient communication. Advanced data-processing technology is not necessary to create for the information-based organization, but it must be remembered that the technology is an enabler that in some respects will outperform established communication structures.

Drucker points to the tasks performed by the middle management in the traditional organization. Their base for performance has mostly been that of communicating the strategies and goals of the top management to the floor, while reporting back the results of the various operations carried out. The base itself was typically a hierarchical command-oriented structure allowing for little or no lateral information exchange beyond what the middle management itself found advantageous. Focus on knowledge specialists and autonomous groups require a different and more expertise-driven type of exchange that makes the traditional middle management role obsolete. The advent of the computer and the computer network has enabled a new type of communication that promises good support to scattered groups of expertise while at the same time it challenges the traditional organizational structures. Both increasing external pressure, driven by global market dynamics and the emergence of the knowledge worker have created a snowball effect that amplifies the need for more computer support in all areas of information treatment. 15 years ago most computers were focused on doing what they had always done before, but faster. Today the computer is transforming the very aspect of human information processing, the way decisions are made and the way actions are monitored. The emergence of the PC and subsequently *Internet technology* brought computer power to the professional. Previously, it was a tool for the computer specialists who serviced everybody else. Now, most households are able to communicate with each other through a wireless device or an ISDN cable. Still we are in an infant state with respect to organizing our lives and working in such a network. Socializing on the net is becoming more and more common for children, but is still a rare thing for many adults.

Chapter 3 Building the Technical Structure of KM

The aim of this chapter is to look at what tools are presently available to support peer-to-peer communication in a knowledge network. It tries to highlight important aspects of both communication and information processing. *Content management* refers to the task of managing the ingredients accumulated in document repositories and databases. Search and retrieval techniques play important roles here. As does the ability to aggregate and refine the content so that it fits the decision processes that experts are involved in. A third type of computer service stems from an area of computer science called *Artificial Intelligence*. This aspect draws attention away from the transaction-oriented part of information processing, and focuses on human knowledge and perception directly. Several computer programs can replace humans in very knowledge rich areas even when the input is incomplete and unstructured. Such programs not only extend the capabilities of a professional, but extend his/her presence in a computer network, often by encoding part of the knowledge that he or she possesses.

The world Toffler described to us has become real. What he clairvoyantly called the Web at the time already engulfs us. Everywhere we go we find people connected to both wired and wireless networks. E-mails are passed at lightening speed across corporate divisions. Open Web browsers have become a common sight in most offices. We see people dashing down the street clenching their mobile phone while talking to a colleague on the other side of the world. Again we see the same type of people fully absorbed in front of their laptops or palm-sized computers while waiting to board the plane that will take them to the customer whose web site they are just reading.

Regardless of who we are and where we go, we are surrounded by an abundance of on-line data in both structured and non-structured form. The amount and availability of such data is exploding. Yet our capacity to pay attention to all this remains almost constant.

The real challenge for both organizations and individuals is to keep updated on things that are of concern. This applies to the Internet as well as the corporate Intranet. How to find the right information in the form that is needed to perceive and act is another big issue. Another related question is how to maintain a sustainable overview despite rapid changes. All this calls for support that can alleviate the situation and increase our capacity to take advantage of this wealth of new information that is made available to us.

Working with the shipping industry for a while we have estimated that there are approximately 15 – 20 million pertinent documents available on the Internet (Autumn 1999), 5 years ago there were none.

The number is likely to increase for several reasons. There is no real cause for believing that the Internet will not recruit more subscribers. On the contrary there is a tendency to channel more and more of the publication effort of a person or a company through the World Wide Web. The publication process has become more efficient causing more people to publish spending less time. Once voice-based computer interfaces become robust enough we will see an even steeper increase in the available documents in all forms because the time to produce them will decrease and the number of producers will vastly increase.

The e-*business* part of the Internet will add to the complexity of the picture. Thousands of on-line catalogues will fight for attention. Despite an overwhelming offer it will still be hard to track down the right product, not to say the best offer.

Existing *search engines* are fighting the battle to index and "bottle-up" the whole Internet. There have been reports of search engines indexing 300 000 million and more documents. In addition to the scale-up problem they are faced with two other threats. One is the increased diversity of the net and the ambiguities that go with this diversity. State-of-the art techniques used by most search engines are not able to cope with that. Accuracy falls short of most people's satisfaction. Another issue is the need to update existing links. Volume is not enough if the rate at which links go obsolete does not decrease. On the contrary content revision has become an asset for attention on the net both for individuals and companies as for any other professional news-feed service. The most rapid rate of index update (May 2000) that we know of is 6 million in a day [Personal communication, 2000]. Even with today's volume of 300 000 million indexed documents it will take almost two months to make a complete run-through. This means that even the best search engine will also fall behind publication dates by an average of a month or two. If the publication rate increases by 10 % per month this backlog will increase to 6 months in one and half years with existing search engine technology.

Today it is fair to say that professionals are really being connected regardless of time and space. Yet their personal information processing capacity remains the same. In a sense the computer has outperformed the human. It is like the novice servant who has learned to cook. Once a set of popular recipes has been internalized the servant keeps serving us day and night, regardless of how much we are able to digest. Since everyone is beginning to get a servant of his or her own, there are so many delicious pieces out there, but it is hard to process. This is the modern challenge of information processing and lies at the core of sound knowledge management.

Chapter 3 Building the Technical Structure of KM

In this chapter, we focus on how information technology and AI can support the infrastructure of a knowledge management system through a number of technological components. Most technology needed for knowledge management already exists. The need is the effective integration of this technology supported by organizational enablers that can make it deliver business results. We will discuss various components that help develop the existing infrastructure into the requisite info structure that is required for effective knowledge management.

3.2. The computer network as a knowledge conversion enabler

Nonaka and Takeuchi's four phases of knowledge conversion can be thought as a kind of life-circle of organizational knowledge (see Figure 3.1). This knowledge life-circle hinges on the distinction between *explicit knowledge* and *tacit knowledge*. Explicit knowledge is formal knowledge that can be packaged as information. As discussed in Chapter 2, it can be found in the documents of an organization: reports, articles, manuals, patents, pictures, images, video, sound, software, etc. It can be also found in the representations that an organization has of itself: organizational charts, process maps, mission statements, domains of expertise, etc. Tacit knowledge is personal knowledge embedded in individual experience and is shared and exchanged through direct, face-to-face contact. Tacit knowledge can be communicated in a direct and effective way. By contrast, the acquisition of explicit knowledge is indirect: it must be decoded and encoded into one's mental models, where it is then internalized as tacit knowledge.

In reality, these two types of knowledge bear equal weight in the overall knowledge of an organization. Tacit knowledge is practical knowledge that is the key to getting things done, but has been sadly neglected in the past. For instance, the recent spate of business process re-engineering initiatives, where cost reduction was generally identified with the laying off of people has damaged the tacit knowledge of many organizations. Explicit knowledge defines the identity, the competencies and the intellectual assets of an organization independently of its employees. It is organizational knowledge, but it can grow and sustain itself only through a rich background of tacit knowledge.

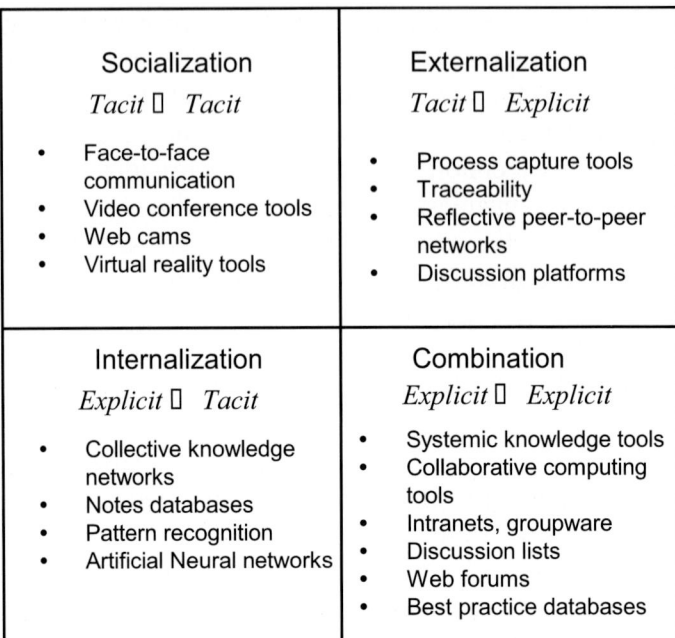

Figure 3.1: Knowledge conversion model [Nonaka and Takeuchi, 1995]

Knowledge that does not flow and does not grow will become obsolete and useless. By contrast, knowledge that flows, by being shared, acquired, and exchanged, generates new knowledge. Existing tacit knowledge can be expanded through its socialization in communities of interest and of practice. While new tacit knowledge can be generated through the internalization of explicit knowledge by learning and training. New explicit knowledge can be generated through the externalization of tacit knowledge, as happens, for instance, when new best practices are selected among the informal work practices of an organization. Existing explicit knowledge can be combined to support problem-solving and decision-making, for instance by matching intellectual capital in the form of patents with marketing data showing customers' preferences for new products. Under this view, knowledge management can be explained as the management of the environment that makes knowledge flow through all the different phases of its life-cycle.

The KM architecture goes beyond the purely social characterization of the environment given by Nonaka and Takeuchi, and tackles issues directly related to the management of the IT infrastructure. Indeed, in today's information-driven society, much of the environment of an organization is given by its IT infrastructure. Thus we have asked ourselves: how can such an infrastructure effectively contribute to an environment that makes knowledge flow? To answer this high-level question meaningfully, we have broken it into smaller, more specific pieces, namely:

- What kind of information technology can contribute to make knowledge flow and support its conversion from explicit to tacit and from tacit to explicit?
- What kind of information technology can best support the explicit knowledge that an organization has about itself?
- What kind of software is needed to support the exchange of tacit knowledge in organizations of knowledge workers?
- How can we use IT to manage the bulk of explicit knowledge contained in the collections of documents of an organization?

These items point to the quality of modern information processing rather than exercising recipes that produce results that we cannot absorb.

Many thriving companies, such as Coke, Statoil, Norsk Hydro, Microsoft, Philips, Buckman have recognized and accepted knowledge as the primary strategic assets. These companies recognized the need for effective and efficient creation, location, capturing and sharing of their knowledge as well as the need to bring that knowledge to bear on their problems and opportunities. A little knowledge is of much more significance than gigabytes of data stored in your company.

3.3. Basic consideration for a KM system

3.3.1. A life-cycle of knowledge

Before you go into the technical structure of your knowledge management system, you have to understand the knowledge functions in your organization. Below we list some knowledge functions in the life-cycle of knowledge:

- Transform data and information into knowledge
- Identify and verify knowledge
- Capture and secure knowledge
- Organize knowledge

- Retrieve and apply knowledge
- Combine and interact knowledge
- Create knowledge
- Distribute and sell knowledge.

Transforming information into knowledge involves the synthesis and conversion of useful data and information into knowledge. For instance, rules of thumb acquired over years of experience and learning may result in knowledgeable shortcuts that help in the decision-making process. Other types of knowledge (i.e., procedural, declarative, episodic, meta-knowledge) need to be identified in the organization and verified as recent knowledge. Once knowledge is identified, it should be captured or acquired and then secured within the organization. Once captured and secured, it must be organized in a way in which others in the organization can retrieve this knowledge and apply it to their situations. They will also combine this knowledge with knowledge of their own within the context of their situation. This will result in a synergistic way of creating new knowledge for the organization. This knowledge would then be distributed within the organization or to a repository and possibly sold. New knowledge would be learned, captured and secured within the organization and then the cycle would continue.

3.3.2. Selecting technology

Table 3.1 provides a technology selection map that can help guide the technology selection process while keeping the actual need in focus.

Table 3.1: Knowledge process and technology enablers

Knowledge objective	Technology enablers
Find knowledge	Knowledge bases in consulting firm; search and retrieval tools that scan both formal and informal sources of knowledge; employee skills; yellow pages.
Create new knowledge	Collaborative decision-making processes; Decisions Support (DSS) tools; rationale capture tools; Notes databases; decision repositories; externalization tools.
Package and assemble knowledge	Customized publishing tools; information refinery tools; push technology; customized discussion groups.
Apply knowledge	Search, retrieval and storage tools to help organize and classify formal and informal knowledge.
Reuse and revalidate knowledge	Customer support knowledge bases; consulting firm discussion databases; past project record databases and communities of practice.

3.3.3. *Connecting professionals and information sources*

In the recent past, firms tended to rely on external repositories of knowledge such as market intelligence databases for bringing in new knowledge with which they could run the company and make decisions. However, with the increased penetration of digital work using personal computers, work done by employees is already in a form ready for electronic manipulation. Companies are therefore creating internal repositories of knowledge bases of market knowledge, customer relationship management knowledge, profile knowledge, product development knowledge, and collaborative knowledge repositories.

While it is easier for raw inputs such as spreadsheets, meeting notes and design documents to be converted into a storage-friendly format, another problem arises: Companies have not been able to standardize on specific platforms and operating systems in a perfect manner. Some employees work on UNIX machines, some on Macintosh, some on Linux platforms, and most others use Windows systems as their primary work environments. Some companies also use incompatible networks across organizational units. When companies try to integrate whatever structured content exists throughout their organization, this effort poses a serious challenge.

Lotus Development Corporation, a subsidiary of IBM, has long touted its Notes system as a perfect collaborative solution. While the value of such a system cannot be undersold, even with Lotus's recent Web integration efforts, there are better alternatives, such as the Web, as a basis for a collaborative environment.

Although solutions like Notes require less up-front development time because of their more comprehensive out-of-the-box attributes and have capabilities like replication, security, controls, as well as development tools tightly integrated with them, the Web-based Internet might require a higher investment in the development stages. Tools like Lotus Domino can allow Notes databases to be shared over the Web; the Web provides a universal platform for the integration of structured knowledge across any existing platform or a combination of platforms. Many companies that embraced Notes early on probably believed that a good plan is better than a perfect plan tomorrow.

Increasingly high levels of integration of multimedia capabilities into Web browsers along with guaranteed backward compatibility allow easier representation of informal content than is possible using proprietary technology such as Notes. Since tens of thousands of companies are developing Web-based applications compared to essentially one company developing Notes, it is more likely that cost-effective, innovative tools will first emerge for Web-based knowledge management systems. There is also a significant level of competition in the market for Web-based tools, which favourably shifts the balance towards this base in terms of price competitiveness. The table below is a comparison of the key characteristics of Lotus Notes and the Web protocol-based Intranets as a primary knowledge-sharing platform.

Table 3.2: Comparison of key characteristics

Characteristic	Notes	TCP/IP	Comments
Architecture	Proprietary	Open/ evolving	The WWWW consortium is placing an increased focus on developing the Web as a powerful collaborative platform
Security	High	Low by default	Can be enhanced with a variety of security tools
Authentication	Strong	Stronger if used in a Windows 2000 type	Windows 2000 (the successor to Windows NT 4.0) provides strong authentication and security features for use in distributed

Chapter 3 Building the Technical Structure of KM

Characteristic	Notes	TCP/IP	Comments
		environment	environment such as those built around Web servers and wide-area networks.
Direct (initial) cost	Moderate to high	Close to none	The Internet is basically free. The only direct cost is that of a service provider, which most companies already have, You still need someone to build the application, or you can buy it from someone.
Development cost	High	Low	You can use existing Web development skills within the company to build an Intranet with a minimal number of inexpensive tools.
Technological maturity	High	Low	Web protocols are still evolving. However, most popular browsers support plug-ins to add newer capabilities to the client software.
Employee training cost	High	Low	Employees are often familiar with the Internet and the Web browser interface.
Legacy integration	Low	High	Wrappers can be written to allow access to legacy data through a Web browser.
Cross-platform integration	Low	High	HTTP acts as the universal protocol that brings together content across all platforms that might be in use in your company.
Development time	Fast	Slower	While Notes development and customization is not always fast, it is usually faster than developing an Intranet with similar functionality.
Out-of-the-box solution	Yes	No/sometimes	Software vendors can customize generic Intranets for quicker development.

3.4. The vital integrator: The World Wide Web

Besides the reasons for choosing the Web over other proprietary technologies as a collaborative platform that we discussed above, several more are worth mentioning. A few essential technology components needed for this integration are discussed below.

3.4.1. Client software

To provide Intranet access and collaborative work support for employees, you need to install a Web client on each PC, workstation or mobile computer. If you plan to use the Windows environment to run such a client, you will need to configure it in a way that allows it to access the Internet through a TCP/IP stack with Windows sockets. Support, in the form of plug-in applications, will be needed to review video feeds or audio through the connection. Similar functionality, usually available by default on most Web browsers, is also needed for non-Windows operating systems such as MacOS. If Microsoft's Windows environment is used as the primary operating platform, most of the socket-level linking is accomplished automatically by the operating system.

3.4.2. Server software

To use the Web as your company's knowledge management portal, you will need to develop a Web server. Although server space can be rented from an ISP on a time-priced basis, it is preferable to eventually move it in-house because security is often a driving concern. Moving such operations in-house, however, often translates to increased costs. Companies such as Buckman Labs have successfully used services provided by CompuServe to run their knowledge management efforts for several years. The best, if not the most inexpensive, strategy will be to base such a server on a Windows platform and run IIS (Internet Information Service) on it.

3.4.3. Server hardware

Companies have traditionally run servers on UNIX machines. With the advent of low-cost yet very powerful PCs, this balance has started shifting towards Windows-based machines such as Windows NT and Windows 2000-based servers (although Linux is a notable contender). A single-processor PC with 500-MHz processor and 256-Mbyte RAM was the minimum, low-end configuration recommended in late 1999. If significant traffic is expected, consider running Windows NT or 2000 along with Microsoft's IIS on a multiple-processor form over any others

Chapter 3 Building the Technical Structure of KM

for the sake of customer support warranted by a large user base and a sustainable upgrade path.

3.4.4. Gateways

In order to extend access from the Intranet and collaborative environments within the company to the Internet and beyond, you must install a company-wide gateway to the Internet. A dedicated server is the best choice for a gateway. Installing such a gateway (which might already be in place in your company) brings up security and accessibility issues that need to be seriously considered and addressed.

A connection for the knowledge management network for mobile employees and tele-workers can be established by means of a modem and registering those employees as valid users with an Internet service provider; you need not go the extra mile by installing dial up lines. Dial-up lines tend to be more expensive in the long run, both to operate and maintain, especially if your employees travel extensively.

3.4.5. GroupWare versus Web-client interface

Even if your company is currently using GroupWare-based collaborative tools, it might be a good idea to gradually move toward a generic Web-based structure such as Intranet. Products such as Notes already provide a fair level of Web connectivity, but the underlying core is still proprietary. Such proprietary systems might be good to begin with, but such focused dependence they do not bode well for an open knowledge management system in the long term. The Web is the unquestionable choice for the matter.

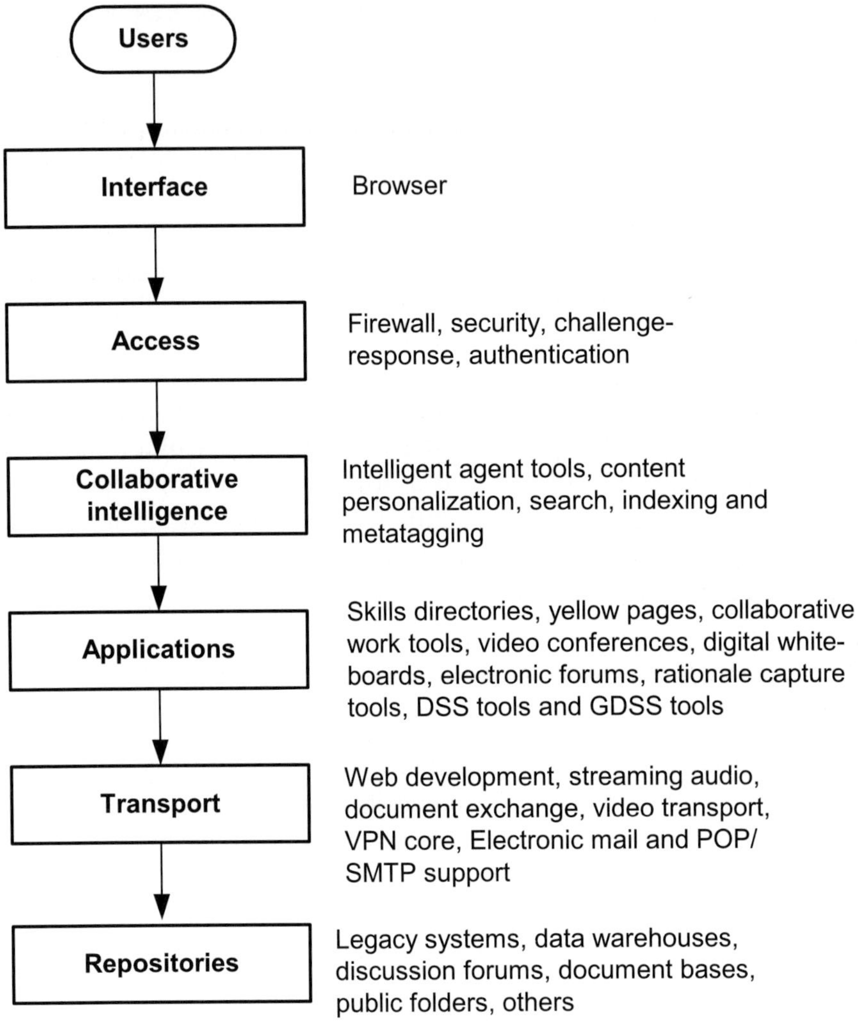

3.5. Technology components of the Web-based KM architecture

Layer	Components
Users → Interface	Browser
Access	Firewall, security, challenge-response, authentication
Collaborative intelligence	Intelligent agent tools, content personalization, search, indexing and metatagging
Applications	Skills directories, yellow pages, collaborative work tools, video conferences, digital whiteboards, electronic forums, rationale capture tools, DSS tools and GDSS tools
Transport	Web development, streaming audio, document exchange, video transport, VPN core, Electronic mail and POP/SMTP support
Repositories	Legacy systems, data warehouses, discussion forums, document bases, public folders, others

Figure 3.2: The six layers of the KMS architecture

3.5. Technology components of the Web-based KM architecture

Before we actually develop a knowledge management system, we should take a look at the technologies that constitute the infrastructure of a KM system. The six layers of knowledge management system architecture that will help you build your knowledge management system are illustrated in Figure 3.2. Some overviews on this figure are as follows:

Chapter 3 Building the Technical Structure of KM

- The interface is the first layer, presenting simplicity to the user. This component masks the complexity of your organization and the underlying processes used to deliver information. The interface provides a universal view to documents, e-mail, calendar, people, etc.
- The second layer is the access layer – the gateway to information within your organization.
- The third layer is collaborative intelligence – products and programming that provide filtering of information, search across many repositories, personalization, discovery and delivery of knowledge, and agents who know and act on user preferences.
- The fourth layer comprises the many applications that provide the "value-add" or "show-me" layer. These applications and technologies provide users with productivity enhancements and improved ways of doing their work. This layer includes authoring and publishing tools, site analysis tools, document management, discussion databases, competitive intelligence knowledge bases, calendars, employee yellow pages, web site analysis tools, sales force automation and executive Balanced Score Card application.
- The transport layer is made up of your Intranet Web development, e-mail, streaming technologies and collaborative tools.
- The sixth layer consists of repositories: data warehouse, legacy systems, document repositories and more.

3.6. The interface layer

The interface layer is the topmost layer in the knowledge management system architecture. The purpose of interface layer is to build a universal view of the enterprise, and to pave the path for, and eliminate barriers to information. Think of the interface as an application. You will make use of icons, tree controls, personalized navigation and graphic design. You are attempting to build a universal "view" of the enterprise – a window to the repository of "truths" about your organization, products and customers. Let us first examine the requirements for the collaborative platform that such a layer must be based on.

3.6.1. Selection criteria for the collaborative platform

For effective collaboration across the enterprise and the smooth sharing of information and knowledge, the collaborative knowledge management platform must satisfy the following set of needs:

- Effective protocol
- Portable operation
- Consistent and easy-to-use client interfaces
- Scalability
- Legacy integration
- Security
- Integration with existing systems
- Flexibility
- Structure.

3.6.2. Steps to get you there

- Hire a talented, dedicated interface designer
- Determine early if the interface will be browser-based or an alternative client-side application.
- Factor in usability testing and scalability
- Work with your IP (Internet Protocol) organization - MIS (Management Information System) to design tree controls and icons.
- Understand the underlying applications, search and results. Knowing the format in which information will be presented will help immensely in the design.

3.7. Access layer

3.7.1. Why is this important?

The purpose of the access layer for a KM system is to protect and secure the information. Your company is a knowledge network where the boundaries are being redrawn (Figure 3.3). Organization charts, department walls, and cubicle walls have been replaced by *firewalls*, time zones, and competing technologies. Your employees, supplies, business partners, and customers and their hunger for information transcend the physical boundaries of the organization. The demands for products, market intelligence and lessons learned about new products are mounting. The traditional security model breaks down while "wide-open access" is not acceptable to corporate board.

Chapter 3 Building the Technical Structure of KM 85

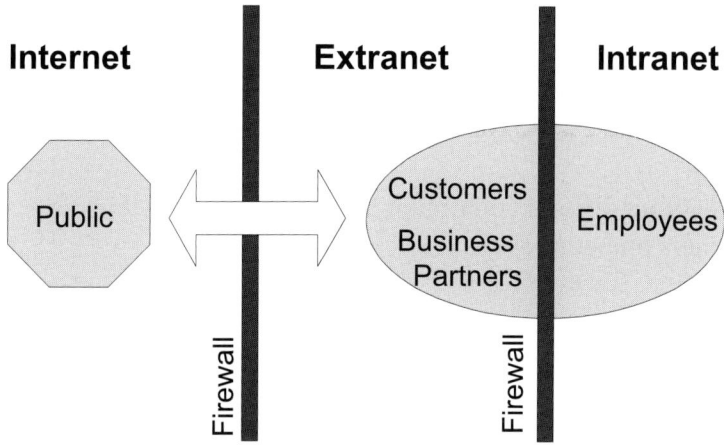

Figure 3.3: Network access model

To strike a reasonable balance, your policies for access and the technical architecture must meet the demands for access to information while balancing legal and information security concerns.

3.7.2. Things to consider

- Access to information is based on profiles derived from the knowledge audit.
- Choose technology for providing access (direct access? Virtual private network? NT security? Password protection? Extranet? Dial-up? Dedicated lines?)
- Who will manage security groups, passwords and sign-on?

3.7.3. Steps to get you there

1. Establish a cross-functional team to define access methods based on the findings of the knowledge audit. The team should consist of IT, legal, and key departmental stakeholders such as marketing, HR, and customer support. Spread accountability, but drive home the importance of closure.
2. Finalize data classification issues and risks. Be concise here. This will help construct the blueprint for IT. IT will require a well thought-out business plan.

3. Assess access methods and associated costs. This may impact the way in which you design the architecture. Dial-up vs. virtual private network could impact performance.
4. Determine how network access costs will be passed on to business partners.
5. Market your efforts; communicate your plans to business partners, customers and employees.

3.8. Collaborative intelligence and filtering layer

The effectiveness of interactive networks such as knowledge management systems is not only dependent on technical ability and reliability that is the infrastructure, but also on conversational robustness. This has been referred to as infostructure: the extent to which the system provides a language structure and the resources that people use to make sense of events taking place within the network. The infrastructure underlying the intelligence and filtering layer supports the necessary transition from infrastructure to infostructure. The aspect of taking infostructure into consideration along with the infrastructure is a crucial determinant of whether users will actually appreciate your system in preference to other sources and use it; the lack of this is the killer antidote for any KM system.

Given the present situation it is proper to ask what can be done. Getting the right information when you want it can yield tremendous benefits for the organization as well as the individual. We have been preoccupied with the business-related aspects of the net for several years and we have observed three main concerns among business management. These are:

- The need to improve collective awareness and perception in order to take advantage of upcoming opportunities and avoid threats.
- Improve reuse and information sharing. One apparent benefit may enable a project to boost performance and withstand time-critical demands. For a full organization it may boost information real information and knowledge flow across organizational boundaries.
- The need to gain other people's attention.

Given the situation described in the previous paragraph the list above constitutes an overwhelming challenge even for a large company. The difficulty of getting your message through to those who need to know and the challenge associated of sorting out what is important is magnitudes larger than what has been experienced before in other media such as television.

The answer must be based on three principles:
- Focus on the interest of the individual
- Focus on autonomy
- Focus on content

3.8.1. *Information feeds*

For a capitalist company or for-profit business, it is important to avoid the "philosopher's trap" by getting entangled in the bottomless issues that lie at the heart of knowledge management. Instead, use clear models or building blocks that define key concepts and provide direction for analysis, action and, most importantly, for results. Develop practical working definitions and move on. The focus, at least in the beginning, needs to be on solutions that can find, summarize, interpret, and analyse large volumes of data and conceptualize information efficiently and effectively. Table 3.3 exemplifies sources and types of feed that a marketing knowledge management system needs.

Table 3.3: Source and types of feed

Source	Examples
Customer knowledge processes	1. Feedback from customers. 2. Knowledge of new product development projects in customer companies. 3. Potential needs of customers; possibly new needs. 4. Level of customer dissatisfaction.
Marketing-research/ development connections	1. The level to which the market data is used by your company's development teams. 2. The level to which marketing departments actually use insights provided by development staff. 3. The extent to which your new service/product development efforts jointly involve ideas from both these parties. 4. Evaluating of one party's products (e.g. marketing plan evaluation by development staff), and vice versa.
Competitor knowledge process	1. How well are competitor information sources integrated within your internal information systems (e.g. online bookstores that allow buyers to compare prices for their selections with their competitor's prices in real time)? 2. Is the analysis of competitors' information systematic

Source	Examples
	throughout the development process for new products and services? 3. Do you use customer evaluations of your competitors' products as a benchmark for your own products or services? 4. Do you regularly examine the IT support that your competitors use?
Market performance	1. How does your product perform in comparison with other competing products? 2. How do customers rate your service in comparison with your competitor's services? (in terms of quality and value). 3. How well are information sources about product markets in general integrated with your planning and development support systems? Your Intranet?
Technology change	1. Rates of obsolescence of your product/service/methodology? 2. Is your market's underlying technology rapidly evolving or mature? 3. Are sources of this information linked to the information systems used within your company? How well?

3.8.2. *Infrastructural elements of collaborative intelligence*

The *collaborative intelligence* layer of knowledge management system builds on several possible combinations and permutations of technologies: Artificial Intelligence tools, intelligent data warehouses, neural networks, genetic algorithms, expert systems, case-based reasoning applications, rule bases and intelligent agents. To understand which of these technologies fit with your own knowledge management system and how they can be integrated, it is essential to understand their role in the context of knowledge management. According to a cognitive process we may use the term APKA in order to divide between the various steps in the *cognitive process* that includes awareness, perception, knowledge and action. What tools fall into the various steps? Some examples are listed as the following:

- Awareness: Push/pull technology, videoconference, Data warehouse, etc.
- Perception: Artificial Neural Networks, Genetic Algorithms, search support, etc.

- Knowledge: Fuzzy logic systems, data mining, expert systems, etc.
- Actions: Automated and semi-automated systems like expert systems.

We will now go into more detail considering some of the technologies, which can be used in developing a knowledge management system in your organization and company.

3.8.2.1. Driving decisions with data - data extraction and aggregation

We have been a data-rich but a knowledge-poor society. We might have all the necessary raw data, even cleanse it in data warehouses, but rarely do we convert it into knowledge that makes the difference. Data warehouses take only one step – they bring together data from disparate sources and at least organize it in part.

Figure 3.4 illustrates a typical data warehouse running in conjunction with an *online analytical processing* (OLAP) system. As the figure shows, a data warehouse is of little use unless the data is converted to meaningful information and applied when needed. Even if this data is used every time a relevant decision is made, it still represents only a fraction of the knowledge assets that the firm has and does not account for expertise that has not been explicated in databases and files.

Data-driven decision support is only one aspect of assisting decision-making with what is known, more specifically, what is known explicitly. Data representations, such as hyper-cube data models in multi-dimensions, help immensely in supporting decision making with concrete data from the past.

3.8.2.2. Data warehouses

While we do not want to get overly involved in discussing the *data warehouse*, let us examine how a data warehouse falls into place in the scheme of things in a knowledge management initiative. Many companies often have multiple databases existing throughout their hierarchy. A data warehouse becomes the big unifier of all these databases. A data warehouse becomes especially useful when you need to look at several different databases at once, combine their content, make it possible to run queries simultaneously across all of them, and reduce data clutter that can otherwise fast overwhelm decision makers. The key characteristics of a data warehouse and its relative fit are summarized in Table 3.4.

3.8. Collaborative intelligence and filtering layer

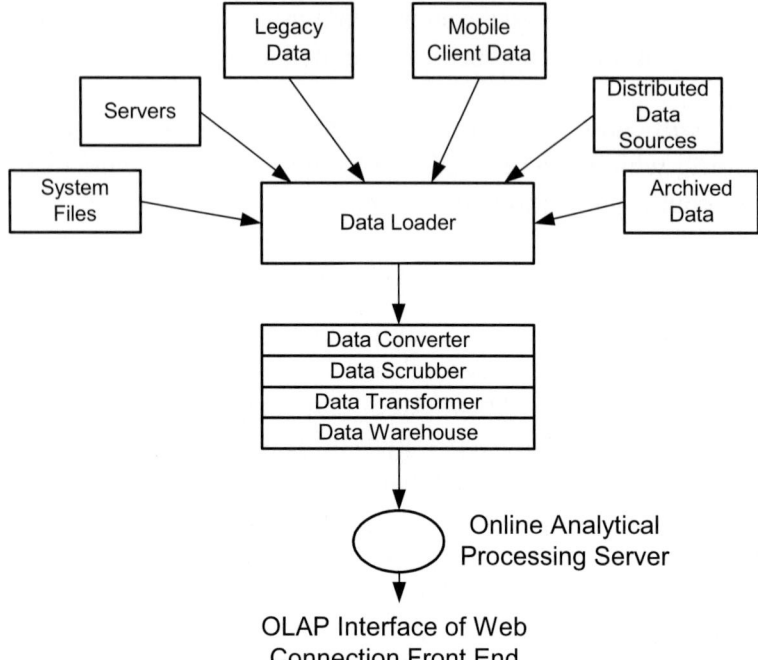

Figure 3.4: OLAP interface or Web connection front end

Table 3.4: Characteristics and relative fit of a data warehouse in the KM infrastructure

Characteristic	Level	Drawback
Response time	Low	Data might not be real time
Scalability with growing needs	Medium	Depends on initial design optimization.
Flexibility of use	High	None
Ease of use	High	Needs a good front end and interface for use
Retrieval of data	Medium	The user needs to navigate through the interface and find the relevant data that helps make a decision.
Processing overhead	High	Not a relevant concern if the size is not too large. Parallel processors on x86 architecture and NT platforms make it very viable. Cost might not be a major concern.
Accuracy	High	Depends on the quality of data scrubbing. Accuracy is higher than the sources since "bad" data has been cleansed out.

Chapter 3 Building the Technical Structure of KM

3.8.2.3. Artificial Neural Networks (ANNs)

Introduction to ANN

ANN offers a powerful and paralleled computing architecture equipped with significant learning abilities. Because the models of ANN are based on biological neural networks, they are able to analyse complex and complicated problems. Today, ANN has undergone a significant metamorphosis becoming an important reservoir of various learning methods and learning architecture. ANN learns from experience and previous examples. They modify their behaviour in response to the environment, are ideal in cases where the required mapping algorithm is not known and tolerance to faulty input information is required. They have been successfully used in many applications such as system modelling, pattern recognition, classification, predication, novelty detection, robotics and process control. ANN algorithms are most frequently used in agile manufacturing systems particularly to increase the learning ability of the systems.

Structure of ANN

ANN contains electronic *process elements* (PEs) connected in a special way. A PE (shown in Figure 3.5) is a simple device that approximates the function of a biological neuron.

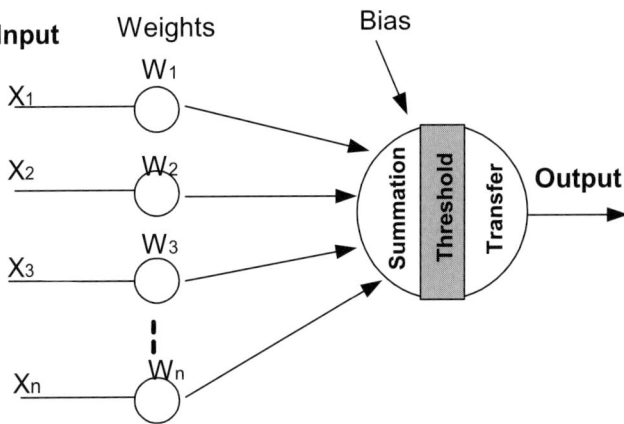

Figure 3.5: A processing element

- *Inputs, bias and outputs*

Each PE can receive many input signals simultaneously, but there is only one output signal that depends on the input signals, bias, weights, threshold and transfer function for that PE. The input signals of a PE come either from the outside environment or the outputs of other PEs and form an input vector **X**, given by:

$$\mathbf{X} = (x_1, x_2, \ldots, x_n)$$

Some PEs have an extra input called bias which represents other influences from outside the network. Some input signals may be more important than others, so there is a weight vector corresponding to the input vector:

$$\mathbf{W} = (w_{i1}, w_{i2}, \ldots, w_{in})$$

These weights express the relative strength (or mathematical value) of the initial input data or the various connections that transfer data from layer to layer. After a PE receives all its inputs, it computes the total input (summation) being received from its input paths according to these weights. The commonly used method is to use the summation function to find the weighted average of all the input elements to each process element. A summation function multiplies each input value by its weight and totals them together in a weighted sum:

$$\text{summation} = \mathbf{WX}^T$$

If bias exists, another term should be presented when computing **summation:**

$$\text{summation} = \mathbf{WX}^T + \mathbf{Bias}$$

- *Transfer (Transformation) function and threshold*

The summation function computes the internal stimulation or activation level of the neuron. Based on this level, the neuron may or may not produce an output (the output of the network is the solution to a problem). The relationship between the internal activation level and the output may be linear or non-linear. Such relationships are expressed by a transfer function. Some networks use the threshold value in determining the output of the PE.

The four most frequently used transfer functions are linear, ramp, step and sigmoid functions where the sigmoid function is the one that is most commonly used. A number of interconnected PEs constitute a neural network structure (shown in Figure 3.6) that can be categorized into three types:

Chapter 3 Building the Technical Structure of KM

- *Input PEs* are those that receive input from external sources to the system.
- *Output PEs* are those that send the signals out of the system.
- *Hidden PEs* are those that have their inputs and outputs within the system.

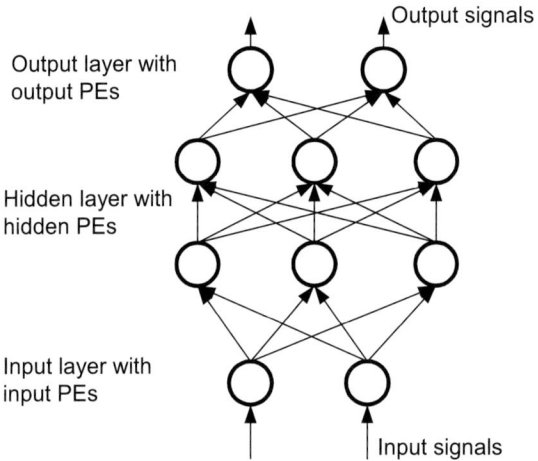

Figure 3.6: A Multiple-Layered Feed Forward ANN

Network learning strategies, classifications and characteristics

A general definition of a learning process can be described as:

Learning is a process by which the free parameters of a neural network are adapted through a continuing process of stimulation by the environment in which the network is embedded. The type of learning is determined by the manner in which the parameter changes take place (Simon Haykin, 1994).

Different ANNs learn in different ways (Figure 3.7) depending on *learning rules* (a prescribed set of rules for the solution of a learning problem) and learning scheme (a model of the environment in which the ANN operates).

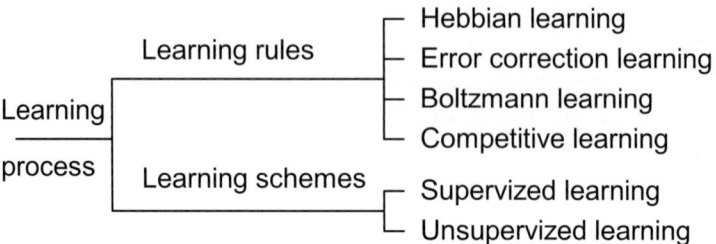

Figure 3.7: Learning process

Hebbian learning comes from the biological world, where a neural pathway is strengthened each time it is used. Error correction learning takes place when the error (i.e., the difference between the desired output and the actual output) is minimized, usually by a least squares process. Competitive learning, on the other hand, occurs when the artificial neurons compete among themselves, and only the one that yields the largest response to a given input modifies its weight to become more like the input. *Boltzmann learning* is a stochastic algorithm derived from information theory and statistical thermodynamics that is known as simulated annealing (Van Laarhoven and Aarts, 1987).

Besides learning rules, different learning processes are also often mentioned including the following two major learning schemes:

- *Supervised learning scheme*

Supervised learning uses a set of inputs for which the appropriate (desired) outputs are known. An external teacher exists in this scheme, and the weights are changed according to the desired outputs. Some famous supervised learning schemes are perceptron, back-propagation and the Boltzmann machine.

- *Unsupervised learning scheme*

In an unsupervised learning scheme, the network will change its weight matrix according to the local information and/or internal control mechanism without the presence of an external teacher. That is, only input stimuli are shown to the network. The network organizes itself internally so that each hidden processing element responds strategically to a different set of input stimulus (or groups of stimuli). No knowledge is supplied about what classifications (outputs) are correct, and those that the network derives may or may not be meaningful to the person training the network. However, the number of categories into which the network classifies the inputs can be controlled by varying certain parameters in the model. In any case, the final categories should be examined to assign meaning and to determine the usefulness of the results. Some famous unsupervised learning schemes are the Hopfield learning method, adaptive resonance theory (ART1 and ART2) and Kohonen self-organized learning.

Usually, ANNs can be classified according to:
- *Structure*: such as one-layered structure (or even structure with only one PE) or multiple-layered structure (shown in Figure 3.6).
- *Input and/or output signals*: the type of input/output signals to/from an ANN might be binary or real valued.
- *Interconnection degree*: such as fully connected or partially connected between different PEs.
- *Direction of information flow*: such as forward-feed or backward-feed (recurrent).

There are also three general types of ANNs that are mostly used in knowledge discovery:

- *Standard Back Propagation (SBP, supervised)*

This is a fast feed forward network using back propagation for training. It is one of the most versatile and consistent ANNs available, and is used to model patterns within data and therefore has wide and extensive application across many areas, including decision support, process modelling and diagnosis.

- *Radial Based Function (RBF, supervised and unsupervised)*

The optional RBF supervised ANN offers an advanced fast classification alternative to SBP. For example, training time is fast with large number of variables and it can train with contradictory samples in the data set.

- *Self-Organizing Maps (SOM, unsupervised) or Kohonen Networks (KOH).*

This tool provides one of the most popular forms of self-organizing maps. It is used in the classification and grouping of data sets, and may be used for data filtering and cluster visualization. Again, various properties of the network can be altered as required. A wide range of views of the classification during and after training provides an understandable feedback of progress. The key characteristics of Artificial Neural Networks are summarized in Table 3.5.

Table 3.5: Key characteristic of ANNs and their fit in the KM system architecture

Characteristics	Drawbacks for KM applications
High accuracy	Requires learning and pre-processing data.
High response speed	Degrades as the net becomes complex.
High tolerance for "bad" data and noise	Requires pre-processing of data for the network to treat it correctly.
Mediocre flexibility	The neural networks need to be retrained if it is to be used to a new application
Low processing resource requirement	The computer needs to be boosted if large amounts of data are fed.
Limited scalability	Data is needed.
Limited need for domain expert	Data needs to be pre-processed.

3.8.2.4. *Fuzzy Logic Systems*

Introduction to FLS

The philosophy of Fuzzy Logic (FL) may be traced back to the diagram of Taiji that was created by the Chinese before 4600 BC. The study of Fuzzy Logic Systems (FLS) began in the 1960s. In the 1970s, fuzzy logic was combined with expert systems to become a FLS, which with imprecise information mimics a human-like reasoning process. FLSs make it possible to cope with uncertain and complex manufacturing systems that are difficult to model mathematically. A fuzzy logic system basically consists of three main blocks: fuzzfication, fuzzy inference mechanism and difuzzfication.

Fuzzfication

Fuzzfication is a mapping from the observed crisp (numerical) input space to fuzzy sets defined in the corresponding universes of discourse. The fuzzfier maps a numerical value denoted X into fuzzy sets represented by membership functions (MBF) in U.

Fuzzy sets
A *fuzzy set A* is a collection of elements defined in a universe of discourse labelled *X*. It generalizes the concept of a classical set by allowing its elements to have partial *membership* (usually $\in [0,1]$), and the degree to which the generic element *x* belongs to *A* is characterized by a

Chapter 3 Building the Technical Structure of KM

membership function $\mu_A(x)$, which associates with each element $x \in X$, a number $\mu_A(x)$ representing the grade of membership of x in A, and is designated as:

$$A = \{(x, \mu_A(x)) \mid x \in X\}$$

Associated with a classical binary, crisp set is a characteristic function, which returns 1 if the element is a member of that set and 0 if it is not. The fuzzy membership function generalizes this concept by allowing elements to be partial members of a set, reflecting degrees of uncertainty about the information.

Membership function

Each linguistic term, such as *cool*, *medium* or *hot*, is represented by a membership function and the set of all these terms determines how an input variable is represented within the fuzzy input (shown in Figure 3.8).

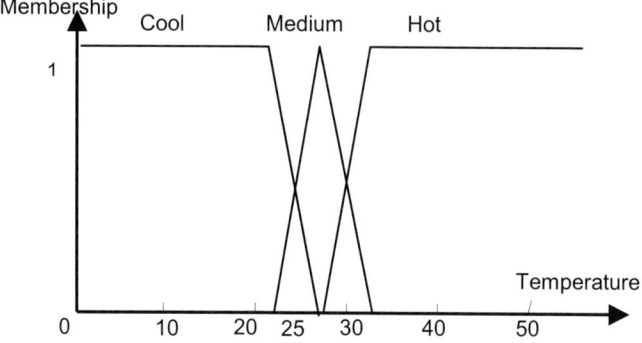

Figure 3.8: Membership functions for temperature

The *support* a fuzzy set A is the set of inputs that have a non-zero membership function value, i.e. the support for fuzzy set "cool" is:

$$\textbf{\textit{Temperature: }} \mu_{cool}(t) > 0$$

For example, a temperature x with 22.5 degrees can be regarded as belonging to fuzzy set "cool" with a membership grade of 0.5 and at the mean time it can also be regarded as belonging to fuzzy set "medium" with a membership grade of 0.5. Besides the triangle and trapezoid functions used in Figure 3.8, other commonly used membership functions include Gaussian functions, S-curve function and B-spline functions of different orders.

Fuzzy inference mechanism

Fuzzy inference mechanism is the fuzzy logic reasoning process that determines the outputs corresponding to fuzzified inputs. The fuzzy rule-base is composed by IF-THEN rules like

> **IF** Process time is Low
> **AND** Queue length is Long
> **AND** Slack Time is Zero
> **AND** Machine breakdown is Very Small
> **THEN** Selectibility factor is Medium

Each fuzzy rule defines a fuzzy implication between condition and conclusion rule parts. Using fuzzy sets, the behaviour of the object can be represented as the form of fuzzy relations. These relations are composed of fuzzy expressions that are connected by fuzzy logical operators. Three important logical operators are commonly applied in a fuzzy relation: *intersection (AND), union (OR) and complement (NOT)*.

Intersection (AND): Fuzzy intersection of fuzzy sets A and B is generally described by the relation:
$\mu_{A \wedge B}(x) = T\{\mu_A(x); \mu_B(x)\}$ where T is the operator for fuzzy intersection.

The standard fuzzy intersection is defined by the relation:
$\mu_{A \wedge B}(x) = min\{\mu_A(x); \mu_B(x)\}$

Union (OR): Fuzzy union of fuzzy sets A and B is generally described by the relation:
$\mu_{A \vee B}(x) = S\{\mu_A(x); \mu_B(x)\}$ where S is the operator for fuzzy union.

The standard fuzzy union is defined by the relation:
$\mu_{A \vee B}(x) = max\{\mu_A(x); \mu_B(x)\}$
Complement (NOT): Fuzzy complement of fuzzy set A is generally defined by a function: $\mu_{\neg A}(x) = 1 - \mu_A(x)$

Chapter 3 Building the Technical Structure of KM

Defuzzification

Defuzzification is the process of representing a fuzzy set with a crisp number. Internal representations of data in a fuzzy system are usually fuzzy sets. But the output frequently needs to be a crisp number that can be used to perform a function such as commanding a valve to a desired position in a control application or indicating a problem risk index as discussed in next section. The most commonly used defuzzification method is the centre of area method (COA), also commonly referred to as the *centroid* method. This method determines the centre of area of fuzzy set and returns the corresponding crisp value. The centre of sums (COS) and the mean of maximum (MOM) methods are two alternative methods in defuzzification.

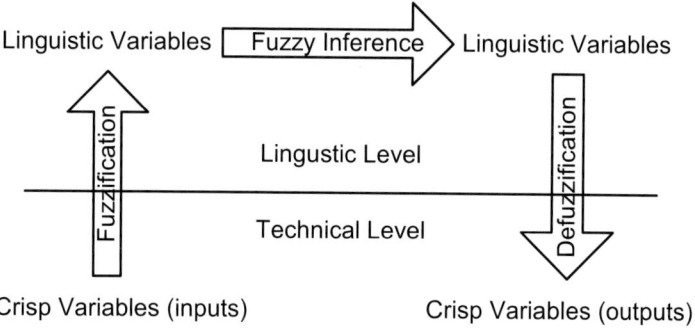

Figure 3.9: Structure of a Fuzzy Logic System

Figure 3.9 shows the complete structure of a FLS. Once all input variable values (crisp) are translated into respective linguistic variable values, the fuzzy inference step evaluates the set of fuzzy rules that define the evaluation. The result of this is again a linguistic value. The defuzzification step translates this linguistic result into a numerical (crisp) value. Table 3.6 summarizes the fit of Fuzzy Logic System within the knowledge management technological framework.

Table 3.6 Characteristics and relative fit of FLSs in the KM infrastructure

Characteristic	Drawbacks for knowledge management
High dependence on domain experts	Fuzzy rules and membership functions using human type language and linguistic variable describe the system. Extensive inputs from domain experts are needed. Very often, fuzzy rules are explicated only to a limited extent, since much of it is tacit.
High speed of development	*If - then* rules can be developed at a fast pace only if knowledge can be elicited from experts in a thorough manner. This often takes up the largest chunk of development time.
Transformation from complex problem into simple problems	As the system complexity increases, it becomes more challenging to determine the correct set of rules and membership functions to describe system behaviour.
Use of heuristic algorithms	Heuristic algorithms can cause problems mainly because heuristics do not guarantee satisfactory solutions that operate under all possible conditions.

3.8.2.5. *Genetic Algorithms*

Introduction to GA

Genetic Algorithms (GA) were first introduced by John H. Holland in the 1960s and were developed by Holland and his students in the 1960s and 1970s (Holland, 1975). The basic idea behind GA is to evolve a group (also called *generation*) of possible candidate solutions (also called *chromosomes*) to a problem at hand, using several operators (such as *crossover*, *mutation*), which are inspired by natural selection and evolution theory proposed by Charles Darwin. Besides GA, there are two other similar strategies available: evolutionary programming and evolution strategies. The distinctive trait of evolution strategies and evolutionary programming with respect to genetic algorithms is that in the latter the simulated evolution takes place at the genotype level that is at the level of coding sequences, whereas the former puts the emphasis on phenotype adaptation.

A GA is an iterative procedure that maintains a constant population size and works as follows. An initial population of a few tens to a few hundreds of individuals are generated at random or heuristically. During each iteration step (generation), the individuals in the current population are evaluated and given a fitness value. To form a new population, individuals are selected with a probability proportional to their relative fitness. This ensures that the expected number of times an individual is chosen is approximately proportional to its relative performance in the population, so that good individuals have more chances of being reproduced. This selection procedure alone cannot generate any new point in the search space. GAs traditionally use two genetic operators (crossover and mutation) for generating new individuals i.e., new search points. Crossover is the most important re-combination operator, which takes two individuals called parents and produces two new individuals called the offspring by swapping parts of the parents. Through crossover the search is biased towards promising regions of the search space. The second operator (mutation) is essentially background noise that is introduced to prevent premature convergence to local optima by randomly sampling new points in the search space.

GAs are stochastic iterative algorithms without converge guarantee. Termination may be triggered by reaching a maximum number of generations or by finding an acceptable solution. The following general schema summarizes a standard genetic algorithm:

Produce an initial population of individuals
While termination condition is not met do
   {
   Evaluate the fitness of all individuals
   Select fitter individuals for reproduction
   Generate a new population by inserting some new good individuals and by discarding some old bad individuals
   Mutate some individuals
   }
   End while

GA is basically a global searching and optimization strategy. Compared with other traditional searching or optimization techniques such as hill-climbing methods, which depend solely on local information to decide the best direction the next step should move. GAs use global information, perform parallel searches and do not require local gradient information, which enables it to find globally optimal or near globally optimal solutions. Some major characteristics of GAs which distinguish them from other conventional methods are listed as follows:

Direct manipulation of a coding

Genetic algorithms manipulate decision or control variable representations at a string level to exploit similarities among high-performance strings. Other methods usually deal with functions and their control variables directly.

GAs deal with parameters of finite length, which are coded using a finite alphabet, rather than directly manipulating the parameters themselves. This means that the search is unconstrained by the continuity of the function under investigation, or the existence of a derivative function. Moreover, by exploring similarities in coding, GAs can deal effectively with a broader class of functions than many other procedures.

Evaluation of the performance of candidate solutions is found using objective, payoff information. While this makes the search domain transparent to the algorithm and frees it from the constraint of having to use auxiliary or derivative information, it also means that there is an upper bound to its performance potential.

Search from a population, not a single point

By searching from a population, GAs find safety in numbers and by maintaining a population of well-adapted sample points, the probability of reaching a false peak is reduced.

The search starts from a population of many points, rather than starting from just one point. This parallelism means that the search will not become trapped at a local maxima - especially if a measure of diversity - maintenance is incorporated into the algorithm, for then, one candidate may become trapped at a local maxima, but the need to maintain diversity in the search population means that other candidates will therefore avoid that particular area of the search space.

Search via sampling, a blind search

Genetic Algorithms achieve much of their breadth by ignoring information except that concerning payoff. Other methods rely heavily on such information and with problems where the necessary information is not available or difficult to obtain, these other techniques break down. GAs remain general by exploiting the information available in any search problem. Genetic algorithms process similarities in the underlying coding together with information ranking of the structures according to their survival capability in the current environment. By exploiting such widely available information, GAs may be applied to virtually any problem.

Chapter 3 Building the Technical Structure of KM 103

Search using stochastic operators, not deterministic rules

The transition rules used by genetic algorithms are probabilistic, not deterministic. A distinction that exists between the randomized operators of GAs and other methods is simple random walks. GAs use random choice to guide a highly exploitative search.

In the past thirty years, GAs have been successfully applied to many areas such as rules learning, feature partitioning, fuzzy controller design, function estimation, software testing and many others [Goldberg, 1989]. These areas share a common characteristic. Although these problems can be different in terms of form and concrete objective, they can usually be transformed into a search or optimization problem in a huge searching space or with too many possible solutions that conventional techniques usually cannot find satisfactory results in an effective way. Table 3.7 summarizes the fit of GA tools within the knowledge management technological framework.

Expert reasoning and rule-based systems

The accounting profession has accomplished tasks on the basis of rules. Take a hypothetical example of what your tax accountant goes through when he/she has to deal with the inland revenue each year: If a person's annual income is NOK 400 000, then his/her tax rate is 35 per cent with a minimum deductible amount, and so forth. Similarly, engineering departments have often followed rules for design and development. However, problems in business that tend to involve a higher level of creativity and innovative off-the-block thinking might not seem to fit well into such problem-solving and analysis schemes.

An example of rules might look like this:

IF	(Retail price of generic TV is at least 25 % lesser than a name brand TV)
AND	(Warranty period is same)
THAN	(It will sell)
ELSE	(It will not sell)

Such rules applied in business, often existing as rules of thumb, can be easily embedded into systems to help make decisions better, more accurately and faster. Their value becomes even more incontestable once they are integrated into a large grouping of tools that will constitute the technology enablers for your company's knowledge management programme. While the examples above are unrealistically simple, actual rules tend to be far more complex and do very well once they are programmed into systems. While all automata can be used to make sense of information that can be run through these techniques, it frees your employees to spend their brainpower on other knowledge tasks, such as socialization, that these techniques cannot address.

Table 3.7: The relative fit of GA-based tools in KM technological framework

Characteristics	Drawbacks for KM
Medium to high accuracy of solutions	Limited and relatively specialized applications.
High response speed/fast problem solving	May deteriorate as the problem increases in complexity.
Development speed of typical solutions based on GAS is fairly high	Solutions tend to be fairly specialized and have a narrow application domain
High levels of embedability	Tools based on GAs tend to be highly dependent on software and the nature of the problem. While this specialization probably improves the performance of the tool, it also severely contains its usability in other problem domains.
Low to medium ease of use	A majority of popular commercial tools available are for non-Windows platforms that are typically not used in most business environments.
Limited scalability	Computing resources often fall short of a complex GA-based solution. Some tools are available for Windows NT and Windows 2000 platforms and take advantages of the multiprocessor capability that NT brings to the low cost, high performance x86 microprocessor family.

Although rule-based systems look neat, their application is rather restricted. They only work well when the following five conditions are simultaneously satisfied:

1. You know what the variables in your problem are.
2. Your can express them in a measurable terms (such as numbers, dollars, speeds).
3. The rule to apply actually covers most, if not all variables that are encountered.
4. The rules do not overlap and conflict.

5. Your rules have been validated to some extent. In other words, you have more reason than creative thought to have come up with these rules.

Rule-based systems are in diametric contradiction to GAs. In GAs, you specify universal conditions under which solutions are considered good, but you cannot apply expert knowledge on how to solve the problem. In rule-based systems, you can bring in expert knowledge, but you cannot specify any universal conditions that denote a good solution. An example of such a situation is credit rating systems. In the rating of the creditworthiness of a person, rules allow the application of specific expert elicited dictum, but no criteria can universally suggest whether the person is creditworthy or not. Similarly for auto insurance, rule-based systems can apply the universally accepted (for insurance industry) and empirically validated rules that risks are higher among males who are single and under 24; however, no universal condition determines the risks of an applicant.

Rule-based systems can be expensive to develop because much of the development time and resources are spent eliciting knowledge for an expert. However, much of the knowledge is tacit and as you would expect, not all of it is explicated. Table 3.8 shows rule-based system and their relative fit in the KM infrastructure.

Table 3.8: Rule-based systems and their relative fit in KM infrastructure

Characteristics	Drawbacks of using in a KM system
High dependence on domain experts and specialists	Extensive inputs from domain specialists are needed. Very often expert knowledge is explicated only to a limited extent, since much of it is tacit. First cuts on elicitation of this knowledge range from poor to acceptable and rarely ever rise to the level of perfection.
Higher speed of development	Rule-based systems can be developed at a fast pace only if knowledge can be elicited from experts in a through manner. This often takes up the largest chunk of development time.
Low levels of scalability	As problems being addressed become complex or evolve over time, rule bases need to be refined. If rules change over time, experts often need to be brought in again to revalidate the rules in use.
Slow response speeds	If the datasets grow large, rules grow more intermingled and complicated. This can often pose a serious challenge to the computing power in use. As problems get complicated, a multitude of rules needs to be matched,

Characteristics	Drawbacks of using in a KM system
	which again degrades the response speed.
Low to medium flexibility	While small bases are quite flexible, as the problem becomes more complicated or involves new variables, the inflexibility of the system becomes an apparent disadvantage.

3.8.2.6. Case-based reasoning

Case-based reasoning is a promising candidate for the knowledge management infrastructure. This approach allows companies to take advantage of previous problems or cases and related attempts to solve them. When faced with a problem, a case-based reasoning system searches its case bases (i.e. a collection of previous cases) for past cases with attributes that match the current case in hand. Figure 3.10 illustrates the inner workings of case-based reasoning system in simple terms.

The user defines a new problem on the basis of some attributes. Based on the attributes, a search engine searches through all the available cases. Cases that are closest to match the case at hand are then retrieved. These cases can be used to further refine the search to retrieve even closer matches.

The consulting industries have been successfully using this approach for consulting assignments. Using past knowledge gained from projects, consultants often, with a bit of justified exaggeration, reduce the task to a simple match and cut-and-paste job. Solving the problem by analogy makes the process of arriving at the solution faster, better, and easier than it would have been had the consultant started from scratch. The distinguishing characteristic of case-based reasoning that makes it a very good fit for a knowledge management system is the fact that concepts are stored as real images and the context of past decision is retained to a satisfactory extent. This helps overcome one of the biggest problems – losing the context of solutions when they are reached and recorded.

Chapter 3 Building the Technical Structure of KM

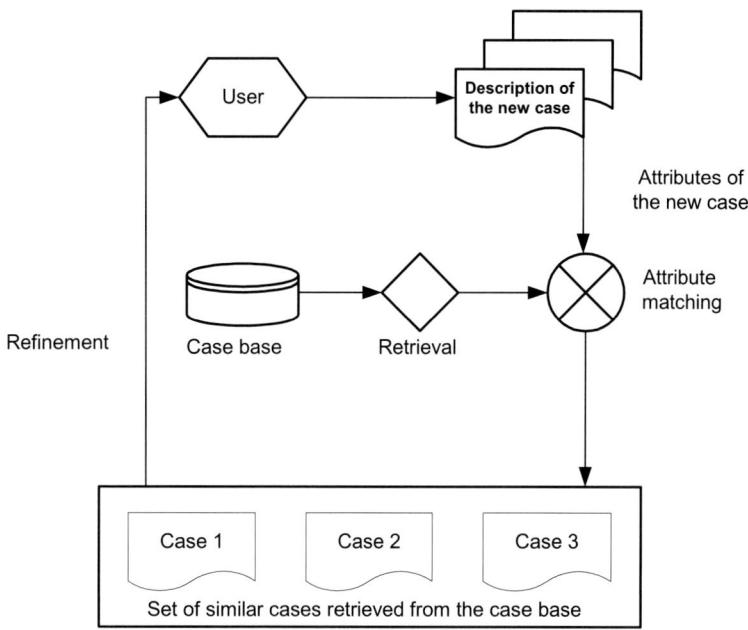

Figure 3.10: The basic idea behind case-based reasoning

Case-based reasoning also works very well with other decision-support technologies, allowing sufficient room for integration of case-based reasoning with several other components within large KM system. Case-based reasoning tools work especially well when the choice is between basing a decision on some data or no data at all. However new or crude a case-based reasoning system is, it always gives a solution. As new cases are added, the case-based reasoning becomes increasingly powerful and accurate.

However, a drawback is that a case-based reasoning system needs thorough initial planning. You must include all possible attributes that you might even remotely anticipate the need for later. If you add attributes later on, older cases that have those attributes will not show up in the search-and-retrieval process unless those attributes are explicitly added to old cases as well. Table 3.9 provides the characteristics that determine the fit of case-based reasoning in KM infrastructural decisions.

Table 3.9: Characteristics of Case-based reasoning in KM

Characteristics	Drawback of using case-based reasoning in a KM system
High level of independence from specialists and domain experts	An expert must fine-tune the attribute matching and retrieval criteria.
High accuracy of solutions	Accuracy is not high to begin with. It improves as more cases are added to the case base.
High response times	As more cases are added to the case base the performance of a case-based reasoning system can degrade. Attribute definition and indexing need substantial forethought to prevent serious problems due to growing case density.
High levels of scalability	Case-based reasoning systems offer a high level of scalability and lend themselves to work in distributed environments, such as across enterprise networks, rather easily. However, the attributes are not easily scalable, and all possible future attributes should be predefined at the outset, when possible.
Unaffected by noise	The retrieval cases will not be affected by the presence of "garbage" or noise in the input case attributes as long as the case base is populated with a sufficient number of cases.
Low ability to handle complexity	As the number of attributes increases, case-based reasoning begins to show weaknesses. First, all attributes in use now might not have been defined in the old cases. Second, the interactions between multiple attributes cannot be judged accurately even if the case base is well populated with cases.

3.8.2.7. Videoconferencing

Videoconferencing enables people to exchange both full-motion video and audio across a distributed network. Although videoconferencing technology has existed for several years, most of the available solutions needed dedicated networks. Videoconferencing requires high bandwidth in the network, since each frame contains about as much data as an equivalent still picture file. Typically, 30-80 frames of video need to be delivered every second to deliver reasonable quality video. Lacklustre bandwidth availability prevents these frames from being refreshed several times every second: The refreshing rate can be slowed down so much that video content delivery might begin to resemble a series of independent

Chapter 3 Building the Technical Structure of KM

delayed static pictures following each other. Although videoconferencing can, at best, be frustrating if you try it over a dial-up connection, faster connections such as a T1 or ADSL line allow for usable-quality, real-time conferencing through the Internet and without the expense of a non-PC conferencing system. Many newer commercial video cameras are optimized for videoconferencing over low bandwidth networks.

3.8.2.8. Push or pull?

A push approach to knowledge delivery actively sends relevant actionable information to the recipient. A pull approach, on the other hand, requires that the recipient pulls out the needed information from the repository. This is an important choice that needs the right balance, since neither approach can serve all users' needs equally well. The important point here is that the users should be able to choose between these two delivery methods.

3.8.2.9. Technological fit

A critical differentiator among the tools discussed so far is the level of knowledge needed to successfully use and apply a particular technology or tool. Some tools require a high level of domain knowledge from the user, whereas others assume that the user is a relatively passive observer in the process. The second dimension is the amount of time that is needed to find a solution with a knowledge management tool in the specific business application domain of interest. As illustrated in Figure 3.11, the two dimensions of these tools can guide their selection.

3.8.3. Level of knowledge granularity in objects

Since a knowledge management system is intended to be a mechanism for securing corporate knowledge, it needs to be populated with knowledge object. However, these knowledge objects can be specified at different levels of detail. A key failure point in the design of a knowledge management system is not deciding at the beginning on the right level of knowledge. Let us take a look at a knowledge management system in a diagnostic clinic. The knowledge elements or object can be classified at different levels of detail and the level of increasing granularity represents the depth of detail that a KM system deals with (Table 3.10).

3.8. Collaborative intelligence and filtering layer

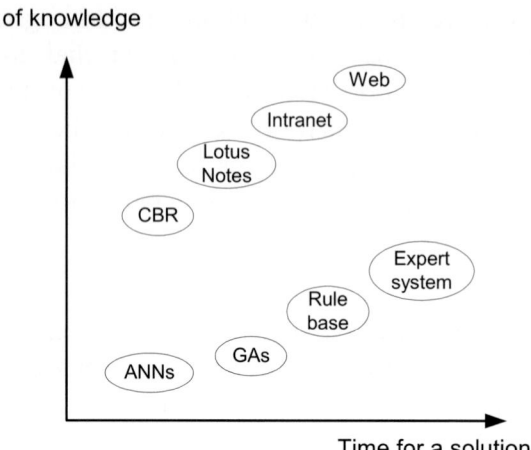

Figure 3.11: Technological fit of knowledge-based reasoning tools

Table 3.10: Level of increasing granularity in a KM system

Knowledge object	Example of such an object in a clinical (diagnostic) knowledge management system.
Knowledge domain	Internal medicine.
Knowledge region	Neurology.
Knowledge section	Brain diseases; tumours.
Knowledge element	General diagnostic strategies.
Knowledge fragment	If the symptom reported by the patient is continual headaches, then consider the possibility of a brain tumour.
Knowledge atom	Excessive and continual headaches are a symptom.

Too high level of granularity will result in the loss of knowledge richness and context; too low a level will cause unnecessary drain on network. Storage and human resources raise the cost and reduce the value of the object. The key lies in selecting the right level of molecularity of knowledge that will be stored in your knowledge management system: the level that strikes an optimum balance between the two opposite extremes of too much detail and too little detail, both of which can render knowledge only marginally useful.

3.8.4. Infrastructural elements for searching, indexing and retrieval

Indexing and retrieval capabilities of a knowledge management system determine the ease with which a user can find relevant knowledge in the

Chapter 3 Building the Technical Structure of KM 111

system. Searching, indexing and retrieval are essential parts of content management, which is an important element in KM. Four types of navigation strategies can be developed in varying combinations: Meta searching, hierarchical searching, attribute searching, and content searching.

3.8.4.1. Meta searching

Meta searching allows the user to determine the focus of the search. The main purpose of a Meta search function is to minimize the time spent in locating a general category for a piece of potential knowledge within repository

This concept is illustrated in Figure 3.12. If the user types in a keyword "Business", what exactly does the user mean? If this simple keyword returns subcategories as shown in Figure 3.12, users can potentially avoid the trap of going in the wrong direction altogether. They can focus on what the word business means in specific context of their task and continue the search process in a more focused manner, using the other strategies we discuss. Meta searching provides a clearer view of the bigger picture as well as context clarification.

Figure 3.12: An illustration of meta-categorical searching

3.8.4.2. Hierarchical searching

If the broad category has been successfully identified, the user can then dig deeper into the repository without running the risk of going in a totally wrong direction. A hierarchical search strategy organizes knowledge items in a fixed hierarchy. The user can follow or traverse links within such a structure to efficiently locate the right knowledge element in a timely manner.

3.8.4.3. Attribute searching

Searching by attributes uses a value input by the user. This attribute value is matched against closely related values attached to documents and pointers such as skills databases.

3.8.4.4. Content searching

Content searching is the least efficient of the search strategies. The user enters an arbitrary item, keyword or text string.

3.8.4.5. Combining search strategies

In order to enable effective searches, it is possible to use all or several of these search and retrieval strategies in parallel.

3.8.4.6. Search engines

Search engines have been focused on a lot in the context of the WWW. Most people are acquainted with Yahoo, Infoseek, Alta Vista, AllTheWeb, AskeJeeves and Google. Several of these can also be bought for the corporate Intranet. Good search engines are essential when data repositories get connected. Once the electronic link is established access from a computer through the network is possible. Yet, the whereabouts and the contents of these easily fall into oblivion. Search engines that have access to the net and the repositories provide considerable support. The traditional search engine is typically focused by the use of search keys that match keywords used for indexing the content by the search engine itself. Both the index and retrieve operations are typically based on word statistics. The frequency of words in a document will determine the dominant keys used to index and retrieve the document. And extension to this technique is called proximity statistics that also take into account the co-occurrence of two words within a distance of each other in a text. This will determine the association between two terms used to support search queries involving more than one keyword. This approach uses no knowledge about the document or data stored. It simply looks at the statistics of words. Although impressive retrieval speeds can be achieved, the accuracy is often very poor. The lack of semantics associated with the query-retrieve association makes the search data-oriented rather than knowledge-oriented. This implies that there is a poor match between the intentions that the user has and the semantics embedded in the hits found. Moreover the traditional search engine indexes the container and less the ingredients for the same reason. This implies that it will get the document and only the paragraph or a summary of the document. In the context of knowledge management this yields only basic support.

Another aspect is the inherent pull operation associated with search engines. If you need something you have to go and find it. Subscription or efficient push technology where the information finds the decision maker is not prevalent at the time of writing. This is also associated with the concept of personalization. Drucker states things clearly. Knowledge is by definition personal. Hence the search schema needs to suit the individual in order to leverage data to a knowledge level. We will briefly explain this.

Evolutionary history both within nature itself as well in socio-economic systems has shown that entities such as organisms, products and services with no specialized capabilities crumble when faced with specialized competition. Search and navigation aids do not need to encompass the whole Internet if they provide for the part that is pertinent to the individual's needs and interests. Search speed must not be measured in terms of query response. A query that yields 100 or 20 000 hits will require significant amount of post-processing. The search effort is not completed before the data gathered is prepared to suit one or more clauses associated with a decision. To process 20 000 hits in order to build a platform for a decision process may take several days, even weeks for one person. If the process of fetching pertinent material can be automated and if this automated process is also able to deliver the proper essence in a form that yields proper attention then a tremendous gain in search time has been achieved.

In order to achieve both the above, focus on content is essential. Content addresses aspects of semantics and pragmatism. Most search engines do not address content, but expressions. This implies that they look at simple word patterns based on rather simple word statistics. This often leads to ambiguities. All ambiguities cause various degrees of noise in a search situation. More novel approaches have addressed similar expressions in terms of more sophisticated pattern recognition techniques.

This enables efficient clustering of similar documents, while the content itself is not addressed. In a subtle way these approaches may also cater for a degree of pragmatism since they maintain focus on verbal expression. Thus, they may incorporate writing style more than content.

In the Internet world, a more advanced category of search support has emerged. This captures and mimics user behaviour and in this way builds semantics into the hyperlink systems. Such a concept is based on a voting principle that yields a cybernetic effect. The principle is simple. Given a query the user's response to the query is recorded. If several people respond in the same manner, then that must be the proper action. Next time the same or similar query is presented to the system this history is reused assuming that the intent behind the new query is similar to the one that satisfied others. Although it is cunning it has nothing to do with content analyses. Moreover it builds on a self-fulfilling prophecy in that it cleanses the population of possible hits always assuming that the interest of the majority is the interest of the individual. In theory such a search tool will wind up with only one alternative since the refinement of the population is a function of the alternatives presented and voted for.

In order to support the content and search aspects required for good knowledge management a new generation type of technology must be defined. This will have to be inherently knowledge oriented, focusing on semantic structures rather than bit patterns. It must address the principles defined here to support the individual. Due to its importance we will address this type of technology in a separate chapter. But note that it is especially suited to handle the important information feeding tasks described next.

3.8.5. *Tagging knowledge elements with attributes*

Since searching works primarily on the basis of textual string matching, it is important that content – both formal and informal – is tagged with a proper set of attributes. More advanced tools are available for pattern matching in drawings, photographs, etc., but these are not always a feasible option for two reasons. First, these tools are still in their initial stages of development and work within highly specialized categories of informal data (rather than information or knowledge). Second, these tools are more expensive and complicated to implement when compared to traditional, commercially available search tool solutions. Consequently, a company must define its own set of attributes to tag knowledge content with. Although many of these attributes can be common to a company and its partners, the need for such clear-cut definitions cannot be

Chapter 3 Building the Technical Structure of KM

overemphasized. A basis of tagging attributes is listed in Table 3.11, which is explained afterwards.

Table 3.11: Tagging attributes for knowledge content in a KM system.

Attribute type	Tagging attribute
A	Activities
D	Domain
F	Form
T	Type
P	Products and services
I	Time
L	Location

3.8.5.1. Activities attribute

The activities attribute refers to the organizational activities to which the given knowledge element related.

3.8.5.2. Domain attribute

The domain attribute tags the knowledge item to its subject matter. This attribute is the primary attribute that drives the meta search process. Your company has probably already identified the broad domains of expertise and skill areas that constitute it.

3.8.5.3. Form attribute

The form attribute defines the physical representation of the knowledge element. This attribute is tricky to define. You can begin with a basic set of values such as:

- Paper
- Electronic
- Formal (file, Word document, spreadsheet, etc.)
- Informal (multimedia, sound, videotape, etc.)
- Collective
- Tacit or mental knowledge
- Pointer (to person who has solved a problem of that nature, etc.).

If information is available in other forms in your company, then add them to this basic "starter" list. The pointer attribute value is similar to the concept of employee skill databases, where you might perform a search for "Web-database integration experts," and detailed contact information for all employees matching that attribute set will show up in the results. This is especially useful when your company's offices are geographically distributed or there are many employees.

3.8.5.4. Type attribute

The type attribute is more relevant to formalized knowledge that is captured in electronic or textual form such as a document or a report. It specifies what type of a document that knowledge element is. Such values can be standardized across multiple companies, such as your company and its supplies. Suggested starting values for this attribute, which can be later extended to account for tacit knowledge types, are:

- Procedure
- Guidelines
- Protocol
- Manual
- Reference
- Time line
- Worst practice report
- Best practice report
- Note
- Memo
- Failure report
- Success report
- Press release/report
- Competitive intelligent report

Beginning with these values, you can add other relevant types that are applicable to your company.

3.8.5.5. Products and services attribute

The products and services attribute specifies the products and service to which the knowledge element relates. This list should be kept specific and non-overlapping. A consulting company, for example, might have, among others, the following attribute values:

- Strategic consulting
- Implementation consulting
- E-commerce consulting

3.8.5.6. Time attribute

The time attribute is useful for time-stamping events and knowledge elements. Time stamping is done automatically for files, but that time stamping marks the creation of that object, which might have a value different from the actual creation of a knowledge object.

3.8.5.7. Location attribute

Use the location attribute to specify the location of pointers that track people within and outside the company. Not all knowledge elements will have a value assigned to this attribute, but it can be used to narrow searches by location.

3.8.6. Push/pull revisited

After attributes and tags for knowledge elements are assigned, delivery based on push technology becomes remarkably viable. The term push delivery should not be confused with Web-based active-push services such as Netscape Netcaster or Pointcast running through browsers or active desktops. Push technology for knowledge management systems should provide employees with a variety of options for both retrieval and delivery.

If some employees do not prefer push delivery, they should be provided with an option to pull content on demand, such as through a search conducted via Web browser or desktop client interface.

A pull-based mechanism for knowledge retrieval can aid decision-making throughout problem-solving processes surrounding the delivery of new products and services. Experiential knowledge can help you answer questions like:

1. Have you faced this problem before?
2. What was done?
3. Did it work?
4. What solutions were considered but rejected?
5. If a fundamental assumption that formed the basis of an earlier decision was to change. What would happen?
6. What criteria formed the basis of the last decision?
7. Who has worked on related projects in the past?
8. Where can we find them now?
9. What were the assumptions at that time?
10. How have they changed?

In any case, using the Web as a primary push or pull delivery mechanism will help your company leverage and fully utilize your mixed hardware and platform set in use throughout the company, across multiple locations, and in real time.

3.8.7. A short summary

Collaboration support can expedite problem solving and task accomplishment in current situations. Using the approach initiated in this chapter can lead, in the most optimistic case, to one or more of these potential benefits:

- The process-centred and product-centred view of KM is effectively integrated to make well-reasoned and accurate decisions.
- Highly-paid workers spend less time looking for information needed to make decisions.
- The decision-making process is streamlined and expedited.
- Tacit knowledge is leveraged and put into action.
- Tacit knowledge begins to be externalized.
- Ad hoc teams are built with a proper blend of skills regardless of the geographic distribution of employees.
- Experiential knowledge is leveraged in making new decisions.
- Sub-optimal product or service quality is avoided by smooth flow of actionable information and knowledge throughout the company.
- External knowledge is applied on a relevant and timely manner.
- Costly errors resulting from repeated mistakes are avoided.
- Valuable knowledge does not become a victim of the information glut.
- All relevant knowledge is integrated into the existing work environment.
- Work process and outputs are systematically organized.
- Knowledge continues to evolve, grow and remain relevant.
- Active sharing, creation, distribution and sharing of knowledge become a reality.

3.9. Applications layer

Knowledge-enabling applications are the applications that come together to provide the "added-value" or "show-me layer". The purpose of knowledge-enabling applications is to create a competitive edge.

The applications layer provides users with productivity enhancements and improved ways of doing their jobs. This layer includes authoring and publishing tools, site analysis tools, document management, discussion databases, calendars, employee yellow papers, Web site analysis tools, sales force automation and executive Balanced Score Card applications.

The list of applications provides a framework for you to get started. This is where the rubber meets the road in KM; infrastructure is a commodity, and the network is a given. Now you must leverage your infrastructure to create a competitive edge for your organization.

While creativity could expand this list a hundredfold, we have chosen a handful of applications that will allow you to get started and begin to produce value quickly.

3.10. Transport layer

3.10.1. Why is this layer important?

In order to implement knowledge architecture across your enterprise, you will continually re-evaluate your existing technological network. Your company has become a network of relationships. You have moved from a concern for transporting transactional data and accounting transactions to a concern for transporting intellectual assets (knowledge) across the network to the right people at the right time. Your network may be moving e-mail, documents, video and audio clips, news and many other types of content.

We look at the network backbone to provide traditional connectivity across the LAN, WAN, and Intra/Extra/Internet, and now, to support the collection, organization, and sharing of information. Collaborative tools provide an economical way to bring expertise and knowledge to bear on a specific problem or situation, at specific point in time.

People have been collaborating for a long time, of course, by using e-mail and the telephone. In aircraft cockpits and hospital emergency rooms, collaboration has been a matter of life or death for years. There is nothing new here for business, except perhaps some technological twists that can improve the retention and sharing of solutions developed in previous situations.

3.10.2. Relevant items
- Network traffic
- Impact of videoconferencing

- Bandwidth issues related to streaming of web-based training modules, audio and video
- Connectivity speeds (keep offline users in mind when designing)
- Open systems that support streaming, HTML, scripting, URLs, graphics and multimedia
- Search tool that can search forums
- Ability to allow for live presentations and that can be moderated

3.11. Repository Layer

The main purpose of the repository layer is to store the data, information and knowledge that are relevant to your organization. The technical architecture we have been describing should now result in you integrating the loosely connected systems, databases and file systems in your organization. It is likely that you will be faced with mining information from legacy sources, as well as those "fresh" data sources cropping up throughout the organization today (Figure 3.13).

This is potentially a large project. You may want to consider a full-time data architect to help you here. To save time and be assured of moving forward, focus your efforts on "controlled" sources of information, those having KAs, editors, or administrators that are in charge of publicly shared, but not catalogued, documents. In such a case, you may want to include information only in certain directories or, alternatively, designate the ownership to an individual KA.

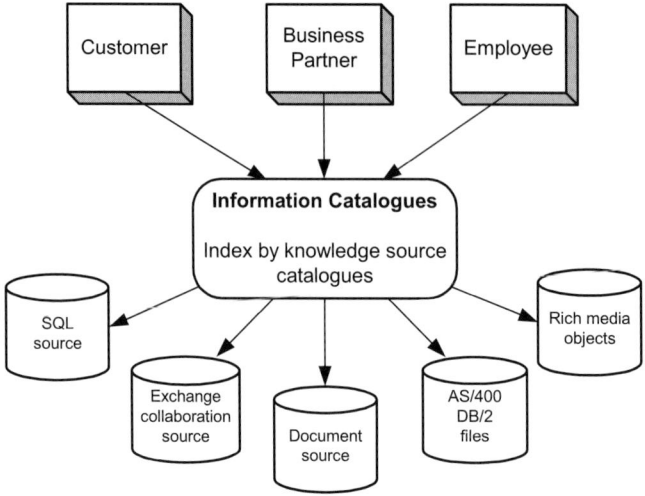

Figure 3.13: Repositories of information

3.11.1. Things to consider

- Inventory data sources.
- Do you have controlled or uncontrolled source of information? Be selective.
- Architect database schema that allows easy extraction of fields in a database.
- Single-source repositories.

3.11.2. Steps to get you there

1. Employ the service of a data architect.
2. Establish schema that integrate with the access model.
3. Create data architecture based on integration of disparate sources.

3.12. Conclusions

Knowledge management must be implemented in a organization or a company via a knowledge management system. In this chapter, we have focused on how information technology and AI can support the infrastructure of the knowledge management system through a number of technological components.

The technology components of Web-based knowledge management system architecture consist of six layers: The interface layer, the access layer, the collaborative intelligence layer, applications layer, transport layer and repositories layer. Most technology needed for knowledge management already exists. The need is the effective integration of this technology supported by organizational enablers that can make it deliver business results. We will discuss various components that help develop the existing infrastructure into the requisite information structure that is required for effective knowledge management.

The technical infrastructure of knowledge management presented in the chapter provides you with a general methodology for building your knowledge management system. In the following chapter, we will present some theoretical aspects about what creates real communication in knowledge management.

3.13. Lessons learned

Most technology needed for knowledge management already exists. The critical part is determining the best mix of available tools and integrating them in your knowledge management architecture. Beer in mind the lessons about these infrastructural components while determining this mix:

- **Choose IT components to find, create, assemble and apply knowledge**
  Since content comes from a variety of sources both within and outside your company, the optimal choice of components must let you create, assemble, find, and apply knowledge in a cost-effective and timely manner.

- **Pick one: Web or Notes**
  Customized implementations of proprietary technology might seem to be easier to implement than Web-based Intranets with equivalent functionality; using open standards such as Intranets holds more long-term promise both in terms of cost containment and incremental development. Choosing the Web option over other options can potentially lead to tighter integration of commercially available complements such as Case-Based Reasoning system and push delivery mechanisms.

- **Identify and understand components of the collaborative intelligent layer**
  Artificial Intelligence, data warehouses, Artificial Neural Networks, Genetic Algorithms, Expert Systems, rule bases, and Case-Based Reasoning are some of technologies that provide intelligence for the knowledge management system. Understand how these tools and technologies work and when their use is appropriate.

- **Optimize knowledge object granularity**
  Granularity of knowledge (represented in terms of knowledge objects or clements that are specified in descending order as knowledge domains, regions, sections, segments, elements, fragments, and atoms).

- **Create knowledge tags and attributes**
  Domain, form, type, product/service, time and location tags automatically classify content along several dimensions. Using

standardized tags allows uniformity in the retrieval and storage of content. Defining such tags up front also helps you determine the right mix of components for searching, indexing and retrieval.

REFERENCES

1. Applehans, W., Globe, A., and Laugero, G., (1999), *Managing knowledge – A practical web-based approach,* Addison Wesley Lengman, Inc.
2. Borghoff U. M. and Pareschi, R., (1998) (Eds.), *Information technology for knowledge management*, Berlin, Springer-Verlag.
3. Davenport, T. and Prusak, L., (1998), *Working knowledge: How organizations manage what they know,* Harvard Business School Press, Boston.
4. Drucker P., (1988), "*The Coming of the New Organization*", Harvard Business Review, Jan-Feb.
5. Goldberg, D. E., (1989), *Genetic algorithms in search, optimization & machine learning*, Addison-Wesley, Reading.
6. Nonaka, I. and Takechi, H., (1995), *The knowledge creating company: How Japanese companies create the dynamics of innovation*, New York: Oxford Univ. Press
7. Personal communication R&D department of FAST Research & Transfer, (2000), Oslo.
8. Schreiber, G. et al., (2000), *Knowledge engineering and management – The commonkads methodology*, The MIT Press.
9. Tiwana, A., (2000), *The knowledge management toolkit*, Prentice Hall PTR.
10. Toffler, A., (1991), *Powershift: Knowledge, Wealth, and Violence of the 21st Century*, Bantam Books.
11. Wang, K., (2000), Computational intelligence in manufacturing, *Keynote speech at ICME 2000*, Hongzhao, China, June 2000.

CHAPTER 4

INFORMATION, KNOWLEDGE AND MEANING –
SOME THEORETICAL ASPECTS ABOUT WHAT CREATES REAL COMMUNICATION

> **Objectives**
>
> - Emphasize that communication is more than transmission capabilities.
> - Discuss a possible incompatibility between the western mindset and a culture required for effective knowledge sharing.
> - Understand that articulation of knowledge is language dependent.
> - Discuss relativism and indicate that this extends beyond physics and into the human perception of truth and meaning.
> - Show that concepts are understood through knowledge of what they can do and how they are used.
> - Specify the requirements of a computer-based system that can capture concepts and knowledge of human behaviour.

4.1. Introduction

In this chapter, we will highlight the fundamental elements that must be observed in order to establish an effective knowledge-sharing environment. As we have pointed out in the previous chapters, knowledge sharing is about communication, both lateral and vertical. The new possibilities that arise with an infrastructure that encompasses computers, networks and software that drive the signal transmission across vast distances at lightning speed are prerequisites for what we want to achieve in knowledge management. The need to tie together various divisions and departments of a company and all their busy workers has been highlighted in the previous chapters. E-mail, Internet and Intranets, data warehouses and content management systems are all support for leaders, in principle, to extend their span of control to far more than the classic 6 – 7 units that were common before as well as employees information processing capacity. The network and the asynchronic form of communication that an e-mail system, both wired and wireless, offer increase people's availability. We have addressed the information overload issues that follow this and there are many initiatives that try to cope with this. Once looked upon as a blessing, many employees feel that 100 e-mails a day swamps them. They simply get into information overload. Today such a reaction is typical for people who have little or few traditions for initializing social contacts across a computer network. But there is a growing evidence that this is about to change. A group of younger people, faced with the same issue – 100 e-mails a day – replied that it is fine. In fact many commented that it was a little on the low side since it was important to "be in the loop". There is an emerging trend that young people initiate social contacts through the net, and that getting many SMS messages and e-mails were a tokens of being popular. That indicates being aware of what is going on and being able to influence the turn of events. Managers who still belong to the first group have not yet recognized this social anthropological phenomenon. But it breathes life into the vision behind systems long before the types of observations highlighted here were made.

Despite differences in attitude stemming from age distinction, there are several more individually oriented mechanisms that determine the quality of communication. For years, managers have failed to really acknowledge that background, context, culture, situation and values determine good communication. Many negotiators have felt despair when their counterpart walked out from the meeting room, refraining from signing the contract which was so close at hand. In deep afterthought they have pondered about what they did or said to offend their partners or to simply reinforce a misunderstanding that was meant to be resolved. And yet, this was eye to eye. This problem is amplified more in the text-oriented, remote, impersonal and asynchronous world of computer-based communication. The situations like "what I said is not what I meant" or "what you read is not what I really intend" are commonplace. Failure to convey effectively what is meant with respect to a goal, a task to be done or a requirement may be disastrous. Misunderstandings can create instant losses and weaken a company's position for years. Failure to convey the real essence of a strategy may end in bankruptcy. A computer system that should support knowledge sharing must observe this, avoid misinterpretations and highlight real meanings. That is fundamental, yet is not well understood by everybody.

In the sections that follow, we will attempt to highlight what mechanisms exist that makes this so hard. In order to do that we will address issues that take us deep into the history of philosophy, since communication between people is about our existence as social individuals.

4.2. Goal

In traditional *information theory* [Shannon, 1948], communication circles around channel capacity and signal transmission exposed to noise. A discourse on communication must be based on this. Yet it provides a very limited view on communication. *Knowledge sharing* is about communication insight and understanding. At the core of this, there are two important elements beyond the signal itself, semantics and intention, the latter applying to the pragmatics of linguistics.

As pointed out earlier, cooperation of autonomous groups and the use of the new communication technology demand a stringent focus on how we communicate. Although e-mails and SMS messaging have both increased everyone's accessibility, such communication channels tend to be overemphasized in terms of effectiveness. Meaning and intention are often difficult to convey through e-mail without careful authoring. Most companies and individuals can document core experience and misunderstandings arising from the use of wrong words. When we talk face-to-face, our words and phrases are accompanied by a complex body language and important points emphasized by regulating the tone and pitch of our voices. Conveying a complex body of knowledge is difficult. Tacitness is largely dependent on the available vocabulary and practice in using this. Most people handle structural descriptions well during everyday life. That is, most people are well acquainted with the task of describing what things look like and often how they are put together. Yet in describing how things perform expressive difficulties often arise. We tend to use images and metaphors to understand and describe how things behave in a particular context avoiding the direct description of the action itself. "Works like a hammer", "swims like a fish", "jumps like a frog" are typical examples of that. Images like these are much more meaningful to most people than elaborate verbal descriptions of how a hammer performs and the way a fish moves. The task of conveying knowledge is a rich, skilled activity and is demanding in terms of words. The result is often doubtful. Few people learn how to play golf by reading a book. If you have ever tried to assemble a model plane by means of a verbal description alone you will know how difficult it is. Even massive use of diagrams may not convey sufficiently the knowledge elements that distinguish a novice from an expert.

In this section, we focus on meaningful communication. Our claim is that knowledge is inherently subjective and that the task of communication is an act of meaningful co-involvement. Passing on insight is not so much the act of building up a transaction which is carefully passed on to the receiver. It is more the act of creating a bridgehead where the terms produced by the speaker stimulate concepts in the minds of the receivers. If the stimulation is good, communication is established. We will try to establish a less traditional view of information exchange; a view that we believe to be absolutely essential in order to support efficient knowledge sharing. In the subsequent discussion of FAROS, these issues are revisited in more practical terms. FAROS embodies many of the principles that we emphasize here. By using work processes, FAROS creates a bridgehead for conveying know-how – the way expertise is applied (rather than what that knowledge is). In doing so, it applies an iconic type of graphics that is simple and standardized, yet able to highlight contextual and subjective elements.

4.3. What governs communication and knowledge sharing?

Language, knowledge and our perception of the world are closely related. In order to create a foundation for our theories, judge historic and present initiatives with respect to information extraction and knowledge sharing, we will briefly discuss some philosophical aspects that address the human ability to perceive the world, experience it and express a view of the same world. Essentially, we will attempt to justify our position for the subsequent evaluation of different historic initiatives to *natural language processing* (NLP), communication theory, information retrieval and text understanding. Basically what we claim is that a major set of initiatives in development of knowledge-based systems and knowledge management initiatives have struggled and sometimes failed simply because they have adopted a classic scientific approach. The success of modern mathematics in the natural sciences such as physics has reinforced the notion that more mundane and qualitative aspects of the world can be modelled by formalisms that are neutral to both the individual and the context alike. The use of formal logic and the application of normalized language formalism have created the basis for multiple systems development. Although this is attractive in terms of organizing knowledge and information and rationalizing the processing of such, it creates a divide between the real world problems and many of the systems developed. One well-known issue debated for years within the artificial intelligence community is the frame problem, which defines a limited and protected world within the systems that can be operated and problems understood and solved. Once the frame issue is violated the performance of the system falters. The issue then becomes mapping the real world onto the artificial through a process that is called world representation. Consequently the advantage gained with strict formalism is lost through the difficulty of creating good world representations. Several systems have faltered during the scale-up process rendering no practical benefits due to this problem.

Another aspect that classic science imposes on systems development is the need to make things objective. The issue of replication of use, both with respect to full systems and stand-alone knowledge bases, is intimately related to the desire for objectiveness. Moreover, several systems that we have studied apply a very mechanistic way of analysis mostly following a linear pattern of processing. Again, such a process is true to the scientific traditions staked out by Descartes and others. Here we advocate a more holistic approach to analysis using non-linear approaches that are inspired by nature. This does not mean that science and philosophy cannot offer other approaches to the issues at hand. On the contrary, modern physics and art do introduce measures of relativism that we feel are important to acknowledge when working with communication and knowledge sharing, especially across a computer network. We also claim that subjectivity poses no threat to the possibility of replication. On the contrary it has profound effects about how to appreciate language as a means of addressing knowledge and for communication among people. We also take the stance of key authors in the field of knowledge management [Nonaka, 1995] that claim that the articulation of experience is language dependent. *Tacitness* is a consequence of internalization through processing of sensory and mind impressions as well as a lack of vocabulary that sufficiently expresses the concepts internalized.

All of this raises the issue of how to approach computer-based activities such as search, e-mail exchange, portal building and document management. It influences our way of thinking about structuring and reusing knowledge. It helps us to explain the success of recent advances in statistical natural language processing. It also helps us to define a theory that can support the pursuit of intelligent text understanding by means of computers that lies at the core of content management and peer-to-peer interaction.

4.4. Language and concepts

John Locke was the founder of British empiricism. He claimed that things existing in the real world are objective in nature. Even if the sensory perception of things is illusory, it is undoubtedly evident that something can be perceived. People's sensory perception capabilities are their primary source of many ideas. There is another fountain, the reflection capabilities of our mind, from which experience furnishes the understanding with new ideas.

Gottlob Frege is said to be the father of *analytic philosophy*. He built a pure language of mathematics by introducing strict terms and definitions of the numbers. Basically he created a language of modern logic that was without ambiguities. His work departed from established work of Descartes and his like. But he was again a pure rationalist. He discarded all aspects of intuition and meta-physics. This, he believed, obscured the essence to be communicated. His efforts spun off results that had profound effects on other philosophers' concept of language. Basically, this was because he was the first to distinguish between meaning and reference. He claimed that the semantics of a sentence is purely a claim. Its reference in the real world provides its true value. Put in a popular form, the source for understanding depends on how well you are able to relate terms to the real world. Without this reference to the reality that a person is familiar with it is impossible to capture meaning. In this manner Frege was thus able to explain how people can have a different set of opinions of entities in the real world, without necessarily disputing the real world itself.

4.5. Understanding concepts depends on what they do and how they are applied

There is no standard interpretation of a concept. Yet, a good start is to look at what it does or makes. For those modelling with flowcharts, frustrations related to the modelling tasks are often wiped out when students are taught to focus on what an entity does rather than what it is. The FAROS approach is actually based on this.

Husserl was the father of phenomenology and focused on the relationship between thinking itself and the world. Husserl addresses the human perception of the world and the notion of experience. This gave rise to consciousness of experience and its effect on our ability to perceive the world. Husserl emphasized that intention is the token of all consciousness. The fundamental aspect of intention is the will to act or the action itself. This is important to understand in terms of communication. In order to interpret the meaning of something we should ask what it actually could do.

Husserl gave rise to the ideas of another philosopher, Heidegger. Heidegger used Husserl as basis for the notion of "being in the world" (German: "Dasein"). "Dasein" defines relationships between different things in the world. Heidegger proposes then that observation and being is basically inseparable and thus places the observer in the midst of the action. There is no such thing as a detached spectator of the world. Hence Heidegger points to important aspects of subjectiveness related to our perception of the world. If we trust Heidegger on this point it implies that there is no such thing as objective experience. Experience is an extension of the self. It is a particular person's special relationship to the rest of the world. Both Husserl and Heidegger are important in order to understand the purpose of both ontologies and data. *Ontologies* define the knowledge of world entities. It implies a person's structural perception of the world around him/her.

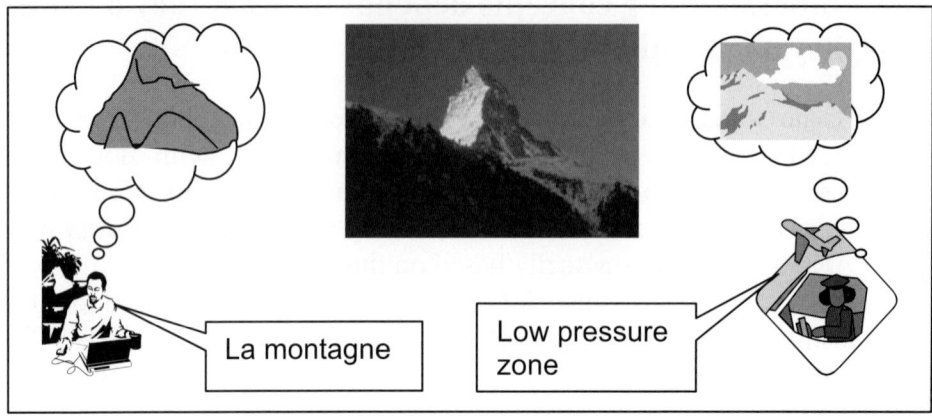

Figure 4.1: Difference in perception of the world, the author and the pilot

Given that we accept the view of Heidegger, it is imperative to acknowledge that two people can never gain exactly the same view of the world. In order to share ideas of the same world they need to find ways of sharing their experience of it. Naturally, one way of doing this is through an ordinary dialogue. The challenge is then to map what they have experienced onto the knowledge of the other observer. This challenge is amplified not only by the different impressions of the world, but also the environment that developed the language to articulate at least part of what they experienced. We see that Frege's reference model constitutes a basis for this. It also tells us that our experiences form the concepts in our mind (Figure 4.1). This again forges our ways of communication. Language must be used to bridge experience. But daily language itself contains the type of ambiguities that Frege worked hard to remove from the language of logic. Hence we are faced with three types of mismatches: the subjectiveness of experience that yields a type of subjectiveness in expression and an expression that uses a language that is prone with ambiguities and incomplete references.

4.6. Language meaning depends on how we use it

Another modern philosopher was Wittgenstein. His early concerns were tied to the task of describing phenomena. At that time Wittgenstein used logic as formalism for natural language, whereas Frege had already demonstrated the power of a pure formalism for logic. Wittgenstein tried to show that language was as an image of reality that corresponds exactly to logic. During his career Wittgenstein developed his ideas about language and he became firm in his belief that we had to attempt to understand the concepts that language addressed and not the language itself. Clearly there is a distinction between the word and the concept [Wittgenstein, 1968]:

> *"You say: the point isn't the word, but its meaning, and you think the meaning as a thing of the same kind as the word, though also different from the word. Here the word, there the meaning. The money, and the cow that you can buy with it".*
>
> *-- Wittgenstein --*

Wittgenstein clearly expresses concern about words as the holder of a meaning that is faithful to the world concept that it addresses. Clearly this is not so. We know very well that a word can have several different meanings. This is daily a cause for misinterpretation. It is also the reason that we introduce redundancy into speech. When we try to explain difficult phenomena we often use different words and sentence that point to the same concept. It is also the reason why we raise or lower our voice, point a finger, raise an eyebrow, produce a fry smile and wave our hands when we talk. We simply overload our messages with redundant phrases and body signs to assure that our real meaning is conveyed. This of course, is not easy to do with the existing computer systems.

Wittgenstein was content that the true conception of the world could not necessarily be conveyed by the word alone, but by its use. Hence context came forward as an important issue. "For a large class of cases – though not for all – in which we employ the word 'meaning' it can be defined thus: the meaning of a word is its use in the language".

4.7. Relativism in art and science – a modern virtue in the Western world

According to Miller [2000], the effort of representing nature has always been a central problem for scientists and artists in the Western world. There is evidence that there has been a mutual influence such that the effort and opinions of scientists have been absorbed in arts and vice versa. Miller states that Albrecht Dürer and Leonardo da Vinci, among other Renaissance artists, struggled with mathematical and physiological problems concerning linear perspective.

In the late nineteenth and early twentieth centuries, artists once again became interested in problems of space and time. Miller tells us that Georges Braque, Paul Cézanne, and Picasso were preoccupied with this during their career. It is an interesting historic issue that Braque and Picasso discovered Cubism in Paris at the same time that Einstein discovered relativity in Bern. This stirred heated discussions in terms of objectiveness and subjectiveness. Western art and science, like philosophy, have at times been in dire straits regarding this. In particle physics the issue surfaces in full force with the departure from the Newtonian world image to Einstein's' "new world" order. The same discussion in terms of relativity and observers vantage point can be seen in discussion on art. The concepts of beauty and aesthetics have always been an issue. Miller's objective assessments of aesthetics and beauty attempt to remove subjective elements. The aesthetician Clive Bell (1881-1964) was a British art critic and philosopher of art who defended abstract art. Bell's aesthetic theory was focused on aesthetic experience. He claimed that objective viewing of a painting requires that "we need bring with us nothing from life, no knowledge of its ideas and affairs, no familiarity with its emotions". The circle around Picasso felt an urge to liberate themselves from the traditional observer's perspective in their representation of the world. They were strongly interested in non-Euclidean geometry. The result was Cubism, where the artist tries to interpret the world by moving around and capturing several successive appearances of that world. Consequently a painting will reflect multiple viewpoints at the same time.

Miller also claims that traces of the same discussion on relativism appear in modern linguistics albeit not with the same strong emphasis. Two linguists Edward Sapir and Benjamin S. Whorf were early advocators of this view [Whorf, 1956]. Despite an evident flaw in their fieldwork they gave rise to discussions on conceptual relativism that claim that different cultures with different languages have such different worldviews that they could not communicate with each other. This is a radical view that does not have broad support. Theories of linguistic incommensurability are radical and must be considered a side movement. Yet there is clearly the notion of differences in point of view, but only with a kind of coordinate system that can act as reference across time. Causal theory permits meaning to change while the reference remains fixed. That is to say that the use of the language may change, but the ontology remains the same.

The above paragraphs illustrate that it is difficult to come to terms with the task of representing the world. Yet the emergence of relativism has come forward. Today we cannot escape the fact that Einstein was right. We are also intrigued by the Picassonian expression. Almost everyone who has seen the picture "La Guernica" (Figure 4.2) depicting the terror of bombardment on the Basque town during the Spanish civil war is struck by the drama and the emotion that the picture presents. A close-up view of the various elements of the picture reveals a simple Cubist syntax. To some, this is a far-fetched abstraction that is very remote from the common understanding of a piece of art. Yet, step backwards a few metres and the meaning and the emotion that it stirs emerge through the wholeness of the artistic expression. Move sideways and you will catch a glimpse of a perspective that was not immediately apparent from the first point of observation. Move back and forth in front of the picture and your movement will impose a kind of animated impression of an unfolding drama. This is the genius of Picasso. He makes the audience participants. The experience that we attribute to Picasso is nevertheless a personal one.

Figure 4.2: "La Guernica", Pablo Picasso, 1937

What does this imply for efforts related to knowledge management? First of all, the Western tradition of relativism is new. Our traditions in relative thinking about the world are less than a century old. In most schools and universities in Europe, the Newtonian and Rembrandtian world order still dominates. We think any successful knowledge management effort that seeks to build autonomous professional groups that should be self-adjusting with respect to each other should abandon this worldview. This worldview calls for an objective truth implying that a person or group may hold ownership to the truth. That is the mother of all knowledge sharing failures. *Relativism* implies that we project our personal worldviews and place within a context that allows others to adjust to it, recognizing that the context may in part define a sufficient co-ordinate system for the various participants to understand each other. Truth ownership must thus be abandoned. Even popular claims of past education must let go. In a true knowledge-sharing effort a reference from Stanford is no good, but the experience may be. In order to learn more of this we should look to the East.

4.8. Elements of the Japanese world order

In their seminal work on knowledge building, Nonaka and Takeuchi [1995] regard the traditional scientific approach of the Western world as an obstacle to understanding the tacit nature of people's knowledge and how it can be shared. They throw a critical light on the Western tradition of objectifying nature. They point out that there is a major difference between Western philosophy and Japanese philosophical tradition that could be the major reason for a different understanding of what knowledge types should play a major role. Japanese epistemology has nurtured a delicate and sophisticated sensitivity to nature, it has prevented the objectification of nature and the development of what they call "the Western scepticism". Despite the fact that it is hard to look past a currently common reasoning paradigm, even scientists in the West could support such a claim. On top of that Briggs and Peat [1999] call for a new perception of the world that looks at wholeness instead of considering a separate "objective" truth as standing next to various "subjective" perceptions of the world. Briggs and Peat cite the writer and physicist Fritjof Capra who claims that the human race is experiencing a "crisis of perception". This perception yields a fragmented, analytic view of reality that is inadequate for dealing with our overpopulated interconnected world. He attributes this crisis to the traditional mechanical view of the world in the Western society so strongly advocated by Descartes.

Nonaka and Takeuchi are quite clear about the influence that world perception has on language. Basic attitudes associated with the "oneness of humanity and nature" in Japanese epistemology can also be found in the structure of the Japanese language. Physical and concrete images of objects are indispensable for Japanese expression. Japanese think visually and manipulate tangible images. In Japanese, statements made by the speaker articulate certain concrete images. The Japanese language is characterized by visual concepts that are highly context-specific in terms of both time and space".

To draw this line of reasoning somewhat further: Zen Buddhism formulated the principle of oneness of body and mind. According to Nonaka and Takeuchi, Zen profoundly affected the Samurai tradition. The first principle in Samurai education was being a man of action. Cognizing the world in terms of words is not central in this Samurai and Zen philosophy, something that Nonaka claims has coloured the general thinking in Japanese society today.

According to Nonaka and Takeuchi, the inherent characteristics of the Japanese language reveal a unique view of time and space. The Japanese see time as a continuous flow of permanently updated "present". Many Japanese novels do not have any fixed time point in their plots, and traditional Japanese poems are free from any fixed time perspective. In contrast, Westerners have a sequential view of time and grasp the present and forecast the future in a historical retrospection of the past. The Japanese view of time is more circular and momentalistic. Everything appears and disappears occasionally and ultimate reality is confined to here and now. The Japanese view of space is also free from a fixed perspective, as is clearly depicted in traditional Japanese art. Since the perspective is not fixed there is no need to draw shadows.

A typical Western way of perceiving the world is to conceptualize things from an objective vantagepoint. Opposed to that, Japanese would rather relate themselves to the things and persons that the world encompasses. Hence there is an interpersonal acceptance of the world as it is. A message is often transferred through the use of context, not solely by a self-complete grammatical code. This can be seen from the fact that verbs in the Japanese language do not conjugate with the subject of the sentence. In Indo-European languages, verbs basically conjugate in accordance with the subject because the meaning of a verb is always used in the same form in any context. The perspective of the speaker can thus be shared naturally and smoothly by the group because of the sympathetic nature of the verb".

4.9. Implications of communication and knowledge sharing

Truly traditional Japanese thinking clearly converges with ideas that have gradually emerged in certain camps in the West since Frege. However, this also tells us that as member of the Western tradition we may carry ballast that makes it difficult to approach the knowledge sharing effort in a manner that produces prime results. Other observations tend to point in the same direction. If we look at, for instance, Japanese industrial traditions and in particular their car industries, we find practices that are well established supporting the principles discussed here. "Toyotaism" is about carefully and detailed communication of how to perform work, supported by a culture of mutual help and exchange of know-how. Many Western leaders have been puzzled that their system did not work, even though a similar type worked for the Japanese. There are several things that indicate that such a system was incompatible with the Western mind set and management traditions.

For reasons discussed above, it is felt to be necessary to shift position towards a more holistic, non-linear approach. Inspired by the fact that other cultures place different emphasis on language and dialectics and still communicate we have to revise our opinion of what should be the main carrier of the knowledge that we want share and build. The underlying principle is that the world we live in, interact with and try to understand is dynamic and highly multi-dimensional in its appearances. This is clearly reflected in natural language by the use of prepositional expressions as the common way of pinning down an event or thing in terms of time and/or place.

The way we should proceed in order to capture the essence of experience and knowledge from both people and written documentation resides not so much with the absolute definition of the words applied, but with their usage and the context instead. Simply spoken, shared values and shared backgrounds alleviate the burden of effective communication. This indicates that knowledge sharing is more than expressing things by words and icons, but creating fundamental sharing culture, in terms of attitudes, values, principles, behaviour and responsibility. In fact, we believe that the aspects of common rhetoric are less important to achieve good knowledge-sharing practice. This must be much more action oriented in turn to be effective.

Consequently, this calls for the use of demonstrations and interaction. It calls for involvement of the learner as well as the tutor. It should indicate that a knowledge management system is not a textbook converted to an on-line resource, but an instrument to generate understandings through action and involvement. Clearly this also determines the way we should structure our communication effort. Indeed the principles that we have treated here should lie at the heart of all means for knowledge sharing. Getting connected is just a preliminary step. Building an Intranet is not necessarily an act of communication and even less a step towards knowledge sharing if these principles are not observed.

Chapter 4 Information, Knowledge and Meaning

4.10. Principles to be observed

Based on this we have tried to sum up our discussion into a set of principles to be observed while working with knowledge-sharing efforts. They must be considered maxims that are constantly revised due to increasingly more research in this area. The world is still experimenting.

4.10.1. Context

There seems to be a growing consensus that understanding and speech capabilities are strongly influenced by context and environment. We will not make any claim that language capabilities are not hard wired into people at birth. Yet it is clear that every spoken language is alive and develops in its own way within a community. Understanding the context and a shared view of objectives, situation and values seems to be a fundamental prerequisite for understanding the use of words and icons as well as their meaning.

4.10.2. Expectation- driven understanding

Memories of historic episodes act as references for understanding *entities*. The conceptual representation associated with it is an instrument for language interpretation and interpreting the goals from actions observed. Candidate memory structures can be triggered based on certain key reminders. This initial reminding can retrieve memory resources that can aid in providing full interpretation. Hence it is important that we are able in our communication effort to identify such triggers that stimulate experience. Stories are often good triggers. The imagination that good stories provoke can have profound effect on understanding. The introduction of a key description or action generates expectations of what will follow. Expectations are generated through associations. Associations are in turn dependent on structural relationships between world concepts encapsulated by the memory.

4.10.3. Subjectivity

Understanding is subjective. This follows from the two other items discussed above. Situation and place determine context. People's experiences are never exactly the same. Hence two interpretations of the world will never be identical. Since both situation and place seem to influence understanding it is clear that subjectivity plays an important role.

In addition we could have added the difference in goals and values. People's diverse objectives and both ethical and esthetical values govern their perception. We believe that this will impose great constraints on any perception of the real world and thus the experienced need to understand others. Taxonomies of terms must be related to both context and the way the terms are used as well as to what they address.

4.10.4. *Syntax versus semantics*

Over the past 30 years there has been an ongoing discussion on what focus to sustain, syntax or semantics, in order to pursue good communication. Much faith has been lent to the former. Yet we see a tendency that both are important. There must be significant interplay between syntax and semantic modelling. In fact the whole issue of understanding circulates around the process of establishing a set of meaningful symbols that are related to each other. In terms of written expressions and content management this implies that it is not sufficient to focus on the text alone, but on the whole system of author, author's knowledge, author's goals and constraints, author's world, chosen vocabulary, listener's context and listener's knowledge. The work of Ram *et al.* (1999) is a recent and impressive contribution in this direction.

4.10.5. *Discretization*

In cognitive psychology, symbol theory is very strong. This applies to what is called the ontological assumption. There seem to be enough evidence to maintain focus on symbols. One reason is the language itself. Wolff [1991] points out that young children seem to discretize language according to entities they observe. This is how they organize the world around them. Yet we must not be led to believe that there is a one-to-one mapping between the concepts experienced and the language created, even within the confined world of a small child.

Tacit knowledge may not be a problem of incomplete dialectics, but an issue related to comprehension. It may seem that action-oriented experience can only be really expressed through demonstration. In fact, it may seem at times that even the masters themselves do not consciously conceive the complex nature of a skill in depth. We should not take the ontological assumption for granted, but challenge it in order to get beyond the stage of simple taxonomies and aggregations. Based on this the limitations of glossaries are evident. Dreyfus [1977] calls for caution. We still have a long way to go in order to understand how knowledge should be represented so that it can be made transparent and readily available for others. The ontological assumption implies that everything essential for intelligent behaviour must in principle be understandable in terms of a set of determinate independent elements. There is no evidence yet that this is so. Quite on the contrary the discretization process is difficult and there is no clear criteria that tell us that the discrete knowledge representation is finite.

Our position is thus to keep a sustained point of convergence on symbols and tokens, but not limit ourselves to that. Work in Artificial Neural Networks, pattern recognition, statistics (as pointed out for vector based similarity metrics above) as well as cybernetics have all shown that continuous variable approaches can do well in terms of representing knowledge, and in many cases outperform symbolic systems for certain applications. On a human level it implies that we may not be able to capture the full content of what a person knows. It also implies that we may struggle to find terms that will clearly address the concepts that we think of. These may be part of a continuous pattern or movement that may be hard to describe and explain. This is typical for skills such as golf. A vocal description of how to play golf well can at best be a good introduction. The real expertise lies in the continuous movement of the swing, which the master repeats over and over again and which is so hard for novices to capture.

People's escape is to combine word-based descriptions with mimics and even demonstrations. This is part of our day-to-day strategy and most people use it all the time. This combination is currently more difficult to apply systematically for a computer-based system such as the Intranet. But the use of graphics is one step along this route. Flow charts, for instance, can be fair representations of professional behaviour. However, with the advent of interactive videos, flash techniques and virtual reality the problem may soon be dramatically reduced. The use of active demonstrations and virtual reality techniques in the context of knowledge sharing is discussed later in conjunction with the FAROS system.

4.11. Conclusions

Efficient knowledge sharing is built on good communication regardless of what means of transmission is applied. People use more than speech in order to convey their thoughts and ideas to their peers. Such things as body language and setting create an important framework for mutual understanding. Communication theory and technology have been preoccupied with signal capacity, such as channel breath and speed. Yet communication is more about language. Not necessarily the language that different nationalities use, but the language that stimulates the mind and insight of the listener. People's background and experience differ. Their ability to understand and share depends on how well they can relate their existing knowledge to the new. We have argued that only when we acknowledge that there is no objective in the interpretation of concepts that we are able to build a basis for true knowledge sharing. Common understanding must be achieved through a process of consensus. This represents something new to Western thinking. The traditional pursuit for objective truth in Western thinking might jeopardize sincere efforts to establish a knowledge-sharing culture. The best way to establish mutual understanding of concepts is through focus on what the concepts can do or be used. This contrasts with the more traditional way that defines what the concepts are. Through this approach it is believed that computers and computer networks can serve an important purpose. It is relatively easy to capture the way in which people work and depict this in a simple way. When access to this is given through a computer network efficient knowledge sharing can be achieved. This is discussed in more detail in the subsequent chapters about the FAROS approach.

4.12. Lessons learned

These are the lessons that we think are valuable for any practical effort knowledge sharing:

- **Information, Knowledge and Meaning**
  Communication is more than signal transmission. The principal goal of all communication must be to convey meaning. Masses of data cannot compensate for a single meaningful cue. Perception and experience are subjective and context specific. Communication paradigms that limit the transmission of the context and ignore the subjective side in all communication will not be good platforms for any knowledge-sharing activity.

- **Articulation of experience is language dependent**
  The tacitness associated with expertise can be a real problem for efficient knowledge sharing. Experts are often "knowledge rich, but language lean". They simply have insufficient exercise in articulating

Chapter 4 Information, Knowledge and Meaning 143

their insight. Even then it might be difficult. It is not given that concepts are discrete and allow themselves to be defined and expressed by a one or a few terms.

In order to express expertise it is more important that your effort triggers established concepts in the mind of those you want to share your knowledge with. There is no such thing as an objective perception of the real world. There cannot be any objectiveness about the communication. Common understanding takes place when two minds share the same view of the world.

- **Focus on how concepts are used or what they can do**
  In order to externalize knowledge for the purpose of knowledge sharing it is likely that a focus on what concepts can do or can be applied is the best approach. It is easier to express and can be assisted by simple graphics or in more complicated situations, demonstrations. Action-oriented expressions are much easier to relate to than structurally oriented descriptions and are far easier to relate to than pure definitions.

  People relate to the real world according to what they are, their background and the given situation (time and place) they find themselves in. It is important to recognize that and relate any expression of know-how in terms of that. In the context of a company, it is important to use the overall behaviour of the company as a framework for a common means to relate individual experience with others. It is through a process of gradual consensus that knowledge sharing will prosper.

- **The most important principles**
  The most important principles of knowledge sharing and real communication are related to the following:
    - Context
    - Expectations
    - Subjectivity
    - Syntax and semantics of the language used
    - Our ability to discretize our perception of the world and express that by means of symbols, icons or terms.

REFERENCES

1. Briggs J. and David, P. F. D. (1999). *Seven Life Lessons of Chaos*. Harper Collins.

2. Dreyfus, H., (1979), *What Computers Can't Do* (Rev. edit), *The Limits of Artificial Intelligence*. Harper Colophon Books.

3. Nonaka, I. and Takeuchi, H. (1995), *The Knowledge-Creating Company*. Oxford Reference Book Society.

4. Ram, A. A. (1999), *Theory of Questions and Question Asking*. In Understanding Language Understanding Ed. (Ram and Moorman). Bradford MIT.

5. Shannon, C. G., (1948), *A Mathematical Theory of Communication*. The Bell System Technical Journal, Vol. 27, pp.379-423.

6. Wittgenstein L. (1968). Wittgenstein's Note for Lectures on "Private Experience" and "Sense Data".

7. Wolff, J. G. (1991), *Towards a Theory of Cognition and Computing*. Ellis Horwood, Chichester.

8. Whorf, B. L., (1956), *Language, thought, and reality*. Boston: MIT Press.

CHAPTER 5

MODEL
– THE STRUCTURE AND DYNAMICS OF A KNOWLEDGE MANAGEMENT SYSTEM

Objectives

- Understand the holistic knowledge management model.
- What is the Faros concept?
- What is the knowledge navigator?
- How important are cultural aspects in knowledge management?
- Understand the learning effect and innovation.

5.1. Introduction

A company has to learn better than its competitors and apply that knowledge throughout its business faster and more widely than the competitors do.

John Browne, CEO, BP-Amoco

In Chapters 3 and 4, you have learned about the technical infrastructure of *knowledge management systems* (KMS) and the basic concepts and approaches for knowledge discovery, capture, sharing, transferring and utilization in an organization. This chapter will discuss the purpose and structure of a holistic model of KMS and explain why a holistic model is important for developing a KMS in your enterprise.

Any football coach in the premier league will tell you why a holistic understanding of the game is important. With today's playing pattern, and the players' speed and flexibility, it is not enough just to understand his position in the game, and defend it without understanding the total strategy and tactics of the game. Unless each and every member of the team understand the total picture, how the individual fits the picture, and what processes he has to do to produce results, both he and his team mates will end up being walked over, and wondering what hit them.

You need to understand the whole picture, and how each part fits together to create value, in order to function as a winning team. By *holistic* we mean all-encompassing and inclusive despite individual differences. A holistic model is to give all members of a team access to all relevant data (Just-in-time Just-enough) required to make a valuable contribution to the organization. The vision that guided the development of the Faros model can be called the *Faros vision*. It was both simple and honest:

- Make our colleagues' workday simpler with a better overview of the data and information that formed the basis for work performance.
- Make the value creating work processes qualitatively better, safer and more secure.

But for the vision to come to fruition, the model must encompass all elements of a collaborative process, either between two people, two teams or company wide. Thus, it is not technology per se that makes the model function, it is the people and the way the management chooses to structure its organization. (Although, without technology a business system model with knowledge management inside, would not be able to utilize to the same extent the knowledge sitting around in artefacts and people's minds).

We see clear evidence of a breakdown of tall hierarchies. It has been going on for some time, but over the last few of years visionary leaders have understood the contradiction between tall hierarchies on the one hand, and increased educational level and more effective methods of production, on the other. Thus, two of the drivers for a knowledge-based economy are a better educated workforce combined with more effective methods of production. This is the core of a knowledge-based economy – an educated work force focusing on improvement and innovation fed into the business system.

The vision of future business systems is twofold:

1. Simplify and automate routine work, both production and service activities, managed through the system
2. Prepare the employees for the role of a knowledge workers

A knowledge worker is capable of creating and sharing knowledge for continuous improvement, innovation and organizational change. Just like the coach on the winning football team, the CEO on the winning business team will be using the holistic approach to secure success.

5.2. Background

A *Business System* equals a holistic knowledge management system (KMS) (the two terminologies will be used interchangeable), and is a managerial approach that focuses on an organization's ability to utilize its intellectual capital for *knowledge creation, propagation* and *movement*. The interchangeable terminology between *Business System* and *holistic knowledge management* is primarily due to required accountability between corporate strategy and its execution by the work force. We will primarily use KM or KMS.

This chapter presents an analysis of an established knowledge management system, its processes and functions served by the system. This synthetic model might serve the practical application of knowledge management just as grammar serves a language. As a grammar is best described by language examples, the grammar of knowledge management will be illustrated by examples from Faros. A grammar defines how the building block of a language can be put together. Our building blocks constitute the syntax for knowledge sharing

The *Faros[2] model* is a value chain and work process oriented knowledge management concept based on the principles of a dynamic process oriented business system. In a process oriented KM system, the transfer of information, learning and innovation follows the process/product stream, making the work arena dynamic. This chapter also gives an analytical abstraction of the Faros KMS, which we term the Holistic Faros Model. Knowledge creation is the central theme in a

---

[2] Faros (Pharos) comes from the Greek word Pyr, means fire. In 288 BC, a 3-storey, 100 metre-high lighthouse was built on the island Pyr off the Mediterranean port of Alexandria. Pharos is considered one of the Seven Wonders of the World.

knowledge-based economy. The *Faros knowledge management system* (Faros KMS) was developed initially to support the upstream and midstream work and decision processes in Statoil - The Norwegian state oil company

In 1972, the Norwegian Government decided to establish its own oil company in order to participate directly in the oil industry unfolding on the Norwegian continental shelf. As an integrated oil and gas company, Statoils objective is, either by itself or through participation together with other companies, to carry out exploration, production, transportation, refining and marketing of petroleum and petroleum-derived products, as well as other business. In 2000, Statoil traded some two million barrels of crude and condensate (light oil) every day. With its close to 18 000 employees the company is present in several large global oil provinces, including the Caspian Sea, offshore Angola, and in Venezuela. In Norway it operates several fields, such as Statfjord and Troll, which are among the largest offshore oil and gas fields in the world. The company's net operating revenue for 2000 was USD 23 billion.

Faros was completed at the end of 1999 after more than four years of development. The solution as well as the approach to arrive at the technological realization is generic, scalable, and it is believed to be adaptable to any corporation or business.

Today, most agree that knowledge management is concerned with effectively connecting those who know with those who need to know, and, furthermore, being able to convert personal knowledge into organizational knowledge. There also seems to be an agreement that managing knowledge requires collaborative understanding. Managing collaboration requires special skills, less emphasis on individual achievement, more on teamwork, as well as effective connectivity.

> *KM, therefore, is the discipline required to achieve organizational learning, that is, an organization's ability to share and utilize its intellectual capital (IC) for capturing, creating, delivering and using knowledge.*

The term intellectual capital represents the total assets less tangible assets, i.e., human capital, patents, trademarks and the like [Edvinsson, 1997].

In order to succeed in turning personal knowledge into organizational knowledge, one needs a repository and navigational system for structured and unstructured information, and a philosophy of redundancy. When building Faros, we discovered that the best repository for the collective memory base was the development of a work process model, and the navigational approach was through a so-called "*Knowledge Room*", where we developed "the multiple ways to Rome". Therefore, a knowledge management system (KMS) is the structure required for creating dynamic organizations for learning that results in:

- Rapid response to changing business environment
- Continuous improvement and innovation
- Improved bottom-line results.

Economic historians have termed the period up to the twentieth century the first *Industrial Revolution* (IR), while the twentieth century has been named the second IR. It is suggested that the third IR, starting with the new millennium, should be termed the Knowledge-based Economy or Era [Thurow, 1999]. Due to the Information and Communication Technology revolution, some are calling the new era the Information Economy. This is a fallacy, as information per se does not affect Maslow's law. Information must still be converted to knowledge so that we can grow food and build shelter. *Information and communication technology* (ICT) is just a technical enabler for the organization to create a more effective KMS. As pointed out earlier communication is much more than technology.

The research and development process essentially merged into one flow as we created the Faros concept. Its first element was having the users describe their workflows and information requirements/categorization in "brown paper sessions". Standardized business modelling methods were employed [Porter, 1985]. Interlinked web documents were developed on this basis, including graphic representations and textual information. Mechanisms for review, revision and maintenance were established. Figure 5.1 describes the relation between the "grammar" (model) and the "language" (realization) of knowledge management.

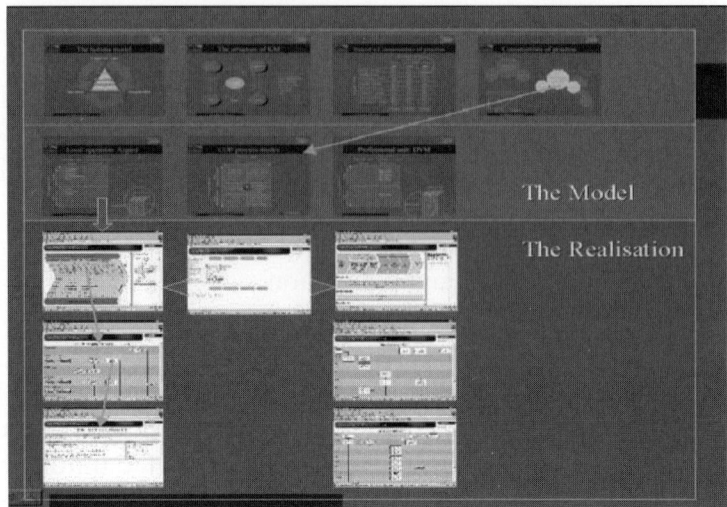

Figure 5.1: Relation between the "grammar" and the "language" of KM

5.3. Ideas and structure of a holistic KM system

Frederick W. Taylor (1911) in the early 20th century was encouraged by reform-minded progressives who sought to improve the lot of the middle classes and their employers. Since the time of Taylorism, the Western world has tried to create scientific management out of social science activities. Moving from owner-manager companies into corporations using hired-in professional managers to run the affairs of the owners, *Taylorism* became the modern business world's first fad.

Taylor's *scientific management* tried to create a revolutionary movement and proposed the reduction of waste through the careful study of work. The Taylor method prescribed a clockwork world of tasks timed to the hundredth of a minute, of standardized factories, machines, women and men. Naturally, ordinary workers resented having to work faster then they thought was healthy or fair. However, in case after case, time and motion studies were not used as the sole basis for setting normative output. Acknowledging that workers could not sustain peak level performances all day long, they used a margin of error or fudge factor of as much as a third to set a more realistic level. This of course, struck at the credibility that Taylor's system was based on scientific laws.

Unfortunately for the continuation of organizational development, Taylorism became so ingrained in both business and business schools, that generation after generation of managers throughout the industrial world thought it literally possible to control human capital by a stopwatch. Since Taylorism, many management fads have popped up only to fall down like an empty balloon.

The holistic KM model recognizes human capital as one of the three cornerstones of a modern organization, creating real value for its owners. Thus, the system must be able to address the needs of the employees and management in a symbiosis required by a world in change. We are not regarding the model as just another fad, but as an answer to a structural change in the market place resulting from the new paradigm - the knowledge-based economy. Below is a partial list of needs to be addressed in a model:

- Accessibility of information
- Unified navigation (a common knowledge room)
- Holistic
- Focused on value creating issues
- Action oriented (dynamic process structure)
- Knowledge production and sharing
- Inclusive in its form regardless of stakeholder's position

The basic concept, therefore, is the design of a system to secure navigational capability aimed at serving each employee of the organization with "just-in-time just-enough" information at the point of decision, and minimize routine work so that human capital can be directed towards improving the value creating processes of the organization. This includes a common navigational metaphor, with a primary focus on the organization's value change. The end result must be improvement, innovation and organizational change resulting in added profitability for the stakeholders.

The structure of the holistic model is aiming at creating a shell where each operating or functional element of the organization is identified, evaluated and illustrated. Through a common navigator (a knowledge room), one is guided through the operating - and supporting work processes down into sub-processes where one finds the relevant process. From here the user of the process can get a description of the individual activities within the sub-process, or links to what prerequisites are needed in order to carry out the activities. All processes are based on, and cascade from, the *management process* in a hierarchical structure. Through the Management Work Process each sub-process and activity is linked to the organization's Vision, Purpose and Strategy reflected in the Management Process.

5.4. The holistic knowledge management model

The ambitious term holistic implies that the model must include and support stakeholders and processes at all levels and all cardinal points in an organization. It must support a flow of knowledge that allows each organizational unit to function according to corporate strategies and requirements, from the production line up to the overall corporate strategy and value. And, it must be able to support an organization in change. That includes effective experience transfer systems both for the operating and expert groups, and a method for developing good practice.

Faros has been created on the basis of a holistic philosophy around the issue of managing knowledge within the organization's integrated value chain. What do we mean by "holistic" and by "managing knowledge"? According to some experts, knowledge cannot be managed. Knowledge can be divided into two elements:

1. Knowledge in the owner's minds
2. Knowledge embedded in artefacts

We consider the first type to be the responsibility of the individual employee, while the second type is the responsibility of management and employees in a collaborative process. The arena for this process is embedded in the concept of knowledge management. Thus, one can only manage knowledge where it is embedded in artefacts, and only in cooperation with the employees for which the knowledge is intended.

Holistic means an organization's ability to develop a KM concept encompassing all units in the enterprise with one common platform. Whether they are operational or service activities, by applying a standard structure for navigating the many rolls and activities, every employee achieves direct access to information, experience transfer and learning. This holistic concept gives transparency, agility and flexibility in the organization's efforts for continuous improvement and innovation of its value chain.

Fundamental elements of the development philosophy were:

- The concept of *Community of Practice* (COP) as described by Wenger (1999), which describes Statoil's organization.
- The Value Chain concept of Porter (1990) with its inherent work processes.

Chapter 5 Model – The Structure and Dynamics of a KMS 153

While designing Faros, we tried to pay attention to the needs in all Communities of Practice's [Wenger, 1999] relationships to the organization's *stakeholders*: the owners, managers, operating and professional employees, suppliers, customers and the society at large. All employees, from the top to bottom, should be able to retrieve any information relevant to serving, collaborating and connecting with, all stakeholders. But only by understanding the information elements' internal relationship and having access to all relevant information and a capacity to act for the good of, and in collaboration with other stakeholders can new and relevant knowledge be created. The reason for this is that managing knowledge does not concern itself only with the knowledge resided in repositories belonging to a few professional thinkers, but to all employees in an organization.

The holistic model must include attributes of the organization that originate in the "production line" and move up to the overall corporate strategy and value (see Figure 5.2). In addition it means that management-oriented concepts such as goals and strategies must be made transparent to the same production lines.

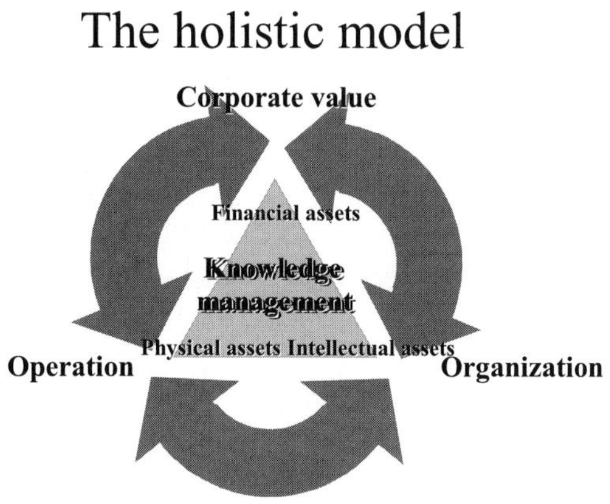

The holistic model

Figure 5.2: The holistic model

5.4.1. The structure of knowledge management

Most commercial production organizations may be divided as *Business Units* and *Service Units*. The holistic approach is to embrace both functions in the approach to Capture, Create, Deliver and Use (CCDU) knowledge.

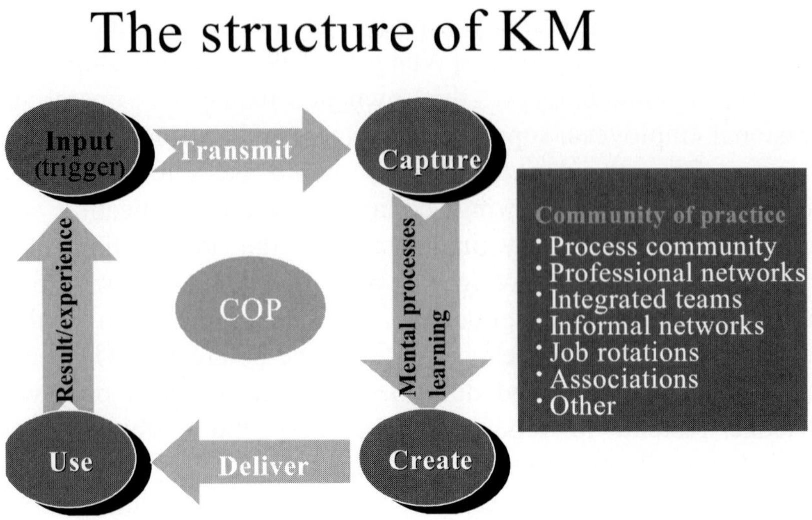

The structure of KM

Figure 5.3: The structure of a knowledge management

Each sequence of CCDU adds to corporate knowledge, and a series of turns may be said to represent a spiral of knowledge. A KMS must serve the function of capturing, searching/retrieving and putting knowledge to use in a new loop.

The spiral takes place within, and among, the Communities of Practice, as can be seen in Figure 5.3. Furthermore, the model is based on the synergy between the operating and service (functional) units (Figure 5.4 and Figure 5.5). While the high level picture is simple, the real problem is in the details. We will now examine some generalized processes at the cross-section between the expert COPs and the business COPs.

5.4.1.1. Local operating situation

Within a *Business Unit* there are both weak (single task operation) and strong (multitask operation by self-supporting units) elements of co-operation, as identified on the vertical axis in Figure 5.4 and Figure 5.5 below. During normal operating conditions, the Business Unit is self-sufficient regarding the functional support offered by the service units.

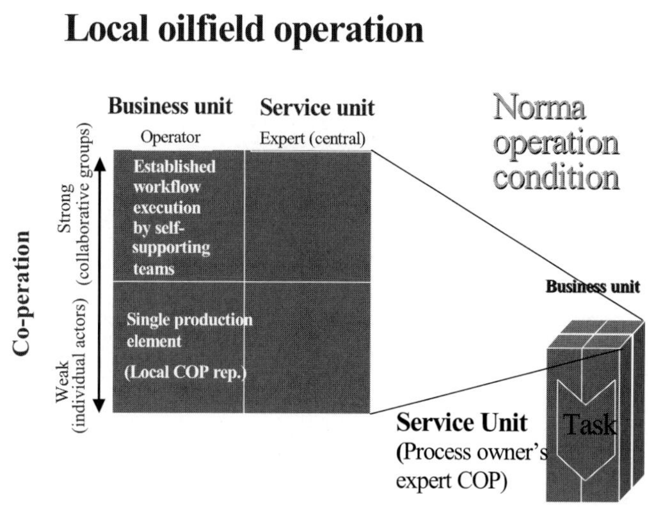

Chapter 5 Model – The Structure and Dynamics of a KMS

Local oilfield operation

Figure 5.4: Local oilfield operation

5.4.1.2. Local service situation

The function of a *Service Unit* is to support the *Business Unit*. This can be done either as a single task (expert) or a multi problem-solving task (team). Aided by technology, the venue for the activity can be either at the Business or Service Unit's place of work. Connectivity and communication is therefore essential when collaborative tasks. Thus, it is not the venue, but the nature of the activity, that dictates the strength of the cooperation within an organization. As we pointed out earlier knowledge drives goal-oriented actions. By focusing on value creating activities we create the basis for making the required know-how to create value explicitly. The KM model based on the value chain and within that, the work process, as one entity, gives transparency to the cooperation, and task responsibility between the various roles, of the value chain.

156   5.4. The holistic knowledge management model

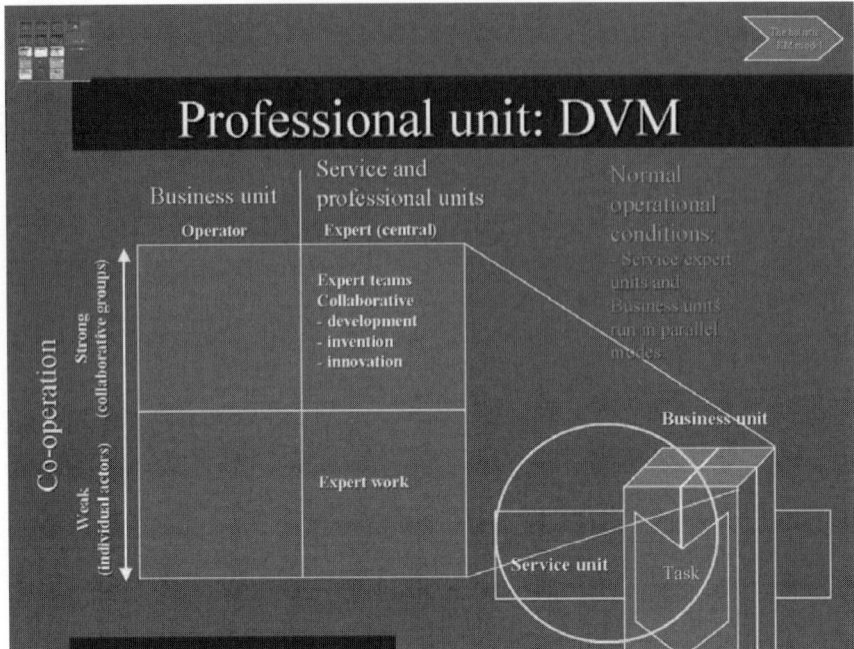

Figure 5.5: Professional unit: DVM[3]

5.4.2. The process model

In Figure 5.6, the process model contains the four modes as seen in Figure 5.4 and Figure 5.5, two within the Business Unit (Transaction and Integrated production) and two within the Service Unit (expert and collaborative problem solving). The four quadrants represent all activities and human capital within the organization. It encompasses a holistic and goal focused model. In a situation of normal operations in a given Business Unit, the two sets of modes run independently of each other.

The process owner is located in the Service Unit, and coordinates the operators' experience with members of the COPs within the given discipline. Depending on the nature of the problem, the solution can be found in a collaborative mode or an expert mode. Once a problem occurs beyond the scope of local solution, a request will go to the process owner to be solved.

If the solution is found to be of general interest, it will be incorporated into the corporate knowledge base through COP vetting. The

---

[3] DVM (in Norwegian: drift, vedlikehold og modifikasjon) meaning operation, maintenance and modification

solution can lead to an improved Good Practice, or a change in the corporate or operating policies. Also low recurrence operating tasks, resulting in statements like "How did I do this operation?" are common issues supported by Faros and collected for improved operating practices.

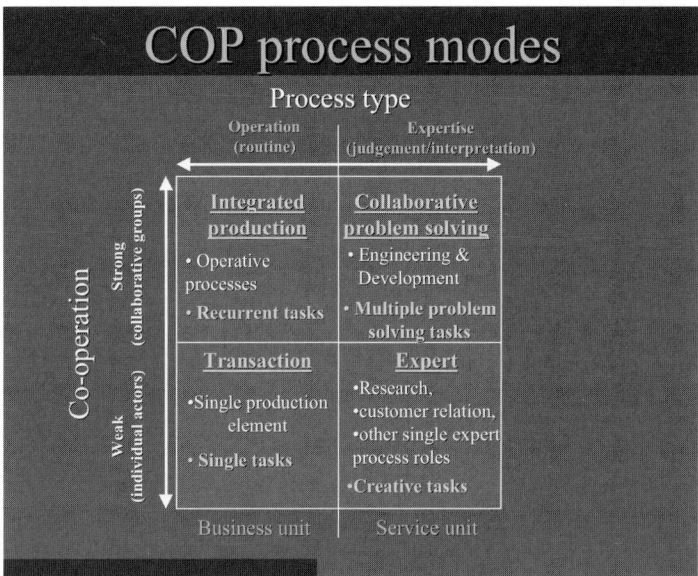

Figure 5.6: COP process model

The four modes discussed above are the Transaction and Integrated Production modes found in the *Operating Units*, and the Collaborative Problem Solving and Expert modes found in the Service Units. While the Business Units are, per definition, responsible for operating the unit's assets through a set of work processes, the Service Units are responsible for developing, in cooperation with representatives of the Business Units, all main work processes to be applied by the Business Units. This is to secure the application of good practice throughout the organization. Furthermore, the Service Units are responsible for developing their own work process. By being responsible for reviewing and adding new good practice to the work process, the Service Units ensure that new knowledge is applied by the Business Units in operating the assets.

5.4.3. *The dynamic model*

Capturing, creating, delivering and using knowledge, embedded in a transparent value chain and work process oriented structure are the basic ingredients in a knowledge system. As can be seen in Figure 5.6 above, the model becomes static unless you add a dynamic process to it. Also by being able to continuously improve and change the company's value chain, through adding new good practice vetted through a feedback loop, you end up with a dynamic model resulting in improvement and innovation of the organization's productive and service activities. This can be seen in Figure 5.7.

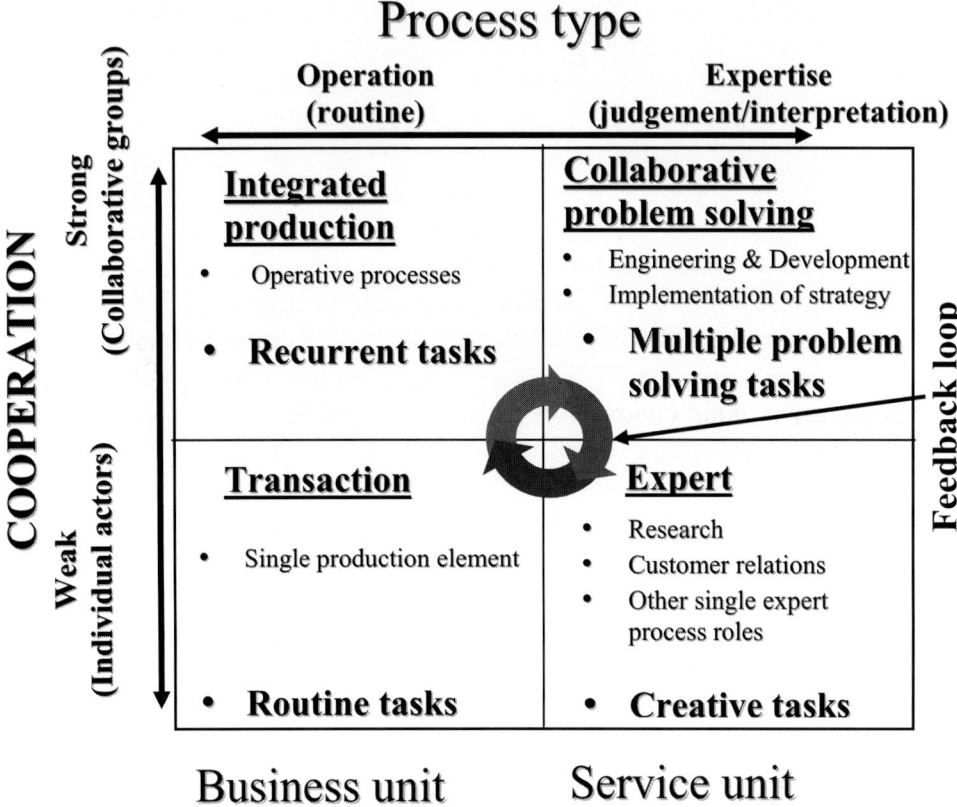

Figure 5.7: COP process model with the "Feedback" loop

5.5. The Faros concept

The basic concept builds on the idea of an employee-owned system. With its knowledge room metaphor as the main navigating entrance, and work process structure as the principle navigator, the model offers a framework for the users to capture, create, share and use knowledge as required. In order for the framework to function, the users develop the content, and fill

Chapter 5 Model – The Structure and Dynamics of a KMS 159

the structure according to the needs of the individual, team and organization. This is made possible due to the system's facilitating methodology. Each employee knows his or her "As is" activities within a process or sub-process. The facilitator supports the users in identifying the value flow of the process, and ways to improve it.

The success of the holistic model is in part due to the system's "ownership". Experience has demonstrated that the employees will not only use the system, they will make sure their colleagues are using it, and improving the value change in the process. The functional success of the model lies in the ability by the user to apply the results on a daily basis, regardless of where you are in the organization, or geographical location.

A knowledge management concept requires the following:
- *A knowledge room:* A common home portal for all members of the organization. This makes it easy to move across organizational boundaries without losing track of how to navigate for knowledge. The room uses a "window" metaphor to find knowledge elements.
- *A process orientation*: The core in a knowledge system is the company's value chain, work processes, workflow structures and the operating instructions.
- *Feedback possibility:* The element securing a dynamic improvement or innovation of the company's value flow is the feedback loop.
- *Navigator*: Here we are using different windows within the knowledge room to navigate for quick access to major knowledge elements. Some of the "windows" in the knowledge room are fixed, while others are adjustable to the need of the individual organizational units.
- *Redundancy*: Going through the various knowledge elements, one can find the same relevant information, depending on which focus the user has. All information must be stored in only one original depository.

5.5.1. Integrating the user

The aim of the model is supporting the individual employee, and his or her team, in creating more value for the organization. The purpose of the model is to create the structure required for a dynamic and profitable organization. At top of any organization is the stakeholders' vision and purpose guiding management. It is the CEO's role to develop the strategy required to fulfil the organization's vision and purpose. When facilitating the users in developing their required KM system from the model, therefore, you need to first secure the work process that management requires in order to deliver the result from the strategy. It is from the management process that all other work processes in the organization will emerge from, both operational and service processes.

Throughout the process of creating the Faros KMS, the facilitating team was closely integrated with the users. This is of particular importance when facilitating the mapping and verification of a Business Unit's "As is" work processes. The facilitator's role is to make sure the users' practice is properly mapped for inclusion in the Faros' *Work Process Navigator*. For the mapping to have relevance to the organization's business purpose, it is essential for the facilitators to secure that all "As is" processes are harmonized with the business' strategy, and evaluated against the process' critical role of in the value chain.

Faros is a user-owned solution developed as a result of unfulfilling promises that IT should be the technology to end all IT-illiteracy among employees. With more than one thousand data bases, each containing thousands of files, the employees started to break under the information overload to the point that thousands of employees demonstrated sign of advanced information bulimia. This was the incentive for developing a *"just-in-time just-enough"* holistic knowledge creation and sharing solution. The setting was to take back the responsibility for developing a functional system offering each and every user, from management down to the post clerk, a model running on, and communicating with, established IT-technology within Statoil.

The users, supported by a focused and facilitated process, developed the structure and contents. The infrastructure and supporting software was built/adapted to the user-generated specifications, and based on the organization's standard IT products. The company operates with a matrix structure, with one set of Business Units and one set of Service Units. The operational work is carried out in Business Units by integrated teams. Managerial and technical problem solving and development activities are carried out in the Service Units. The employees are organized in operational and professional Communities of Practice across business and service units. In the Faros concept we have achieved a mutual transparency between service and operational processes, making activities accessible to all employees of the company.

COPs can concern processes in the organization's value chain, such as operating and maintaining a section of a production unit, however, service employees often belong to a professional group responsible for a function (see Figure 5.7). Examples are catering, information and telecommunications and rotating equipment. Of course, there are both formal and informal COPs, and thus not limited to the examples above.

Chapter 5 Model – The Structure and Dynamics of a KMS 161

However, within the formal structures, the two types of COPS, operating and service/professional, face different types of challenges.

For the professional COPs, it is a challenge to communicate the COP's position, role and mandate in the organization to the rest of the organization. Members of the professional groups must be able to visualize goals, tasks, own work processes, responsibility and authority within the various processes networks in the organization. Furthermore, these employees must provide, for the benefit of other employees, entry points for finding expertise and good practice, ensure experience transfer across organizational borders, develop new good practices based on own and others experience, and secure contiguous improvement and innovation in the company.

It was important for the experts in the Service COPs to secure their needs for communication, retrieval of expert information, and creating new knowledge. In the holistic model we were able to establish expert retrieval methods consisting of two information categories:

- *Structured*
- *Unstructured*

The structured category included methods like "tool boxes" used by the experts while working. We were able to apply the same knowledge-sharing logic to the Service Unit COPs as was developed for the Business Unit COPs. The unstructured category, on the other hand, had logic more in line with chaos, where, according to the Greek philosopher Hesiodo Theogoni, the Universe in the beginning was a vast, unshaped room where all things developed. Here, we successfully used the Corporum content management engine. The search engines and KM utilities are based on ontological principles.

For the operational COPs the challenges are to establish/describe specific work processes for each Business Unit, making their role and tasks transparent in relation to other Business Units, as well as Service Units occupied with the responsibility to support these activities. Furthermore, the operating COPs must make all relevant strategic, operational- procedural- and technical documentation accessible, for application by the employees to facilitate learning and visualization.

5.5.2. Roles for managing work processes

- *Process Owner*(s) is responsible for having the processes and Good Practice developed, and keeping them up to date (reporting to the Service Unit Manager).
- *Process Manager* is responsible for having the sub-processes developed in cooperation with the relevant COP (reporting to Process Owner).
- *Local Process Owner* is responsible for, within each Business Unit, to ensure that all local processes are fully developed (reporting to the Business Unit Manager, and is the Process Owners representative in the Business Unit).
- *COP*, both in the Business and Service Units, is responsible for developing sub-processes, local operating instructions and identifying relevant linkage.

The Process Owner will normally be a senior person in the central Service Unit, with only a few Process Managers under his/her command. The Local Process Owner is a senior manager at the Business Unit, such as the manager in charge of operation. The technology providers are all the experts sitting in the Service Unit. They will normally report to a functional manager, such as the person responsible for certain equipment or technology. While the functional manager is responsible for manpower, it is the Process Owner who is requesting experts to support the COPs in developing a given work process. Once a technology provider is seconded to a Business Unit, he/she reports to the Local Process Owner, or someone else in the Business Unit.

Implementing a holistic system in an organization requires some consideration about the way you work, and the way you would like to work. Furthermore, it will require appointing the responsibility for maintaining the corporate deposit of knowledge. We have proposed the roles as described above because we have found they work, without having to restructure the whole organization.

5.5.3. Availability and focus

There are also some key development issues facing the organization. First of all is the issue of availability and attention. It must be made unequivocally clear by management that one of the most important responsibilities of the Service Units is their ability to supply JIT-JE services to the Business Units. Our findings show that with information overflow, the ability to focus is reduced, increasing inefficiency and hazardous behaviour.

While the responsibility for processes lies in the Service Units, it must be clear that it is the users (i.e. Business Units' employees) who define the work processes within the areas of operation. The process owner must also secure access to relevant information required along the chain of work processes, either operational or functional (service). To facilitate such JIT-JE information retrieval, you need search facilities designed for precise and rapid retrieval, inclusive finding external information and information required in an unstructured work situation.

Another key issue is the question of creating a redundancy of avenues, which give the user a wide choice of ways to one original information source, depending on the context at hand. This is of great importance to most employees. Just like the way the brain functions in various situations, it should be possible to retrieve information via multiple channels.

On the question of experience that is not stored electronically, the organization must be able to find ways and means to make this available so that it can be exchanged. One such method can be through alternative COPs, such as informal networks. Another can be by copying handwritten documents such as "hand over instructions" for last watch to the next crew, systemize these instructions and generalize them for others to learn from. For the users of Faros, it was important to be able to retrieve such information through a system for correlating knowledge/experience to persons where you have a collegial dependency without daily face-to-face conversation.

The Navigator is a *meta-system* available to all Business Units of the company that decides to adopt it. This reuse makes the economics of the system favourable to the company. The Work Process Navigator structures relevant information around a work process. The Internet-based Navigator offers easy access for retrieval, experience sharing and development of good practice, dissemination of improvements and innovations, and learning. Thus, Faros opens up the organization's ability to create new knowledge, using the work process concept as the facilitator. One employee's thoughts, incorporated into good practice, may nourish the thoughts of his/her colleagues.

In today's international business community, information is thrust around the world with a speed never recorded in history before. Furthermore, the level of educated employees is rising, resulting in increased capacity to reason and take action to the good of the organization. This confirms the experience that tall hierarchies are doomed in a dynamic marketplace [Kantor, 1983]. The consequence of this is that an organization, wanting to stay alive in the knowledge economy, must relinquish much management decision-making power, and bestow it on the individual employee, resulting in more employees reporting to an individual manager. The need for a large middle management tier has thus been removed, rendering today's business activities to a flatter structure. For company survival, it is now crucial that the information reaches closest to where the decision will be made and implemented: the new decision-making employees. This means a just-in-time (JIT), just-enough (JE) information system, that is, a KMS.

The self-imposed task of the Faros team, therefore, was to create a knowledge concept capable of delivering all information relevant to a given activity or decision to employees. The concept should identify and develop core technology for easy access to information and multimedia elements, and a navigating concept for the information search.

5.5.4. Redundancy and learning

We wanted to combine the written word with a multimedia impact in order to create a stronger basis for improvement, innovation and learning. After debating these issues during 1996, we ended by formulating the following hypothesis:

> *Learning takes place in the work process.*

The hypothesis became Faros' cornerstone for formulating its vision, goals and product.

After reviewing several visual metaphors, we decided that the Faros *Knowledge Room* was to be a platform for navigation. This created a generic and transparent knowledge structure where the knowledge repositories between the many Communities of Practice (COP) could be compared. *Communities of Practice* is a term developed at the Institute for Research on Learning, and discussed later in this chapter. Operational: the activity of operating and maintaining the production facility of an operating Business Unit. Professional: The research, development, engineering, maintenance and other support given to the Business Unit. Such support can include petroleum technology, construction technology, facilities engineering and catering services. In Statoil, the professional networks are called "*Process networks*".

Through many avenues, such as linking our multimedia-learning lab to the work process, we wanted to ensure that visual support related to the task at hand. Furthermore, we wanted good experience to be shared. An important part of a KMS is the ability to share experience. Through an experience transfer system we wanted to ensure that users' experience was sent, not just to a "data bucket" where it would be stored and never again be required by a human brain, but also to the responsible process owners for further kneading into Good Practice (GP) descriptions. Our experience transfer system was to result in the reuse of information, as well as a collaborative system for developing new GP based on information with the same relevance.

After a discussion among international organizations it was found that "*Best Practice*" for some could be *Worst Practice* for others. Thus we settled on Good Practice. Statoil continues to refer to the Industry's *Best Operating Practice*.

We wanted to create avenues of opportunities for the users to have more than one entrance to find originally stored information. This reflects the brain's capacity to handle fuzzy concepts and many alternative ways to remember and retrieve specific data. We decided that Faros needed to have a plethora of redundancies for searching for relevant information.

Furthermore, both searching for, and securing, relevant information is a challenge for the operational as well as the professional communities (main process owners). Through combining the two types of units (Business and Service) in a seamless and transparent structure, we expected both groups would tap into each other's activities, and thus benefit from being connected to a unified system. The results include a high level of learning and gaining insight for the creation of new knowledge.

5.5.5. *The organization's value chain*

The organization's *value chain* consists of two elements:

- The Business/Operative value element
- The Service/Functional value element

Each element has a set of main work processes, sub-processes and work activity descriptions. While an organization may choose to structure the metaphor [Porter, 1985] of the Operative and Service value chain differently, it is imperative not to differ significantly between the two metaphors. That is because of the recognition and transparency factors.

The Business Units are responsible for developing the operative processes. Figure 5.8 shows Business unit knowledge room, Value chain,

Work process and Operating instructions represented as a value chain. The *Value Chain* means the added value process making up the value flow elements starting with input, via the added value factors of production, to the output. In the "Value chain" window (picture 2 from top) you select a sub-work process listed in the right-hand margin (each of the listings is part of the total work process represented with a name and number in the Value Chain). From the sub-work process one chooses an Operating Instruction at the activity level where the task is described and relevant information is linked up.

There is a process owner for each of the main work processes in the organization's Value Chain (refer to Figure 5.9). Most often, the process owners should be located within a Service Unit, depending on whether the process in question is an operational process (e.g. Maintenance) or a functional one (e.g. Health, Environmental, Safety). This is due to the fact that the *Service Units* house experts within a given area of proficiency, while the operating units house the "hands on experience" that will collectively secure good practice. A work process is a symbiosis resulting from the combined effort of employees who are responsible for operational and functional activities. The expert makes sure that the collective experience is turned into good practice and reflected in the sub-processes that are to be followed by all employees within the given activity. Let us consider an example from offshore operations.

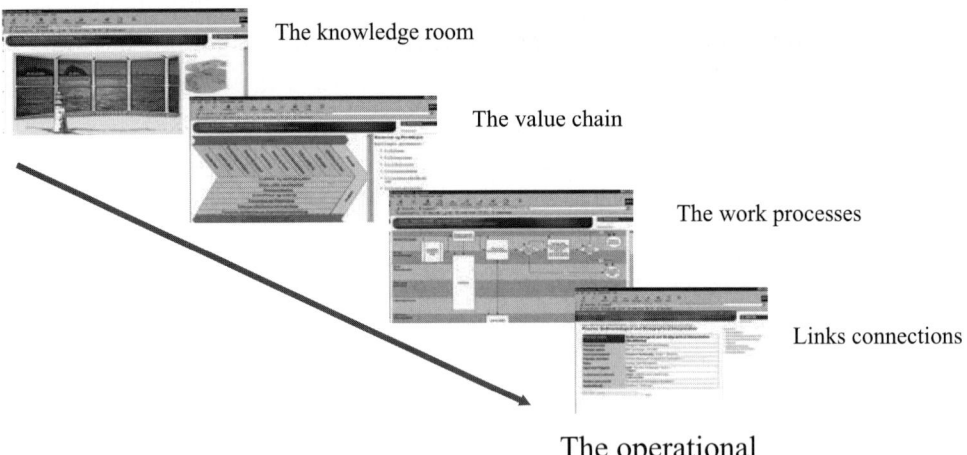

Figure 5.8: The Faros Navigator structure

Chapter 5 Model – The Structure and Dynamics of a KMS

Over the 1990s, there has been an increasing number of unwanted events when operating the oil and gas installations offshore. One of the areas where the unwanted events have increased is in operating and maintenance of cranes on board oil platforms.

PA is the crane supervisor, process owner of the Crane Work Process, and a super user of Faros. He explains why Faros is so important for the learning aspect, experience transfer and security of crane operations: "I was sitting in the crane cabin, about to lift a load from the supply boat to the oil rig when a big wave pushed the boat away from the rig. It was only seconds before the boat would have drawn the crane into the water. I hit the emergency button, releasing the wire from the crane and rushed it into the sea".

The Crane Work Process has links to the Crane operating and maintenance policies, as well as Good Practice documents and technical documentation. Also, there are links to training programmes (accessing from Intranet) developed by the crane COP, learning how to carry out maintenance on the cranes. In order to avoid unwanted accidents, just like the one described above, PA and his COP stayed updated by reviewing the many workflow activities described in the work process. Using video cannon they are displaying Faros Crane Work Process on the wall, drill down into the work flow activities, discussing the many work activities within the work process, and refreshes last time maintenance activities, carrying out a form for after-action review.

As the COP was planning for next work-over, somebody pointed out: "But don't you remember last time (20 months ago)? It took an extra week to get the wire. Either we have to change the routines or allow for an extra week for completing the process. The second alternative means an extra week with an idle crane. That costs money".

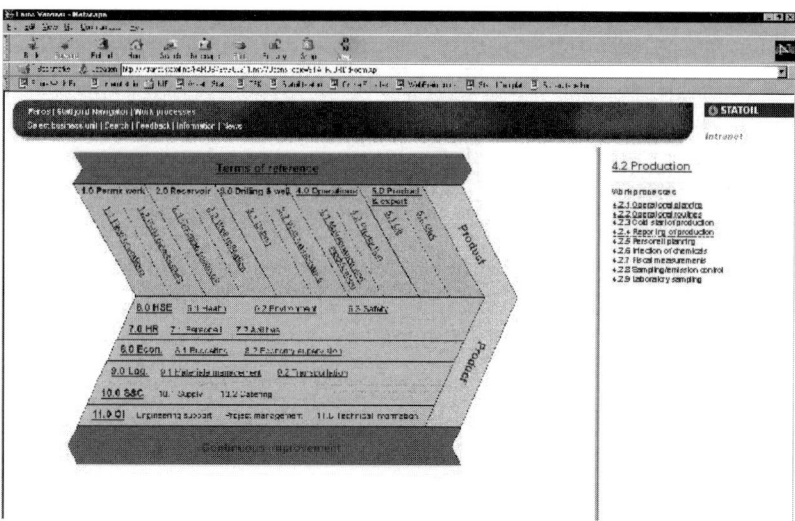

Figure 5.9: The main operating work processes

5.5.5.1. *The main operating work processes*

The purpose of identifying a work process/work flow activity is:

- Creating a common understanding of tasks to be performed within the team's areas of responsibility.
- Mapping activities to identify the "As is" work process activity flow.
- Develop models for more effective workflow ("To be").
- Identify relevant information for JIT-JE retrieval at point of use.
- Identify process owner(s) for up-keep of process and good practice.
- Appoint Process Manager for developing sub-processes
- Appoint Local Process Owners within each Business Unit

The operating teams will be given executive power over decisions and actions taken within its area of responsibility. All coordination takes place at the level of Local Process Owner. For the members of a Service COP, such as a tele- or mechanical expert, working in a Business Unit, he or she must answer to the Local Process Owner at the Business Unit.

In Figure 5.9, the right-hand margin lists of sub-processes originating from the main operating work process "4.2 Operation". One of the sub-processes is 4.2.1 - Planning level 4 (Operational plan). For each main process there will be a set of sub-processes, each with its own process chart. At the bottom of a process hierarchy you will find a set of work activity descriptions, one for each element within the process chart (see Figure 5.10).

The sub process of planning level 4 (operation plan), illustrated in Figure 5.10 below, gives the instruction of the many activity elements in the sub-process. Each sub-process can consist of further sub-processes, should the process be requiring such details. Each sub-process has a set of work activity descriptions. One may retrieve the following information by clicking on the relevant area of the sub-process:

- Description of the process (Title at the top of the sheet)
- Description of the roles and responsibilities of the organization (Left-hand of the sheet)
- Description of work to be carried out and by whom (work process elements)
- At the bottom you will find the process owner(s), date for issue, who developed the sheet.

Chapter 5 Model – The Structure and Dynamics of a KMS 169

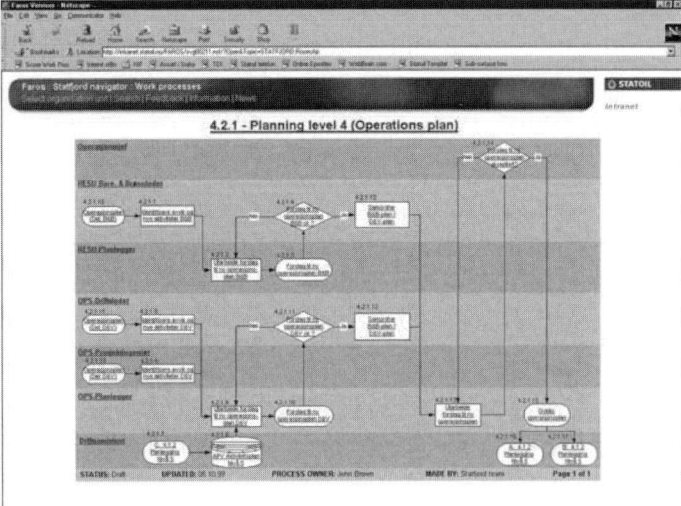

Figure 5.10: Planning level 4 (4.2.1)

It is the responsibility of the COP team servicing this sub-process to identify and fill in all relevant information into this work activity.

Figure 5.11 below represents one of the work activity elements: Description of the process. "Process description for activity 4.2.1.14" gives details of the task to be performed. Further details and more information will be given behind each of the process elements in the sub-process chart.

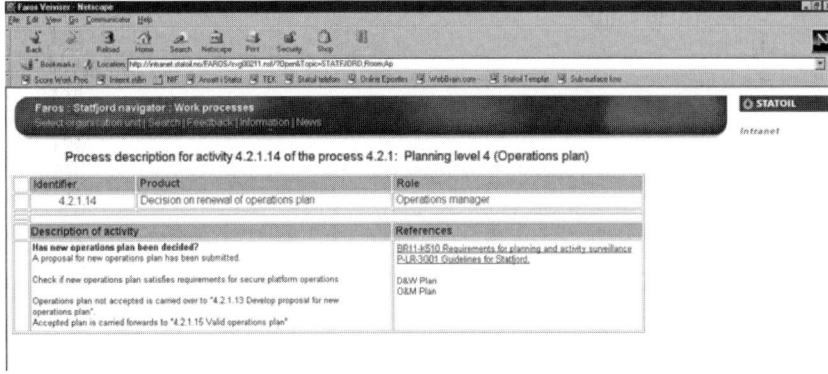

Figure 5.11: Work activity elements

As can be seen from the above figure, the team developing this process has identified relevant information to be linked to the work activity. The information required is linked from the original source. For each document, only one original should be maintained by the organization.

> "Now I really understand what is going on out on the platforms. By studying the many work processes within my area used on the platforms, and going into the sub-processes, I can suggest modifications that support a more effective execution of the task. Furthermore, this new Good Practice can be made available to all platforms all at once".
>
> The main Service Work Process differs from the main Operating Work Process both with regard to the value chain and the information contained on the page. This metaphor reflects the role and responsibility the functional service units have within the organization. However, the metaphor is close enough in resemblance to be understood by the operating people. The importance of being understood by the operating people is vital. They are the ones who request service from the Service Units.

5.5.5.2. *The main service work process*

The sub-process to *prepare plans for development and operation* will be worked on by several of the organization's functional units. The role list on the left-hand side indicates who are involved. Behind each box in the work process is a new sub-sub-process, as shown in Figure 5.12.

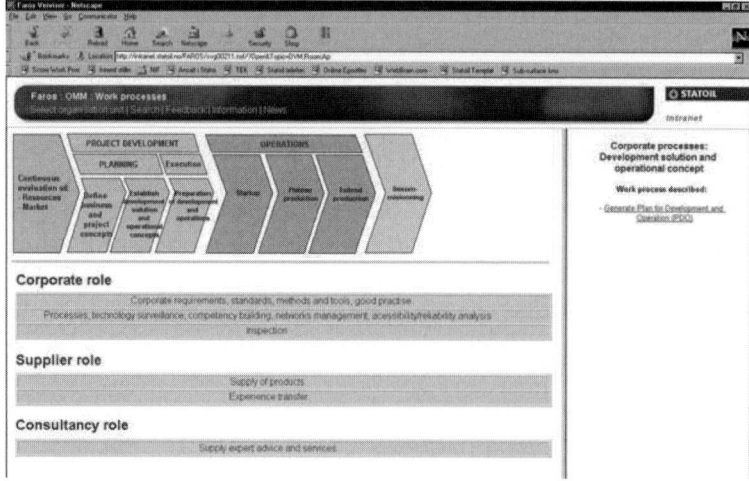

Figure 5.12: FAROS work processes

Due to the large number of Service Units involved in this process, there is a requirement for a sub-sub-process. The process: "Prepare technical annex PDO" seen in Figure 5.13, indicates which technical disciplines are to be involved. Behind each box there may either be yet a process chart, or a description of the job to be carried out, as seen in Figure 5.14. Thus, there are no limits to the degree of detailing that is possibile. The key rule remains, however: keep it simple, and keep the avenue short.

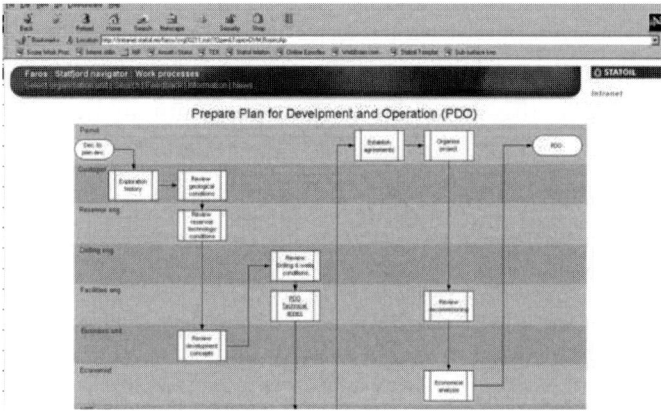

Figure 5.13: Prepare plan for Development & Operation

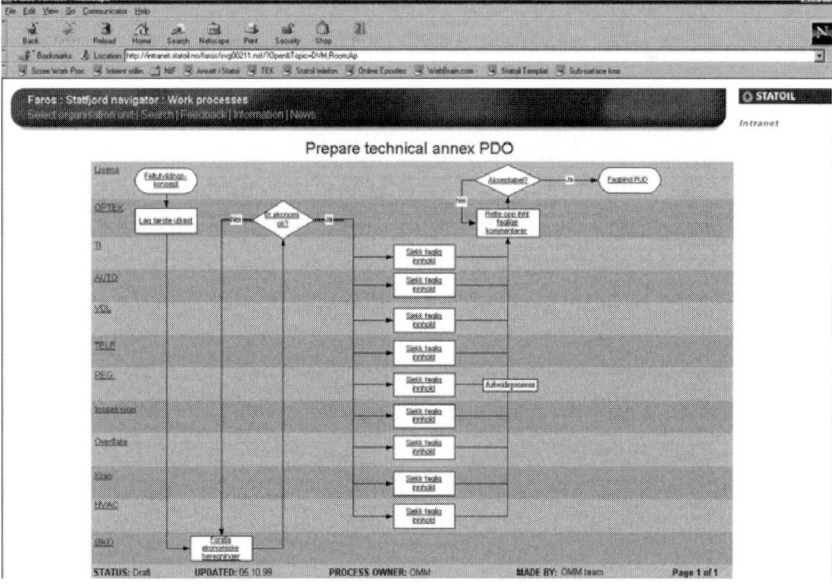

Figure 5.14: Preparing Technical Annex

5.5.5.3. Linking

Operator A (Business Unit) is responsible for operating and maintaining the unit's production system. He needs a piece of equipment on the offshore installation that is required to revise the work process for new equipment to be installed. The Operator is uncertain of the task ahead and decided to call the engineer B (Service Unit) responsible for the installation. Normally either the engineer would travel to the site and the two would discuss the process of operation and maintenance, or the two would exchange documents back and forth. Instead, A called B and suggested they both opened Faros. Here they found the old drawing as well as links to the new drawing, and other links that were relevant. By both looking at the same pictures, and sitting in different geographical locations, they worked through the variants and came up with a new work process.

> Based on the experience of the operators such as A, B was responsible for developing the new work process. Furthermore, B added all relevant links, such as service schedule found on the supplier's home page, the company's policy on operation of the equipment and a video demonstrating an operational element of the equipment. By looking at the same drawing it took the two of them an hour or so to agree on how the additional equipment should be dealt with. B drew up the new work process based on A's experience with the area of description, sent the proposal by mail, and within a day or two, instead of a month or two, the work process was finished.

5.5.6. The feedback function

In order to develop a holistic model capable of dynamically improving and altering, the value creating processes of a firm, you need a method of gathering, processing, and applying experience. This is an issue of tremendous importance, and a constant worry, for management. The main raison d'ètre for providing a *feedback function* is to:

- Facilitate functional network connections
- Allow systematic collection and processing of experience
- Allow experience transfer across organizational barriers
- Develop good practice from experience
- Allow continuous improvement and cross-fertilization between the various operational COPs

We discussed the infusion of a dynamic process to the basic model in Section 5.4.3 above. By adding the experience transfer system (see Figure 5.15 below), a dynamic feedback loop is created; the organization moves its focus from the physical assets to the human assets. The first line of knowledge creation within an organization is the entity's ability to learn from its own experience. The second line is to learn from others. Thus, capture, create, deliver and use "Experience cum Knowledge" is a central element in an organization's ability to grow, improve (and hence survive). Experience acquired through applying the present knowledge to the company's value creation, will result in new insight. This insight is often made at the point of operation. The organization may have many such points of operation, and for each operator functioning in a given setting the experience may be varied. By channelling all experience to the process owner, sitting in a Service Unit, the process owner can develop new good practice from these results.

Once an operator has a problem, he/she brings it into the integrated team. If the problem cannot be solved at that point, it will be transferred over to the service area to be dealt with by the collaborative problem solving team, or the expert as required. By identifying new experience, the expert will participate in creating new good practice, originating in all operating units. The new practice will be linked to the work process used by the operating team(s). This way, the work process becomes the basis for a dynamic KMS.

> A Chief Engineer sighed and said:
> *We have not succeeded in developing a feedback function that is good enough to support the development of Best Practice. If we had had a structure for collecting feedback to be the basis of new Best Practice, we would not have had the fire in the transformer on board the production ship - an accident costing us two million dollars in cost and lost production time.*

Developing Good Practice (Best Practice for some) depends on how the organization has been able to organize its feedback function. Faros took the challenge of the Chief Engineer and developed, together with his people, a system capable of returning feedback from a given work process, directly to the process owner, with copy to the person responsible for the process in the Business Unit where the experience was registered. This has now achieved the following objectives:

- Experience returned to the responsible person in the Service Unit rather than dumped into some data bin never to be recovered.
- Automatic information to others concerned, such as the Local Process Owner, or interested operating units.
- Accumulation of experience within a given discipline at one location rather then stored in a random data bucket.

Once you ensure that more than one person receives a copy of someone's experience, the sender will be more certain that it will be processed, and that something may come out that process. It is the ability of the organization to recognize someone's effort, someone's worth that makes employees want to strive to make the organization good.

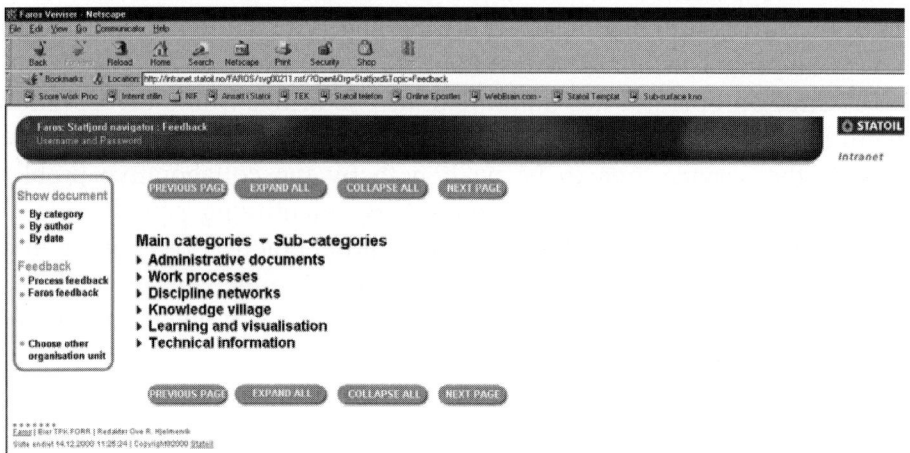

Figure 5.15: Good Practice development process

5.5.7. *The Community of Practice matrix*

While the "bricks" of the holistic model are the COPs, the "mortar" is the work processes flowing along, and across, the value chain. The high level structure (Figure 5.16) of the relation between the Service Units and the producing Business Units is a simple matrix, where members of production COPs require service from the expert COPs. Figure 5.16 illustrates how a standardized Faros solution was "rolled" out into the different Business Units and Professional Units. Although adjusted for individual requirements, we were capable of implementing the system in months rather than years. One of the super-users, belonging to a Service

Unit, but seconded to a Business Unit, gave us the following comments on her very successful implementation of Faros into the Business Unit:

"We had been using 3-4 man months on developing a set of work processes for a Service Unit within a Business Unit". This Service Unit supplied the Business Unit with certain daily tasks. These activities were common to all the offshore installations. "It was time to demonstrate the result to the Service Unit manager, and all the managers responsible for the function within the other Business Units. When the group of managers saw the result, they decided to have it implemented in all the Business Units, making the Service Unit manager the process owner. Those of us being responsible for the development were very proud when the management group decided to apply the system across all of the company's facilities. This way we all share one method of working, making us one community of practice. The duplication saved the company millions every year through copying the processes and ensuring that Good Practice is copied across the Business Units. This is a very effective method of operating facilities containing many hundred workers".

A standardized solution offers a number of advantages:

- Rapid roll-out - standardized process and information modelling allows rapid customization
- Transparency - moving a person from one unit to another: information can be painlessly retrieved in a familiar visual environment in the new position.
- Shared infrastructure throughout the organization.
- Standardized information environment developed into an internal benchmarking arena.
- The learning effect on individual and organization is enhanced due to JIT-JE information.

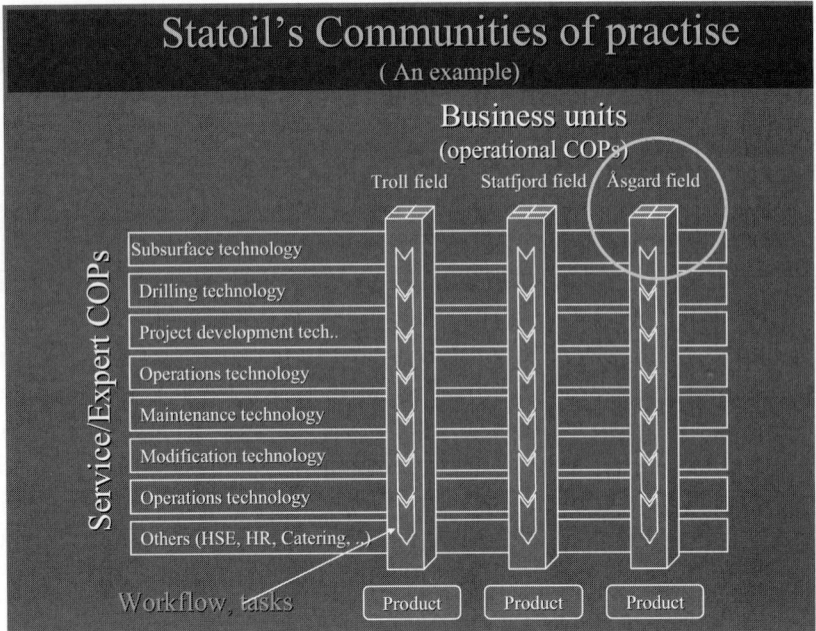

Figure 5.16: Example of Statoil's Communities of Practice

5.6. The setting

The model that we have described is a value and action oriented model of how the company works. The model provides a common means for interaction between individuals and groups that is not easy to achieve otherwise. The model provides an overall understanding of what is going on in the enterprise and how results are achieved. Since the model maps the real world it is easy to relate to. It manages to incorporate both the context of operation as well as its rationale. This caters for good communication and thus effective knowledge sharing.

Knowledge management is a strategic discipline that is well suited for the *knowledge-based economy*. Its goal is to add value through utilizing the firm's knowledge creating potential in a more effective manner, thus securing corporate retention of employees and growth for all stakeholders. In the above we have demonstrated how the model uses the value chain to navigate between linked information, as it relates to the tasks contained within the work processes, and the relationship between tasks and roles and responsibilities when executing the value creating process. The transparency achieved through looking at a value chain as one entity, makes people more capable of sorting the company's critical from the uncritical activities. Linking work processes within a value chain together in an electronic web, we have created the basis for a navigational system capable of offering Just-in-time/Just-enough information to the users of the system.

The avenues of history are littered with stories of those who obtained success through the application of intelligent information before others. In business it is important to have a holistic approach to acting on relevant information. In order to succeed, you need to link the information to the right value adding processes. Take the issue of benchmarking. Your Balanced Score Card identifies competitors that have a more effective value creating process. You need to pinpoint that information with your value chain in order to compare apples with apples. By having a holistic, transparent, concept of navigating in the value chain, this can secure a rapid response time for changing the business approach in a fluctuating business environment. This is a continuous improvement and innovation process impacting the organization's total value creating activities. You are now in a position to change your operating practice, and through such efforts, improve the bottom line.

If you want to build a more innovative, flexible and responsive organization, you transfer decision-making powers out into the organization, removing unnecessary middle layers to get a shorter line of communication. The resulting near-network structure secures a rapid response time for improvement and innovation. That makes the human capital the most important asset within the organization. To get a rapid response time, you need a feedback system for quick experience transfer. The transfer system must be capable of handling reviews for Good Practice development. Both experience and Good Practice must be easily accessible. In order to develop Good Practice, you furthermore need a method of revision, that is, you need someone who is responsible for adding up the experience, organizing a review team, and issuing new Good Practice. This is your process owner's responsibility.

Experience and Good Practice development requires a clear understanding of roles and responsibilities. The holistic model provides such division of responsibility, while structuring the value chain and its many work processes; for linking experience, Good Practice, and other relevant information to the work process structure.

The linking aspect requires navigational redundancy. The need for information is changing relative to both the individual and the individual's situation. In order to build a KMS for the knowledge communities to participate in, and pool their collective knowledge, we have to secure an arena for all members to participate in. The condition for participation is that the system reaches each individual in his or her own present situation. That is the purpose of redundancy. Your search for specific information changes depending on your different needs and situations. There will be different needs, different roles, and different tasks for each individual employee.

Example:
> *If you take the morning flight from Oslo to Stockholm every morning, you observe that your co-passengers have their morning coffee, but no alcohol. During the return flight of the same evening also coffee is served, but this time some of the passengers enjoy a glass of something stronger. The needs have changed. In the morning the shirt, tie and jacket were neatly in place. In the evening the jacket was off, and the tie a bit looser. The needs of the passengers are different at different times, depending on their different roles.*

Being able to find the same, original, information from different starting points is an important aspect of the Faros concept. That way we are able to support the users regardless of their frame of mind. One day your problem is related to a technical issue, another day you have to answer an administrative question. In both cases you need the same Good Practice document. Such a document can always be related to a given work process. Thus, by going into your own work process, you are in a good position to navigate the course to where the right information is stored.

Thus, KM is a strategic discipline, aided by a KMS, making the human resources more effective in operating the organization: KMS is making the employees good in order to make the organization better. Since the introduction of the World Wide Web, we have taught ourselves to browse through information, just like shopping - often aimlessly through the shopping malls. While browsing is the aimless search for something that may be of interest, navigation is the purposeful search for information relevant to a given task. The *Holistic Faros Model* has the aim to structure relevant information around the work process, resulting in both increasing the effectiveness of the operation, and the creation of new knowledge. The organization of information around a work process results in the JIT-JE logic.

The employees often do not check for relevant information on a subject before executing a task. This might be often due to not finding right information, resulting in failing to follow the current policies, or good practice.

> *In developing the model, we decided to turn the "burden of proof" from the employees' responsibility for finding all relevant information, to the company's responsibility for making available all the data that are relevant to a specific work process.*

The work process, thus, became the focal point when seeking relevant information. Although obvious, it is subtle in a way. Navigating in the information space is thus like tracking information according to how it is actually used or produced by the company. Our experience from using Faros is that the system encourages employees to check information relevant to a case or work activity in conjunction with solving the task. The burden-of-proof element does not remove the employees' responsibility for looking up data they know exists. It does, however, secure a level playing field giving all employees the same possibility for performing well.

Through this method of seeking information, the company has secured a vital relationship between the employees' work arena and all necessary information the company says is relevant to it. This way we bring to the decision point all known relevant information that could be in words, pictures, animation or sound. A KMS requires the ability to find and retrieve information in two radically different modes. One mode is to navigate along a structured model (i.e. work process descriptions), the other is to find information elements that do not reside in a model adapted to the current context of the worker (i.e. search and retrieve). These may for ease of expression be termed structured and unstructured information. Finding structured information requires that the model is intuitive and closely mimics the work processes that it is supposed to support. Finding unstructured information requires effective search methodologies and tools.

5.7. The Knowledge Navigator

As a holistic concept, Faros has addressed management needs as well as the needs of the knowledge worker, for both professional and operative employees. The model enables each employee to instantly recognize and understand his or her own and other employees' work processes, regardless of Business Unit association. Based on our vision of how we want information to float to us, and the use of the Web for realizing this we created the *Knowledge Navigator*. The Navigator is a three-dimensional Knowledge Room "entrance" to the information, to give a roomier feeling at the outset of the navigational journey. By way of recognition, the users can make virtual visits to other units and thus identify new opportunities. The Model keeps the user in focus and the threshold of proficiency to the lowest common denominator.

The Faros Knowledge Room, illustrated below, exemplifies the principle behind the Model. The instrument panels can be adjusted to the individual requirements. While we decided to have some windows constant, others could vary between the different Business Units. In the Knowledge Room of the professional network, the model allows for different subjects than what you will find in an Operating Unit. One reason for this is that GP development is the domain of the professional networks. The Knowledge Room then becomes a launching pad for deeper penetration into the work process, and out to the reference information.

Figure 5.17: The visual metaphor

The Knowledge Navigator is an effective way of supporting the user into reaching their world of information. Once you have chosen the relevant window, the next view gives you two sets of information - the value chain and work processes related to the chosen value chain activity.

Without the active participation of the users, one cannot design, build and install a KMS, and expect it to be used. It may function technically, but if it is not used, it will decay just like a forgotten fruit in warm weather. Figure 5.17 shows the structural route of getting from the Knowledge Room to the relevant information behind the work process window. Similar routings have been developed for seeking information behind the other windows.

Technology is not an issue for us in the present context, once the structure of the business has been identified and described, most needs can be covered by the adaptation of off-the-shelf software centred on web technology. Recent generations of technology, like the XML code, promise great opportunities.

5.8. Cultural aspects

For an organization living by its knowledge created by its employees, collaboration becomes a central theme in the utilization of its human capital. In organizations that are ruled by strong hierarchies, where dictates are followed by threats of disciplinary action if there is non-compliance, collaboration will not blossom. If collaboration is not encouraged, KM will not succeed. As collaboration is built on trust, one has to turn to the issue of virtues if KM is to succeed as a value creating discipline within an organization. Respect for fellow colleagues, good will, and the ability to make a difference for the common good, are values to be instilled in the organization in order to secure a positive cultural environment for collaboration. That is the basis for securing a successful working of Knowledge Management.

In order to make the Faros vision come true, you have to create an environment within the organization that is capable of strengthening the culture of serving the needs of its human capital. The virtue of the organization, therefore, becomes one of doing the employees good. Its purpose is to strengthen the employees' capability for:

- Collaborative work practices, including creating and sharing knowledge and delivering and using information
- Establish methods for experience transfer
- Developing system for creating new good practices
- Securing a "Just-in-time/just-enough" (JIT/JE) information retrieval, and redundancy, method, and with the burden of proof on the owner of information.
- Developing good practice
- Developing new products/processes
- Benchmarking (e.g. Balanced Score Card) for improved productivity
- Lifelong learning.

5.9. The learning effect

A lesson from early learning organizations:

> *By building an organization for learning and dissemination of knowledge, capable of dynamic change, the Macedonians and the Vikings became the rulers rather than being ruled.*

A knowledge management system should be able to support the aim of the learning organization, that is, an organization's ability to capture, synthesize, deliver and use information. Its tools are the information and communication technologies, redundancy building, Communities of Practice, work processes and the JIT-JE principles.

In order to succeed with the aim of KM, the organization has to strengthen the culture of serving its intellectual capital. The most important action management can take is to secure a culture of sharing, and reusing, knowledge. And the most important work in this culture is leading through example.

5.10. Innovation

We believe that the Faros Holistic Model makes knowledge creation and transfer possible, by proliferating information from one to many both within, and between, communities of practice. Accelerated learning is of the essence in the knowledge-based economy. Through the use of work processes as the "playground" for the operators, we can better accelerate and improve the learning process. In Chapter 7 you can read about our findings.

5.11. Conclusions

Employees and associates produce around 80 % of the input into a KMS. Only about 20 % are made up of ICT support tools (software and hardware). Consolidations of databases, both indigenous and exogenous, virtual reality systems, learning programs, electronic meetings etc., are all small elements in the KMS' core - the company's main working processes. Mapping how we work, what we contribute, and who the receivers of our intellectual (documents) and physical products are, is the only way a company can get a picture of its internal modus operandi. This is the first step in creating a knowledge-based system. It is the second half, the second step - the application of information into improvements and innovations, or what the economist Joseph Schumpeter calls *creative destruction,* which is the more valuable aspects of knowledge management. However, it will not be possible to achieve the more desirable, value creation of the second half without building the KMS first.

Building a learning organization, one needs a KMS to structure the work. Such a system requires the engagement of management as well as the employees. A KMS requires fewer levels of decision makers, it distributes knowledge from one to many and it ensures that employees know what happens in other areas of the organization by virtual mobility. Experience transfer function due to the systems simplicity. Capturing information for JIT-JE, simplifies the work processes. Navigation through work processes simplifies the operation. It is just like *survival of the fittest*: innovate, propagate and move. In Chapter 6 you will read about how Faros was built and implemented.

5.12. Lessons learned

A holistic model of KMS has been presented. We have learned the following 10 lessons and we believe that the concept of the holistic model is valid to knowledge management systems for a wide range of business organizations, regardless of their business or product range.

Lesson 1: The "raison d'être" of a KMS is to enhance the value of production processes.

- The added value of a KMS can only be optimized by network-based organizations.
- Network structures push decision-making power down and out in the organization.
- The effect of Communities of Practice will be enhanced in a network organization.
- Hence, hierarchical structures should not be sustained.

Lesson 2: The KMS belongs to the users.

- The users provide the requirement descriptions, the contents and make it a part of their daily work.

Lesson 3: The work processes are the cores of the structure of knowledge.

- The tasks at hand determine the requirements for information and knowledge.
- Work processes change with time, experience and technological developments.
- The KMS must be able to change in step and to facilitate the change process.

Lesson 4: The KMS must be dynamic, serving the transfer of knowledge across and within communities of practice.

- Processes must be in place to receive, distil, synthesize and propagate improvements acquired through experience made in business, and in knowledge development projects (R&D).
- Considered feedback mechanisms and organizational responsibilities must be put in place and managed.

Lesson 5: The KMS must be independent of a technology platform.

- Always be prepared to adopt improved technology solutions.
- Keep it simple.

Lesson 6: The KMS must be true to the value creating processes.

- The KMS must be independent of the organization.
- Focus must be on the essential entities that are served by the system, only then can the system support the identification of requirements for organizational development.
- It must facilitate these changes at the same time as it survives any organizational change.
- When organizational bonds and networks break, and people are dispersed, the KMS will be the repository of knowledge that ensures continuity and transfer of knowledge to the new organization.

Lesson 7: The most important repository of information still is in people's minds.

- A technological implementation of a KMS must support access to knowledge residing in people's minds.

- It must help find people with experience and insight, and then help establish contact.

Lesson 8: A KMS must support localization and retrieval of information also outside of the work process-based context.

- Advanced search facilities must be included.
- Redundancy of avenues to information must be created.

Lesson 9: Any organization will be best served by having only one holistic KMS.

- Efficient rollout and maintenance.
- Common "look-and-feel" provides recognition across units and facilitates adaptation to new work situations.
- If you find that your organization requires more than one KMS, it may be time to re-think your organization.

Lesson 10: Technology is just an enabler - the people do the job.

- Technology applicable to a KMS will only in exceptional cases provide more than 20 % of the solution to your KM challenges.
- A KMS is no better than its day-to-day management and maintenance of the system.

REFERENCES

1. Arc Group's KM Magazine, Feb.-July 2000, London, (http://www.ark-interactive.com).
2. Chandler, A., (1961), *Modern organizations*, MIT Press, Cambridge, MA.
3. CognIT AS, Halden, (http://www.cognit.no).
4. Drucker, P., (1984), *Entrepreneurship and Innovation.*
5. Drucker, P. et al., (1985), *Innovation and Entrepreneurship,* New York.
6. Edvinsson, L. and Malonel, M. S., (1997), *Intellectual Capital*: the proven way to establish your company's real value by measuring its hidden brainpower, Piatkus, London.
7. Hjelmervik, O. R., (1987), Entrepreneuring and Turning on the Intrapreneurs, *Scandinavian Oil-Gas Magazine* 1/2-87 and 11/12-87.
8. Kantor, R.M., (1983), *The Change Masters,* p. 76, University of London, UK.
9. *Knowledge Management magazine*, issues 5-10, 2000. The ARK Group, London, www.kmmagazine.com.
10. Porter, M. (1985), *Competitive Strategy*, The Free Press, New York.
11. Porter, M. (1990), *The Competitive Advantage of Nations*, The Macmillan Press Ltd., London.
12. Senge, P. M., (1990), *The Fifth Discipline*, the art and practice of the learning organization, p. 13, Doubleday Currency, New York.
13. Taylor, F. W., (1911), *The Principles of Scientific Management,* Harper Bros, New York.
14. Thurow, L. C. (1999), *Building Wealth*, Harper Collins Publisher Inc., New York.
15. Wenger, E. (1999), Communities of Practice: the key to knowledge strategy, *Knowledge Direction,* vol. 1.

CHAPTER 6

PRACTICE: THE FAROS CASE STUDY

Objectives

- Why does Statoil need a KMS?
- Understanding how the Faros concept can be implemented to build KMS in Statoil.
- Why does Faros go live in Statoil?
- What can we learn from the Faros system?
- Think about the possibility to implement the Faros concept in your organization.

6.1. Introduction

In Chapter 5, we discussed the general purpose and structure of a holistic model of knowledge management systems and showed that it is important for making a successful knowledge management system. The question here is how we can implement the concept to develop a knowledge management system for an organization. The Faros case study will show the practice of developing a knowledge management system.

The *Faros knowledge management system* was completed in July 1999 after almost a four-year development period. Throughout the process, the Faros multidiscipline team was closely integrated with the users. This was of particular importance when facilitating the mapping and verification of a Business Unit's "As is" work processes - the heart of the Faros concept. Here the team acted as a facilitator, making sure the users' practice was properly mapped for inclusion in the *Faros' Work*

Process Navigator. The Navigator is now fully developed into a meta-system available to other Business Units within Statoil. This reuse makes the economics of the system favourable for the company. The Work Process Navigator structures relevant information around a work process. The Internet-based Navigator offers easy access for retrieval, experience sharing and development of good practice, dissemination of improvements and innovations, and learning. One employee's thoughts, incorporated into good practice, may nourish the thoughts of his/her colleagues.

This chapter summarizes the concept's development, building and implementation. Our aim has been to create a system capable of managing a company's intellectual capital leading to improved value creation in a changing environment. The core of all knowledge management (KM) initiatives is to create competitive advantages benefiting all stakeholders, not introduce more information technology. For a company to become a learning organization, its management must treat all human capital as intellectual capital, and make provision for achieving their goals. By acting as a learning organization, the employees will apply their intellectual capital in a continuing search for new, or improved, value-creating opportunities through investing in the relevant knowledge and capabilities needed for the company to succeed. A learning organization will most likely avoid the Damocles' sword of re-engineering every time the market is in turmoil. Such organizations will continue to find ways to grow and prosper organically, as can be seen from the evolution of the Finnish tyre company Nokia into what is now a mobile phone leader.

KM is not an IT system to be bought from the local IT shop and handed to some employees for instant application. Its users must build a well functioning system over time. The Faros meta-system is the formula and recipe for engaging the Business Units' employees in shaping their own KMS, and securing a more robust organization. The organization's culture and its senior management's backing are two essential ingredients for KM to succeed. Unless management backs the initiative, the Machiavellian kingmakers will start their scheming. The Faros example, therefore, is about building a long lasting competitive advantage through communicating, connecting, sharing, collaborating, transacting, accessing, capturing and improving value creating activities. Through the system's navigational capabilities, integrated with the use of multimedia learning support, the company's employees will be able to create a learning organization.

In April 1999 an internal user evaluation report in Statoil confirmed that the completed part of Faros was in regular use by the target users, and functioned according to purpose. Due to a cost/value balancing, the Faros project team has carried out an evolutionary system development that started as a "blue-sky" project late in 1995. Thus, while the first modules have been in use since January 1998, others have yet to be implemented in the various units. The location of Faros' work process element is presently under discussion at Statoil.

Building redundancy to benefit the users' mental maps has been important for the project. The following sections present how we organized the Faros concept to enable the user to find the information from different perspectives and user requirements. We describe the use of Faros as coach, problem solver, information retriever, innovator, business process modelling, electronic learning (e-learn) and partly socializer.

6.2. Creating a knowledge management system

A cartoon depicts the Chief Dinosaur addressing his subordinates. The text reads: "The future looks bleak. The world is in chaos, and we all have a specialized brain the size of a walnut". This is exactly what happened to the retailing organization Woolworth, founded 1879 in the UK. Its last store was closed 1997 in the USA in 1997. According to Williamson [1999] of INSEAD, Woolworth "had refined and polished its economic engine and deepened its narrow range of competence into almost perfect extinction".

Archimedes believed that he could move the world through a fixed point; given a stick long enough to get a firm grip. This is called levering. Although Archimedes may have been able to move the world, few other "world size" feats have ever been accomplished by a single individual. Most major achievements, barring individual competition, are a result of teamwork. The core of teamwork is cooperation and sharing of information, experience, etc., in order to reach a common goal while defending one's own territory. While Archimedes used a stick as a lever, learning organizations are using knowledge management for this purpose. The stick was to Archimedes what the knowledge management system is to the learning organizations. Leveraging your knowledge is the essence of knowledge management. It is the ability to lever ones knowledge that distinguishes the *learning organizations* from the "also rans". By using a knowledge management system as a lever, one secures an effective operation as well as strengthening its ability for innovation and growth. Unfortunately for the dinosaurs, they did not know of Faros.

Faros' purpose is to offer an empowering knowledge system enabling the employees to build a learning organization with the goal to strengthen Statoil as a leading, profitable, energy company capable of serving all its stakeholders in a more competitive environment.

6.2.1. The Faros concept in Statoil

The purpose of all organizations is to achieve wanted objectives. If your desired goal is to harvest the elk population in your area, you set up a hunting party, with dedicated tasks for each member. The most experienced, or best, hunter gets to shoot. Before the shooting can take place, one has to get information as to the whereabouts of the animals. The most intelligent information is that which leads you to achieving your goal faster than your competitors. The hunting party is organized as a flat network organization for quick decisions towards securing the stated goal.

In today's international business community information is thrust around the world with an escalating speed. The hierarchical structure is less applicable for today's business activities and thus has had to yield to a flatter structure. The progress of a business does not hinge on one person making strategic decisions, but on many smaller or larger decisions made by all of the employees along the company's value chain. For this to happen, it is crucial that the information reaches the right person, closest to where the decision will be made and implemented, without undue delay. The consequence of this is that added responsibility is given to the individual employee, resulting in more employees reporting to the individual manager. The need for a large middle management tier has been removed.

Starting up as a "moonlight" project in Statoil (a project without full approval of senior management), the Faros team believed that if the employees were given access to all relevant information at point of decision, as well as information supporting a process of learning while working on a problem, values would be created and learning would take please. Our challenge was to combine the written word with multimedia impact in order to create a stronger basis for improvement, innovation and learning.

After searching for a solution to the challenge described above, we ended up with the Faros Knowledge Room. From the room we created links for navigating in information and between the many communities of practice.

Building on our own experience from searching in vain for information, as well as discussions with experts, we decided that Faros was to have multiple redundancies for finding relevant information. We wanted to create avenues of opportunities for the users to have more than one entrance for finding originally stored information. This reflects the brain's capacity to handle fuzzy concepts and many alternative ways to remember and retrieve specific data.

Below is a list of challenges for both *professional and operational* COPs in Statoil:

Challenges of professional COPs:

- Communicate position, role and mandate within the Statoil community,
- Visualize goals, tasks, work processes, responsibility and authority within the various networks in Statoil
- Entry point for finding expertise and best practice
- Experience transfer across organizational borders
- Developing GP based on experience
- Continuous improvement and innovation based on cross border comparison with the various operating units.

Challenges of operational COPs:

- Work processes (SAP and Business Unit-specific)
- Strategic, operational and procedural documents
- Technical documentation
- Learning and visualization
- Functional network connections
- Systematic collection and processing of experience
- Experience transfer across organizational barriers
- Developing good practice from experience
- Continuous improvement in cross fertilization between the various operating COPs
- The business situation in the functional networks (ability to supply JIT-JE services)

The resulting transparency between the many COPs can be seen from the matrix in Figure 6.1.

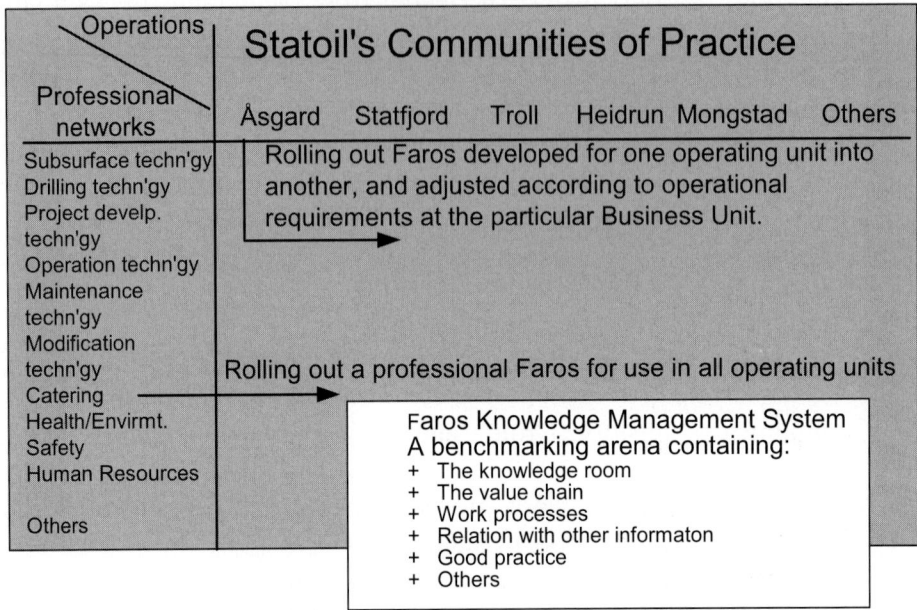

Figure 6.1: The communities of practice matrix

6.2.2. Organizing information

Unlike just browsing on the Web, the Faros team felt that time had come for someone to focus on navigation. To navigate is "to steer, or direct.... or to plot the course for (travelling)" according to Webster's. Thus while browsing is aimless search, navigation is the purposeful search for information relevant to a given task. In our zest for IT simplicity we created the Faros Work Process Navigation concept, which reflects the relevant information around a work process. This way of applying the Web, we believe, has formed a new school in utilizing IT for a more effective execution of the relevant business goal.

We wanted to create an arena for capturing, sharing and dispersing knowledge creating information. We wanted the arena to be transparent, both for operational and professional Communities of Practice, in order to create a common ground for a cooperative work system. And all relevant information for the users was to only be one or two clicks away from a work process. The work process, thus, became the focal point when seeking relevant information.

Employees, it turned out, often did not check for relevant information on a subject before executing a task, and thus risked failing to follow current policies, or GP. When realizing that not seeking information was the norm rather than the exception, we confronted employees with their practice. Their explanation for not searching for relevant information was twofold: Not only did they have problems using the computer systems that were required to find such information, also they did not know in which of the more than a thousand databases they should search. An *intelligent search* could reveal the existence of a policy document, or that a similar task had been done before. Such a search could yield added value in the form of an improved GP, leading to reduced maintenance costs, or even a value creating innovation.

The combination of not mastering the IT and not knowing where to search for information created a major strain on employees, resulting in information anorexia. Thus, it is not always a "Not Invented Here" problem that causes people not to benefit from others' experience or ideas. Despair, from searching in vain, can also be the result of not finding and thus avoiding seeking relevant and new information. They felt victimized by the situation. As mentioned before, to counter this, we decided to turn the "burden of proof" from the employees' responsibility for finding all relevant information that are relevant to a specific work process to the company's responsibility. If there was an item of information, relevant to the task, out there in cyberspace, which the company had forgotten to inform the employee of, the user cannot be blamed for not finding it. The burden-of-proof element does not remove the employees' responsibility for looking up data they know exists. It does, however, secure a level playing field giving all employees the same possibility of performing well.

Through this method of seeking information, the company has secured a vital relationship between the employees' work arena and all necessary information the company says is relevant to it. This way we bring to the decision point all known relevant information, irrespective of whether it is the written word, pictures, animation or sound. We have two types of information: structured, and unstructured.

6.2.3. Structured information

Running an oil platform requires structured work processes. One example is a process for preventive maintenance. In this job there are standard checkpoints for identifying wear and tear, as well as replacing soon-to-break parts. Building an operational work process in Faros, the Operator is to be provided with all relevant links to stored data, knowledge of the equipment to be serviced and the addresses of its suppliers.

The Faros Work Process Navigator makes immediately available all relevant corporate policies, good practice, visualized and textual learning elements, suppliers' information (Internet/Extranet), technical documentation, 3rd party information, and other information in a relationship that is seen as natural for the user in his/her work situation. By both securing information directly (hierarchical search) or indirectly (non-hierarchical), based on a natural relationship transverse of the information silos, all bits of relevant information can flow naturally to the exact point in the process where the employee will be requiring it.

6.2.4. Unstructured information

Unstructured information, on the other hand, relates to activities, which cannot be anticipated in advance. Drilling a new production well requires the drilling team to analyse the geology and hydrocarbon structure, and from the analysis develop a strategy for producing the optimal amount of hydrocarbons. Having planned the well, set the drill, and submerged it halfway down into the geological structure the team runs into trouble. A shallow gas pocket is encountered. The drilling is stopped, and the incident requires new information. Information to solve the case can be anywhere, and must be sought based on the current situation. This then becomes a search for unstructured information.

Finding a methodology for searching unstructured information, we discovered, can have a great effect on the learning aspect of working with uncertainty. By giving predetermined links to relevant structured information, and an effective search engine, such as CognIT's Corporum, for searching unstructured information, we may be able to aid the employees to look in the desired direction. Through a system of predetermined subscriptions for leading sources of knowledge, such as a university and Knowledge Community[4], the very source searched for should be well within reach. I will discuss this further in the following section.

---

[4] We consider Knowledge Community and Community of Practice to be synonyms.

Chapter 6 Practice – The Faros Case Study

6.3. Building the Faros knowledge management system

6.3.1. The Faros Knowledge Room

Our ambition was to enable each employee to instantly recognize and understand their own, and other employees', work processes, regardless of Business Unit association. Based on our vision of how we want information to float to us, and the use of the Web for realizing such a float, we sat out to build the Knowledge Navigator. What should this navigator look like? We decided on a three-dimensional "entrance" to the information, to give a roomier feeling at the outset of the navigational journey. This navigator became the Faros Knowledge Room.

Our first generation Knowledge Room was a closed and darkish room. The feedback from the users was one of confinement. Furthermore, the room metaphor was, according to the users, in conflict with the lighthouse metaphor, a metaphor the users wanted to relate to. At a user meeting we decided to go for a concept where the user entered the top of the lighthouse, looking out on a section of the Norwegian coast. After some further searching we decided to assimilate the knowledge room with the inside of a control tower on an offshore platform. We installed the room with windows to accommodate a view out to where the information was.

It was vital for us to create a feeling of control for the user, and that the user was at ease when navigating for information. We believed that both offshore and onshore employees should be able to relate to the room design. Throughout the whole design of Faros we have had to keep the user in focus, and the threshold of proficiency to the lowest common denominator.

The structure below illustrates how we ended up with designing and organizing the 2nd generation Knowledge Room. From here you can see the instrument panels, in the form of the names of *navigational aids* like "Work Processes", "Administrative Documents", "Technical Documents", "Learning and Visualization", "Knowledge Village" and "Networks". (See Figure 6.2 as you read in Norwegian from left to right). Using Java application for easy navigation, the Knowledge Room is so designed that we can replace/insert new subjects as required. While we decided to have some windows constant, others could vary between the different Business Units. In the Knowledge Room of the professional network: Operation, Maintenance and Modification (DVM), we have included windows such as *Good Practice*. One reason for this is that GP development is the domain of the professional networks. The Knowledge Room then becomes a launch pad for deeper penetration into the work process, and out to the reference information.

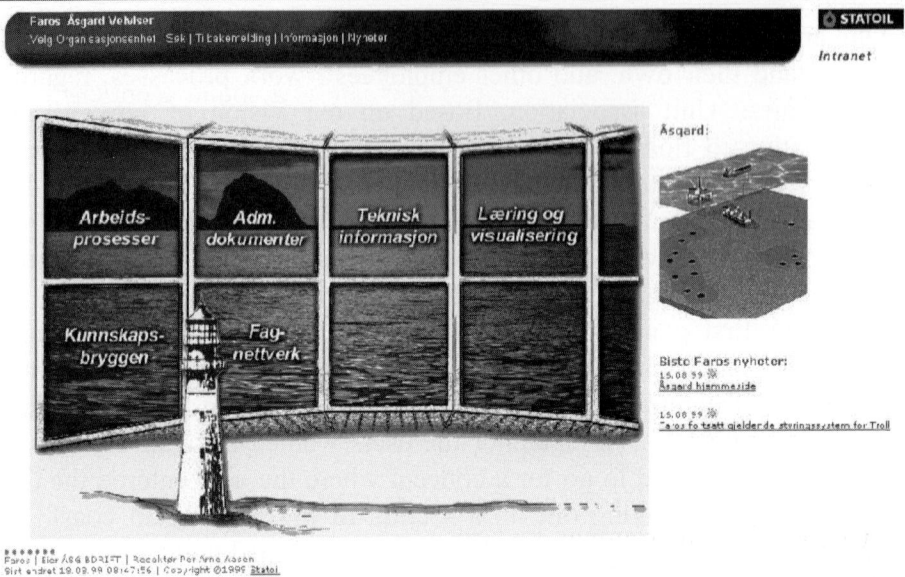

Figure 6.2: The Åsgard Navigator

Another vital element of the navigational tool was the number of "clicks" needed before arriving at useful information. Faros' "two clicks to information" was achieved by combining the Java technology with the Web. The Knowledge Room is an effective way of supporting the user in reaching the world of information. Once you have chosen the relevant window, the next view gives you two sets of information - the value chain and work processes related to the chosen value chain activity.

6.3.2. The Work Process Navigator

From the windows in the Knowledge Room, the user selects the appropriate entry point for information. The portal we consider most important is the "Work Process" area. The Work Process area is the employee's "operating room". It is the heart of their principal functions. When entering this domain, the first picture to occur is the company's value chain, portraying the business process elements. Here the user can get a comprehensive picture of the company's value-creating elements.

This overview helps familiarize the user with the company's many activities, and shows how the hydrocarbons travel from the ground, via production, refineries, petrochemical plants and out into the market.

6.3.2.1. The navigational structure

Not only was the Faros team staffed with top qualified multi-discipline members, but as users we also carried with us a sound scepticism to IT. Our first priority in designing the system was attention to our colleagues - doing them good. Secondly it was to the company - harvesting on its investment in intellectual capital by improving the company's value creating processes. By now we had identified a set of user requirements and an IT technology for easy access to information. Our next challenge was to translate these requirements into a functional navigating structure.

Without the active participation of the users, we could not design, build and install a KMS, and expect it to be used. It may function technically, but if it is not used, it will decay just like a forgotten fruit in warm weather. Figure 6.3 shows the structural route of getting from the Knowledge Room to the relevant information behind the Work Process window. Similar routings have been developed for seeking information behind the other window.

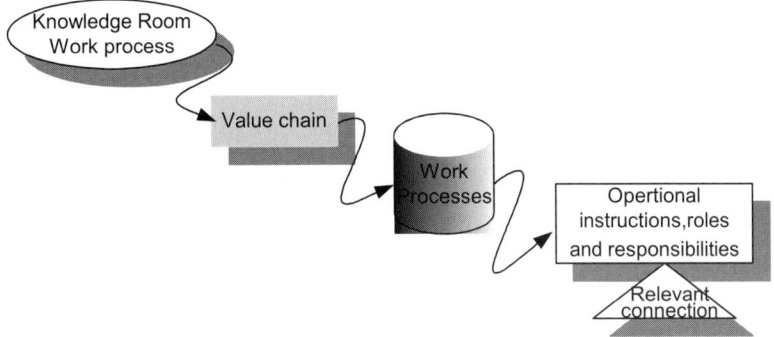

Figure 6.3: Navigator illustration

Figure 6.4 illustrates how we can navigate through the Knowledge Room into the work process, picking up the chosen process, and navigate further into the relevant data storage facilities through a *Web navigator*.

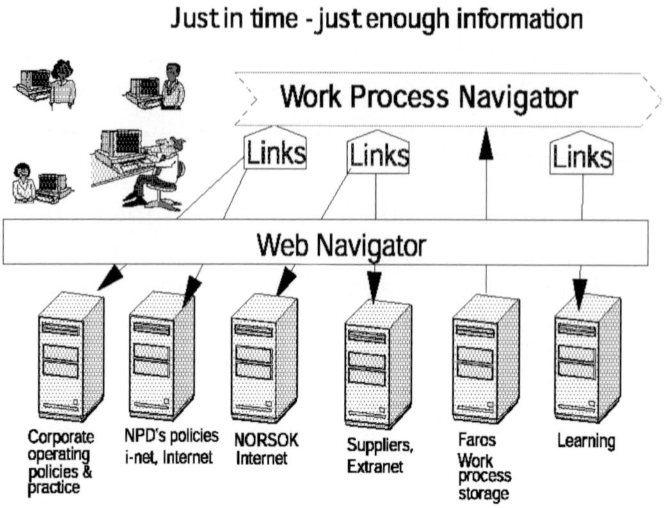

Figure 6.4: Linking illustration

6.3.2.2. The Value Chain

Our second navigational metaphor - the Value Chain, helps the user find the activity to work in. From here the user can select the work process he or she wishes to go into.

We have two basic Value Chain portals. One serves the operating Business Units (e.g. production of hydrocarbons), the other caters for the professional Business Units (technical and administrative service providers to the operating units). Of course there may be variations in the two basic models, but variations relate primarily to the structure and focus of the Business Units' range of responsibilities within the company's value creating processes. Great effort has been made to secure a commonality for easy comparison between the various Communities of Practice. Figure 6.5 illustrates the two types of value chains.

The above picture of the operating unit's value chain was developed as a result of these operating COPs' modus operandi. Their responsibility is to run the installations in the most effective way, and according to Statoil's Health, Environment and Safety standards. To secure both timely and correct operating data, each information link was identified relative to the various activities to be carried out on the facility.

Below the top arrow "Rammebetingelser" (Framework conditions) are found requirements for Industry's Best Operating Practice. In this section we have also created a Management's Arena for coaching. Here the managers can enter an information room where they can identify what

Chapter 6 Practice – The Faros Case Study

competencies are required for a given task, who has the relevant competencies, and who are available for work. Furthermore, you will find information on who has which role, managers' responsibilities and their relevant work processes, and team members identified for cooperative work.

One purpose of the *Management Arena* is to get an overview of who belongs to which activity group, and thus identify which persons participate in the regular meetings going on in the operation. Another purpose is to identify good-performance teams, by evaluating team performance, what they can do together and how they function.

In the Management Arena we have also seen the opportunity of creating an information room for running virtual meetings (based on a prototype product developed by Andersen Consulting), where an individual member can connect up to the meeting in progress while checking into her hotel room a few time zones away. Once installed in her hotel room, our traveller can electronically offer her opinion on the agenda issues left by the other participants in the virtual meeting room. The meeting will vote on the issues the following day, but leave the voting open an extra day for others to vote electronically, if required.

The middle arrow contains the main elements of the operational process securing the hydrocarbons from the ground to the refineries. Behind each value element, a set of operating work processes is found, as can be seen on the right-hand side of the illustration in Figure 6.5. By clicking on 4.1 Maintenance and Modifications (Vedlikehold og modifikasjon), the work processes related to this value element appear in the right-hand section of the screen.

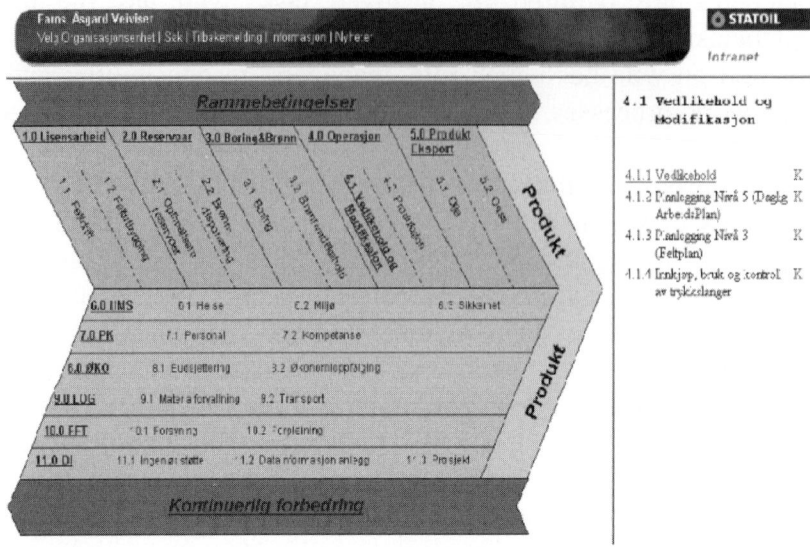

Figure 6.5: Value Chain for an operating unit

At Statoil, the professional networks have been given certain roles in relation to the operating units: Corporate (Konsern), Supplier (Leverandør) and Consultative (Konsulent). For Faros to meet the professional COP's requirements, we had to make sure the following aspects were incorporated into the value chain:

- The members of the professional networks must be aware of relevant work processes, and be capable of identifying – and participating in the development of – preferred work methods and activities within the process areas.
- The system must be capable of presenting complex information in a simple and easy to understand metaphor, through one work process portal.
- The structure of the platform was designed to create common ground from which all professional COPs could discuss challenges, either within their own units or among the other business units, regardless of geographical location.
- Faros' solution is to tie the information structures of the professional COPs to the value chain of the operating units. This will give the operators greater access to their various professional communities and their GP, depending on the relevant problem to be solved. The professional COPs, are now able to study the practice of the operating

units leading to new GP. These transparencies make room for greater cooperation between the experts and the operators, and thus improve the operating units' profitability.
- The system must be able to communicate with external suppliers through the company's Extranet or via the Internet. This allows a supplier and the user of its services to communicate when the information needed is displayed to both of them on their respective screens.

6.3.2.3. Work Process Navigation - the zest for IT simplicity

Our third navigational level: The Work Process is illustrated in Figure 6.6. This was our starting point in developing the Work Process Navigator. First we had to create the "As is" work process together with the users. This mapping and verification of processes was necessary both in order to understand how a given function is performed, and how it can be improved into a "To be" process. Such work can only be described by people who are in operational work. Our job was to facilitate this work, and supply a meta-system through which the organization's KM needs can be materialized.

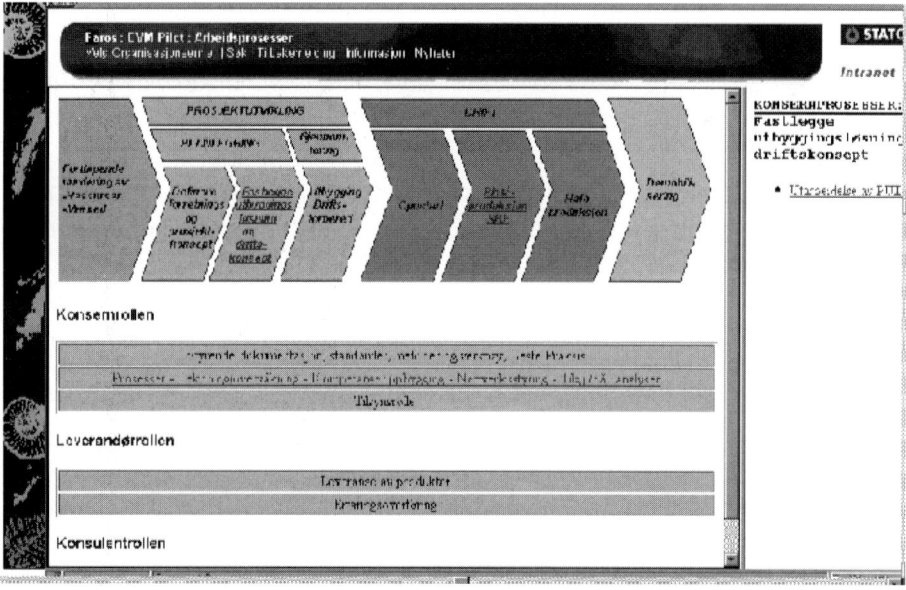

Figure 6.6: Value chain for a professional unit

Our discussion during 1996 concluded that "learning takes place in the work process". We are of the opinion that working through a process activity, will achieve learning while doing. Should a routine have to be changed, for example due to new insight, it can be organized so that "As is" is exchanged with "To be". One consequence of new insight can be a revision of the whole work process, removing or adding whole or part of it. Through this work, the operator has learned on the job. The meta-system has given him a framework where he can record his experience.

6.3.3. Information elements linked to the Faros Knowledge Room

From the Knowledge Room, in addition to reaching the Work Process arena, you can also reach directly the underlying information relevant to the *Business Unit*, such as the *Administrative documents, Technical documentation, Learning, Knowledge Village* and *Networks*. These are the core windows. The respective units may have additional windows such as *Technical Measurement Tools, Good Practice* guides or *Knowledge Mapping*, documents portraying the skills of its individual employees.

Faros contains no additional information outside the work processes and its underlying details as created by the users. All other information is routed via the many links in the system from an original source having a Web interface. From the work process position, the users identify the various connections as the process is being structured. Or, as the work processes are being worked with, new relevant information will be earmarked for a given process. From time to time, the user may want to go directly to the information source without going through a work process. This flexibility, which is known to the IT buff as redundancy, is an important element in a knowledge system. The content of some of these other windows is described below.

6.3.3.1. Administrative document navigation

The administrative documents, operating policies and procedures, are stored in a database called "Delta". In order for us to access these data, we created a web user interface. The policy documents have been organized with the requirements of the regulatory authorities at the top, then the Corporate requirements, the Business Unit requirements and the single production unit's requirements at the bottom in a webified matrix. In addition, access to various standards and codes is given, such as the Norwegian Offshore standards "Norsok".

6.3.3.2. Technical Documentation navigation

Statoil has thousands of technical documentation records. Every platform, pipeline, refinery and petrochemical plant has a set of blueprints stored. To allow the user to access the relevant document, drawing or 2-D model, we commissioned a team from the Technical Assistance unit to prepare a Web user interface between the data-buckets and Faros. This information is stored in various types of media, and as such needs to be coordinated in a common structure. From a given work process the user wishes to obtain the relevant drawing, specification, data sheet, or other appropriate info related to a given piece of equipment.

6.3.3.3. The Learning and Visualization navigation

The Learning and Visualization section was one of the first activities thought of in Faros. Its purpose is to enable the user of a process to obtain visual or textual illustrations when carrying out difficult-to-grasp operations. For a sub-surface production unit we built 3-D structures and converted them to virtual reality. Then we gave them functions so that users can twist, turn, strip and rebuild while engaged in their work process. In a similar way we created animation for anti-collision drilling, safety requirement zones, etc. These are but some of the possibilities we wanted the user to have access to while preparing for a task, either through the Work Process window, or directly into the Learning window. It was of particular importance to be able to illustrate difficult-to-grasp operational situations. Through such illustrations the organization both reduced the training time for an operation, and maintained a higher level of security.

The learning product we built for the Drilling unit contained four modules lasting several hours, and offered an exam and certificate at the end of the programme. We wanted to develop a learning programme that could also be used for short refresher updates by the operator while staying in the work process. This turned out to be a difficult task both administratively and technically. After some trial and error, we succeeded in developing a learning module which the users could connect to for bits of information related to a given work process. This led us to develop the learning module with finite elements, capable of either running a full sequence, with a test and certification at the end, or dipping into a single unit for clarification while being in the flow diagram.

6.3.3.4. The Knowledge Village navigation

Our objective in creating the Knowledge Village was to equip the user with a structure to search for unstructured information. We organized a group to identify how this could be achieved. Since starting the work on the Knowledge Village in the autumn of 1996, many thoughts and attempts have been made trying to structure the unstructurable. We decided on trying to create a concept based on two elements: a story board and a set of links to information pumping, intelligent agents or other useful data related to the users' work and areas of interest.

The Knowledge Village serves the needs of the user of information. The needs of the conveyor and the needs of the user may in rare cases coincide, but most traditional home pages do not provide a tenable, painless and secure avenue for the user to find useful data. Structuring the information is important and useful in some contexts, but mostly in simple and shallow structures that in most cases will not cater for the needs of acquiring information in a complex environment, nor for the needs of speed and convenience. A different approach must be sought from the user's point of view when the requirement for information is complex and unpredictable.

One example of the unpredictable: Marit, the sub-surface manager of an oil field, needs to solve a pressing issue right now. Apparently her case is unique, and thus it is not evident who and what can contribute to new and satisfactory solutions. The problem may seem specific to the individual at the time, as she has not experienced it before, while it may not be specific to the organization as such. As a consequence, the problem can be catalogued and made subject to a process type structure.

Faros is the user's own window towards unstructured knowledge, adapted to the user's own requirements. These will vary according to the element of work, which is undertaken. Identifying and describing these requirements for groups of users and even for individual users will be necessary before the operational environment can be designed. Experience shows that building a required process is in many cases the start of a creative restructuring of workflows and business processes. A strong common requirement will be the ability to search for, capture, share and distribute useful knowledge and to apply it when and where it will make a difference. Ability and agility in acquiring useful information will make a difference both in handling day-to-day tasks and in non-scheduled events.

The concept is based on the potential offered by Web technology to integrate existing technology, data sources and access mechanisms through carefully designed workflow management. The basis for our case is a day in the life of an imaginary team of people working on an oil field asset. A tool for helping the main character, sub-surface manager Marit, is a structured agenda, driving her case to a conclusion and recommended action. In addition to her agenda, she has a search engine, the Corporum, which she can activate as the need for identifying new and relevant information arises. As Marit arrives at work in the morning, a message from the production manager is waiting for her: During the night one of the wells collapsed and stopped producing. Now she needs a structured work process to secure unstructured information that will, by the end of the day, provide relevant information leading to a recommended action to the urgent problem, which confronted her in the morning.

This is one aspect of how we may explore unstructured information in a structured manner. Another way is using the Knowledge Village to tie in to the world's knowledge sites. We are talking of being able to enrol in the pursuit of knowledge at any learning institution. Through a pre-planned and organized learning system, the company can identify those learning organizations within the company's activities that may offer the best training ground through e-learning.

The first courses for the Faros computer-based distance learning concept were to be in core areas, such as field operations, Health, Environment and Safety (HES), sub-sea technologies, field development, *Total Quality Management* (TQM), etc. Through cooperation agreements with external units of expertise, employees could tap into course materials and lectures at will and on demand. Connecting the learning to a work activity would enhance the learning experience.

Together with Professor Rolf Lenschow, former rector of the Norwegian University of Science and Technology (NTNU), and his team, we developed the "virtual learning lab". The first project was a TQM course. Through an external link to the University, we were able to establish an electronic learning arena for the employees to link into at will. The professors could go into the lab, leaving their lectures and pick up the student reports. Unfortunately, as the programme was put into action, the participating employees fell out due to their lack of mastery of the Web technology. The experience is important, however, and a valuable lesson to bring with us now when the technology has made this simpler.

6.3.4. *Use of information technology*

Having created concepts such as the "Knowledge Room", "Work Process Navigator", "Faros Feedback", and "JIT-JE", the team had to find a technology capable of coordinating these issues. In the autumn of 1996 Statoil was fully committed to the Lotus Notes technology. The project team realized, however, that building a KMS on the LN platform would neither give the flexibility we were seeking on behalf of the users, nor the life-long learning idea.

We decided on Web technology in order to secure JIT-JE relevant information for each user. Our aim was to link into any database or data warehouse internally in the organization, or externally to suppliers, authorities, customers, etc., from a work process description. By having the process owners identify what information a certain process required, we were able to secure, through linkage, valuable information for the users of the process.

6.3.4.1. *The Web*

One decision of paramount importance for the project was related to the IT platform. In the autumn of 1996 the decision was made to use the Intranet and Web technology as media for communication. As the reader may remember, the World Wide Web was a very vague concept and in its embryonic stage in 1996, and we were also warned against using this technology, particularly as it was not standard in the company. Before we could apply Web technology, we had to make sure that it could handle the enormous amount of links, documents, drawings and multimedia required.

In order to meet the functional requirements of the users, we had to secure an easy and effective method of finding, handling and disseminating relevant information. We decided that the navigational flexibility the Web offered was more important for the long-term effectiveness of the system than the short-term obstacle of reaching some files stored in databases that did not communicate with the Web. Furthermore, if we were to be able to realize the vision of life-long learning, we had to reach the external sources of competencies, such as universities, suppliers, experts and other sources Statoil's employees could tap into. This, we believed, would be accessible through the Web. Luckily, Statoil implemented the Web during the autumn of 1997.

6.3.4.2. *Visualization*

One of the key ambitions of Faros was to create and connect multimedia elements to the work process. The purpose was easy navigation and life-long learning in order for the employees to do the job right the first time. By doing so we hoped the learning aspect would reduce operating failures and unwanted incidents, and enhance the safety of operation through strengthening HES as the company's stated number one goal. Learning in order to solve a problem is of great significance for any organization. If you can utilize Virtual Reality (VR) technology in such a process, which is the closest you get to the real problem without actually being there, you will get more intelligently run operations and more astute employees. Learning, through connecting multimedia with work operations, will enhance the employees' ability, at all ages, to upgrade their skills, regardless of discipline, in a more effective, satisfactory and benign manner than spending days on end in a classroom listening to an instructor. This is the virtual answer to "Seeing is believing".

We tested out both Virtual Reality (VR) and Quick time VR (QVR) for their ability to animate the operation of a piece of equipment, such as a subsurface production unit. Once we had a test version ready, we tested it on the net. However, that was easier said than done. We then decided to use CD ROMs, and had a few CDs made up for distribution among the users. Again we run into operational bugs making us face the inevitable. The challenges in terms of VR and its relation to IT technology, Statoil's Intranet and the licence fees were insurmountable in the end. While VR gave more control and options for activities such as stripping and rebuilding a piece of equipment sitting on the seabed, other challenges were impossible for us to overcome at the time. The QVR turned out to be a safer and easier technology to use.

6.3.4.3. *Other technical supports*

We had to secure a method of linking documents to each other. Both object oriented systems, and simple systems with drawing applications were evaluated. One important criterion was the user's own ability to operate, change and install new information into the drawings of the work processes. Although the process owners were to be so-called "super users", trained to a certain level of proficiency, we still had to keep it simple. Thus we opted for a simpler software tool rather than more robust object oriented documentation software, which only IT experts could apply.

Operating and servicing a KMS requires two types of activities: the IT role and the Author/Web role. The IT role includes maintaining service on the system, linkage support, server support, etc., and is performed by the company's central IT unit. The Author/Web role is done by the process owners (super users), or owners of information. It entails adjustments, changes and additions to the products stored in the system, as well as linkage to both internal and external information. For the Knowledge Management System to function as intended, each Business Unit must be self-supporting regarding the Author/Web work. The IT element is only a small part of a KMS. Therefore, the system must not be made so complex that each unit needs to hire experts to operate it. Anyone counting on building a system to be maintained by IT experts at user level is shooting himself/herself in the foot. Knowledge is a live commodity, not to be caged in by the dogmatic. The issue of KM is too important to be managed by the IT experts.

Faros has been developed in-house, using a Lotus Notes and Domino platform. However, the Faros concept can be applied to any Web-facilitated technology.

6.4. Faros goes live

6.4.1. Implementing Faros

While building Faros, we created the following applications/products:

- The Faros technology template
- The Faros project directive
- Process-mapping structure
- Standard symbol structure
- Implementing guide
- Business proposal structure
- Operating and maintenance manual
- Knowledge Room

- Work Process methodology
- Work Process Navigator
- Structured
- Unstructured
- Good Practice methodology
- Experience transfer
- Development and dispersing
- Redundancy methodology
- Knowledge Village

The first Business Unit to implement Faros was Troll, with its Troll A gas production platform and a land-based operating unit. With its gas-in-place of 1.2 trillion cubic metres, Troll is the world's largest offshore gas field in operation. On 1 January 1998, Troll's employees were informed through a Lotus Notes mail that they were to use Faros as navigator for the retrieval of operating policies and best practice documents. This message was issued after a 14-month development period. Troll was the acid test of whether or not the concept was user-friendly. After a few introductory snags, the system turned out to be a favourable spot for finding information. It was well received and demonstrated a very low user threshold.

In the summer of 1997 we started to develop the Åsgard Faros, two years before the field came on-stream with its first production in June 1999. The Åsgard field is operated through a management structure of self-managing teams for the operation and maintenance activities. The field development consists of one oil production ship and one gas production platform, in addition to its land-based operating unit. The two offshore units operate 16 subsea production templates in the Norwegian Sea, making it the world's largest subsurface production field. During the operating group's start-up training for running the production ship in mid 1998, it was also trained for Faros application. After a two-day training period the group of operators became fully conversant with using the Faros system.

In the early spring of 1999 we implemented Faros on Statfjord's three operating platforms. The Statfjord field, with its oil-in-place of over 3 billion barrels, is one of the world's largest offshore oil fields in operation. In addition it contains large gas reserves. The Faros work started in the autumn of 1998, organizing initially four processes. Using the results from the previous work at Åsgard, supplied by additional functionality as required by Statfjord, we launched the Statfjord Faros about six months after completing the project proposal. As with the other Business Units, the Faros team was the facilitator for the process owners and super users. Introducing Faros to the operating and maintenance people was done by the process owners through a Lotus Notes mail plus presentation and training on the platforms. Once the system was up and running we found it to be in regular use.

These were the first three offshore operating units that used Faros. We also developed a pilot for the onshore Mongstad refinery, developing the template plus two work-processes related to the refining of fuel. Again, the system proved flexible for yet another type of operation, and the users turned out to be very appreciative about Faros.

In parallel with the operating units we developed Faros for a number of functional units such as Drilling and Well Maintenance Technology, Process Development Technology, Operating, Maintenance and Modification Technology, and Operating Services. Here we developed pilots for several of the units. Due to the many facets of operating the technology units, we left it up to the individual units to expand on the work done by the Faros team. As the users gained experience with Faros, we saw how they benefited from it. Of course some used it more than others. That will always be the case. We also know of employees in other Business Units who use others' Faros.

In addition to each unit installing the concept, and informing its employees accordingly, the Faros team issued a general statement to all users where to find Faros in the maze of Statoil's many data buckets, and how to operate the system. Word of mouth also spread the news in various groups about how to use Faros.

6.4.2. Evaluating Faros: customer satisfaction

In May 1999, a user analysis was completed, where users at the three operating units and some of the professional units had been interviewed. The following was concluded:

1. *User experience*:
   Approximately 70 % of the employees in the units that had implemented Faros were using the system to a larger or smaller degree. Faros was evaluated as both functional and user friendly. Informing the user of its application can, however, be improved on. The employees should also be better informed of why Faros was built, what information had been installed into the system and where user support could be found.
2. *User satisfaction*:
   The IT solution was experienced as good in terms of response time and online time. Printout and interface could be improved upon. Facilitating the work processes was good, and the Faros team was given high marks for its service level. But the project needed a better structure.
3. *Price, quality and service*:
   The price was acceptable. Faros was seen as a high quality product. The service level was good.
4. *Overall recommendation*:
   Faros is a system that is well qualified for mapping and visualizing local work processes and is recommended as the preferred system in Statoil.

6.4.3. The Faros system tools

While building Faros, we also developed process support tools capable of "rolling out" Faros for new Business Units reducing the cost of implementing the concept in a new Unit. This was successfully tested when building the Statfjord Faros. We were able to reduce its development and building time by a factor of four. As we were going into new units, the "role out" time was reduced, and so was the cost. We were able to standardize the system, while staying flexible regarding type of units and type of information.

Due to Faros' funding structure, primarily financed by the individual Business Units, we also had to build a supportive accounting system, making sure that we had the costing issue under control.

6.5. The learning effect

In a new BBC documentary on The Human Body, the episode on the Brain [NRK, 1999] reveals that although each individual has a very small brain, termite colonies are able to build monumental structures. The report offered the following solution:

Signals between the workers coordinate the insects into a co-operative effort. The holistic result is greater than the sum of the individual effort. This is also how scientists have been able to observe that the human brain and its neurones are working in order to accomplish a task. Furthermore, the pattern of social interaction between individuals in the termite society is how Man also has developed his society over the millennia in order to meet challenges.

The essences of a Knowledge Management System are:
- The learning organization: sharing, learning and doing
- Web/Internet for more effective communication
- Communities of Practice (or for some "Knowledge Communities")
- JIT-JE structures
- Building redundancies
- Organizing for innovation
- Faros is the practical approach to this

The source of prosperity is our ability to organize available resources in an effective value creating process. That is the foundation of our survival. As rational creatures we are constantly cognisant of doing work with the least amount of input factors, being it material or immaterial, for each unit of output. In order to reduce the use of material factors, such as land, labour or capital, we need to engage the immaterial factors: the intellectual capital, which all human beings have. This chapter will now present some general thoughts on the issue of KMS and reflecting upon four years of "running with the ball".

It is the intellectual capital of the team and the users of the system, which have been applied to the creation of the Faros concept. Its main purpose has been to strengthen the culture of creating value, through strengthening the employees' capability in:

- Building a more robust value creating process
- Sharing information and experience
- Improving the way we work together
- Creating knowledge and good practice
- Developing new products
- Benchmarking for improved productivity
- Securing life-long learning

Building a knowledge management system has not been easy. As a matter of fact, no entrepreneurial venture is ever a piece of cake. Or, in the words of the 16th century Florentine statesman and philosopher Niccolo Machiavelli, as he describes it in his philosophical document "Il Principe":

> *It must be considered that there is nothing more difficult to carry out, nor more doubtful of success, nor more dangerous to handle, than to initiate a new order of things.*
>
> *For the reformers have enemies in all those who profit by the old order, and only lukewarm defenders in all those who would profit by the new order. This lukewarmness is arising partly from fear of their adversaries, who have the laws in their favour; and partly from the incredulity of mankind, who does not truly believe in anything new until it has had actual experience of it.*
>
> Niccolo Machiavelli the Prince, 1532

Building Faros was also about *intrapreneurship* and *innovation*. It takes time to build the milieu [Hjelmervik, 1987] for an innovative organization, which also is a management responsibility. However, that is a subject for another document.

We have now presented how we organized, created, implemented and tested the Faros concept. Furthermore, we created a transparent system capable of universal application, and rolled it out in new Business Units. Let us now turn to the principles of this experiment, for it has been an experiment. Back in late 1995 we searched many places and were not able to find an example, at least not an example that had stood the test of time.

6.5.1. *Knowledge vs. Information Management System*

We need to corroborate goals and milestones, match them with results created by employees responsible for the results and identify competence-building action.

A knowledge management system is not created in thin air. It is created in response to certain needs. As long as we have had management structures in business, intelligence of the business and its markets has been required. According to Alfred Chandler [1962], the new ownership structure in America hired in managers to organize resources along hierarchical and divisional lines, as can be seen from Bismarck's military concept[5]. The hired President of GM was establishing, and running, the general office, whose purpose, among others, was to collect market and operating intelligence - building and operating a *Management Information System* (MIS).

Actually, MIS was not invented by the new hired hands of business. It is as old as the Roman Empire, if not older. An example is from a historic account of the House of Rothschild, which we are not able to give the correct source, unfortunately. However, the story is an interesting anecdote on the issue of knowledge management. The fortune of Nathan Mayer Rothschild (1777-1836), the English branch of the 18th century Frankfurt money exchange-house, was in large part created by him through applying intelligent knowledge of the market. According to the story he had sent an observer to the Belgian town Waterloo, where the Duke of Wellington met Napoleon in the final hours of the Napoleon-dominated Europe. Once the battle was a fait accompli, the observer rode non-stop for two days, reaching Rothschild in London with the news before anyone else was in "the know". As soon as the London Stock Exchange opened, Rothschild started to sell in a big way. Prices fell dramatically, and then his agents bought up as much of the available

---

[5] The military development according to Prussian general Karl von Clausewitz' *On War*, a leading international military strategist serving under Bismarck.

shares at rock-bottom prices. Once the market knew Napoleon's fate, the stocks on the London Stock Exchange went up, securing Nathan Rothschild's fortune and fame.

As we are moving into the 21st century, it is apparent that intellectual capital is growing faster as a corporate asset relative to the reliance on muscle power. As a matter of fact, there is no other capital more significant for the future of an organization, whether commercial or non-profit, than intellectual capital. Just as the time honoured adage of "putting one's shoulder to" created the industrial miracle, so must "putting one's mind to" be the employees' attitude when the organization is harnessing its assets in the knowledge era.

All intellectual capital is human capital, and is therefore a repository for value creating knowledge. Every employee of an organization has an obligation to apply his or her intellectual capital to the betterment of the employer. However, unless there is a tit for tat in the husbandry of that capital (over and above monetary remuneration), an undercurrent will build up and create a counterpoint in the form of a maelstrom pulling the organization down. The ability of the organization to secure regular fill up of knowledge, or making sure relevant knowledge is reasonably accessible when employees are carrying out their functions, is the acid test for the organization, and "tat" of the equation.

It is in moving from "muscle power" to "intellectual power" that we are changing focus from MIS to KMS. It is no longer enough for the management of economic resources to confine him-/herself to the MIS. If one does, and is not removed by the owners for lack of a clear vision, the market will secure a quick burial of the company. The point is, any company neglecting to keep its workforce updated on the company's continuing value creating processes, knowledge repository, markets, suppliers and competitors, will fail. Not in a far distant future. It may happen tomorrow. A properly structured KMS secures the renewal of the company's competitive advantage - continually. Just like the termites.

6.5.2. *Innovation through a KMS*

It was Peter Drucker who once said that management's two prime tasks are innovation and marketing. If we are to bring the world forward, innovation is certainly an important function, not only for management, but also for the whole organization. But it is management's responsibility to create conditions that will encourage improvements and innovations in the organization.

Lack of a systematic method of organizing access to a firm's collective knowledge repository system, and from that position create new knowledge, insight or experience, will over time render any company obsolete. The fields of broken dreams along the corporate graveyards are amazing. Westinghouse, Amoco, Mobil, Borrough, MG, Rolls Royce, Rover are but a handful of the recent hall of corporate closures. If every leading firm is to follow the Woolworth example, in Professor Williams' words specializing itself into almost perfect extinction, closing shop after nearly 120 years of service to the community, there is your recipe.

On the other hand, should the organization's stakeholders wish it to survive, innovation must follow. In addition to a management capable of creating an innovative milieu in all segments of the organization, timely access to relevant information is an absolute requirement. Work process mapping, sharing of information and cooperative work are some of the elements required for the process to take place.

Managers and other employees in Statoil challenged the Faros team, to develop a process securing experience transfer, hoping that it would lead to improvement and innovation in the operation of the oil and gas fields.

6.5.3. *Information overload*

The information overload issue addresses the JIT-JE principle, which is the fundamental approach of the Faros Knowledge System. In today's world of mass communication, multimedia and the fast pace of society, it is getting increasingly more difficult to get the attention of the managers and their employees. Two studies show this. According to a study by the Institute for the Future [Beck and Daveport, 1999], the average American white-collar worker receives 190 messages every day across various media and 71 % of these workers feel "overwhelmed" by the volume of information they receive. A UK study [Teknisk Ukeblad, 1999] reveals that an employee is disturbed every ten minutes due to electronic information. The communicator requires immediate attention and follow-up, work that is stealing from the employee's productive time.

One of the present authors completed his graduate studies in 1974, and was asked by his new employer to work with the company's corporate strategy team. At that time, it took this international North American based company one year to prepare a business strategy for the executives' late autumn strategy session, lasting some weeks. In 1975 we got our first time-sharing "laptop" computer capable of printing out new strategy alternatives within a few months of starting preparations. Soon the CEO, fascinated by the new technology, was asking for a new printout within two weeks, while asking, "how long does it take you to print out a new case as we are changing the numbers?" The reason: The executive board had discovered that the new machine could answer their "what if" questions, or so they thought. What they did not discover, was that in order for the machine to print out an intelligent answer, it had to be fed intelligent data. They overloaded the employees with futile requests, while the system printed out results of marginal value.

It is getting ever more difficult to sort out the 'need to do' from the 'nice to do' information in the communication age. Intellectual capital will demand information of substance over quantity in order to serve the future challenges of the organization.

6.5.4. Collaborative systems

We did not know how we worked. That is why we sat down to work out the processes in order to have a common point of departure. If nothing else, work processes are a common ground for discussion, before you start looking for new ways to work.

Externalizing tacit knowledge is of the utmost importance for the organization to benefit and prosper from each individual's knowledge and experience. Being able to share, one-to-one or one-to-many, is fundamental to the Faros approach.

Faros has built up its concept around a collaborative form of interaction. This includes recording experience in a way that encourages communication and shared results. This communication is aimed at a two-way interaction between the sender and recipients. Furthermore, through a COP's work process the entire COP, as well as other COPs, can enter opinions derived from experience in using the process. You know that your experience, recorded and forwarded to the process owner, will be part of creating a new good practice, benefiting the team, the COP and the company.

In addition we have seen and heard of how the employees have worked collaboratively, and shared experience, while building Faros. How people have learned while doing by referring to learning elements. How colleagues have been on the phone to each other discussing a given work process, or how an employee has discussed with a supplier a set of drawings connected to a Faros process map. It seems like Faros is creating a basis for creative, collaborative thinking.

Recording of experience must be accommodated in a work environment catering for ease of recording. If users cannot share their experience from the position they are in, the likelihood of ever sending the message is substantially smaller. Any user who has to go an extra step to record knowledge will not do it. This is in accordance with studies conducted in the early 1980s finding out the frequency of visits between colleagues in research laboratories. If the distance was more than 10 metres the frequency dropped from once a day to once a week.

Having observed both employees and managers using Faros for purposes of sharing information in ways that has not been done before, and making a point of it, we saw that Faros satisfies the need for a collaborative work environment. One example is an employee and his boss, sitting in different locations, accessing a drawing linked behind a work flow activity and discussing changes to the drawing of significant ramification, then agreeing on a joint approach for the further work.

6.5.5. The life-long learning organization

A survey made in Unilever Ltd, by David H. Smith shows that several of the technicians were very satisfied about using Faros because they were working in self-managing teams. This requires them to constantly get hold of relevant information.

The same survey confirms that Faros represents a major achievement in creating a benchmarking arena for the development of best practice documents. Over 80 % of the employees repeat mistakes made earlier by themselves or others.

We wanted to combine the written word in a process with a multimedia impact in order to create a stronger basis for improvement, innovation and learning. "Learning takes place in the work process" has now been tested and found workable. Thus, we changed our hypothesis to reality. We believe the Faros concept is supporting the life-long learning ambitions of modern organizations through its work process navigation, and from there out to visualizing examples. Faros offers the framework of integration, participation, engagement and empowerment, all ingredients in creating a learning environment, as proposed by Peter Henschel at IRL. Our hypothesis-cum-vision aims directly at the employer's Achilles' heel – how to secure a life-long learning focus for his intellectual capital, namely its employees.

On another aspect of learning – computer-based distance learning between Statoil and NTNU, a project we started in the winter of 1997, this did not succeed according to plan. Two caveats can be mentioned:

- We observed that there has to be room in the workplace for socializing while learning. This relates to the human behaviour pattern (see box on IRL below).
- Even if everything was working: the technology and linkage to the university were in place, a top expert team was at hand and the study material was ready, there was one side of the equation that was not complete: The "students" had not yet fully bought the idea of distance learning through a computer. It was like preparing for a party without a host. We learned a lot from that experiment.

The challenges for distance learning will of course be reduced with the falling threshold of technology. However, the technology, in our opinion, will only be a part of the remedy. If distance learning is to become part of an organization's "life-long learning" programme, other mechanisms must be put in place. The most important of such mechanisms is management's commitment and understanding of the issue. In the future we will see an organizational structure that is more capable of soaking up nourishment through neural tentacles, where its repository of intellectual capital is located. In a flatter network-based structure, teams will work together and intrapreneurship will lead to competitive advantages for the company. The members will find the openness refreshing and engage themselves in the business of business, rather than in the business of politics. Operating units will continue to use a more hierarchical structure than professional units, partly due to the repetitive work pattern in an operating unit.

It is in this setting that we can see the idea of life-long learning being materialized, benefiting both the employee, regardless of age, and the company, regardless of past performance. Once such a vision takes hold in the company there can be no question of turning back to the old hierarchical structure with one person taking decisions and the rest acting accordingly.

Below are seven principles on the issue of learning developed by IRL:

1. Learning is fundamentally social.
2. Knowledge is integrated in the life of communities.
3. Learning is an act of participation.
4. Knowing depends on engagement in practice.
5. Engagement is inseparable from empowerment.
6. "Failure" to learn is often the result of exclusion from participation.
7. We are all natural life-long learners.

6.5.6. Tacit to explicit knowledge

Volunteering knowledge, as part of the day-to-day work is the most fundamental task of facilitating support for KM. Having received the feedback, the knowledge sharing capability of Faros becomes transparent. In addition it shows how practical externalization of knowledge can be achieved. With this response, and looking back at the response, Faros meets some of the fundamental challenges identified by Nonaka and Tekuchi [1995]. The five basic conditions required at the organizational level to promote the knowledge spiral:

- Intention (reaching a goal)
- Autonomy (freedom at the individual level to act)
- Creative chaos (stimulating internal activities with the external environment)
- Redundancy (intentional overlapping of information)
- Variety (broadest variety of necessary information)

According to these authors, these enabling conditions are introduced into their model for the knowledge-creating process in the organization. Nonaka and Tekuchi demonstrate for the reader how it is possible to transfer tacit knowledge into explicit, which in turn is used to create new knowledge. Botkin [1999] argues in his latest book *Smart Business* that there bare two types of knowledge. One is inside people's minds and cannot be managed; the other is implemented in goods and services, and can be controlled. That is, once you have been able to document knowledge it is manageable and made explicit.

6.5.7. Towards system thinking

Two American animals, a pig and a hen, debated who was most involved in the American kitchen. "I am present on every American breakfast table" said the hen. "I", said the pig, "am involved". All business is about total involvement. You have to involve both the heart and brain to succeed in building involvement. System thinking entails a holistic understanding and involvement on the part of all employees.

Since Faros maps out processes pertinent to the individual as well as the full organization, it provides the individual with a good understanding of his/her role with respect to operational targets or goals. This map is also applied as a grid for all information making it possible for them to distinguish between what is pertinent for each user, and the goals that all are working towards.

According to Senge [1990] learning organizations are set apart by their openness, systems thinking, creativity, empathy, and feedback. He calls such organizational learning "generative," in that it emphasizes continuous experimentation and feedback in an ongoing examination of how they go about defining and solving problems. Through the building and implementation of Faros KMS, the process owners and their team, have been involved in the business process mapping. Through this process they have acquired a better understanding of the company's business practices, management systems, job definitions and organizational structures. But, they have also acquired insight into how the job can be done more effectively in order to produce greater value for the company. Through the Faros Feedback function and the arena for discussion, employees gain experience in cooperative work for the benefit of all involved.

KM is too important to be left to the directors. It must be an integrated part of every employee's workday. The focus is on involvement. This is not only smart business; it is crucial if the company is to husband its intellectual capital, benefiting all stakeholders.

6.5.8. *Information Technology and user threshold*

Faros seems to cover the need for a simple and fast search of user information, given its structure regarding the user interface. Also in terms of future requirements for upgrading or modification the concept will satisfy this need, as average skill is required to operate Faros. Dynamic upgrading of Faros by the process owners requires special IT tools. Furthermore, Faros represents a low user threshold, and an equally low threshold for the updating of information as required.

Faros is built on Statoil's standard IT platform using its Intranet and Web. Many IT solutions, such as Data Warehousing, Data Mining, Infobases, are all part of the vast assortment of meta bases which Faros can link into for in-house information, or go outside the organization for external information.

As they are product suppliers to a KMS, IT systems have not been discussed. However, one of our objectives was to create a system with a threshold that was so low that the novice can use it. We believe we have built a benign user interface structure, and thus have achieved one of our goals.

6.5.9. Infrastructures and costs

Faros has been built through an evolutionary system development plan. We started out with a pilot concept, and then expanded it as we experienced and learned. This has been part of the Faros success. As we have gained momentum, we have also expanded the infrastructure. Today both whole modules as well as individual pieces can be copied in order to create a new business unit module. The cost can be estimated today with certainty when copying an existing module. This makes the dynamic use of Faros predictable, at a low cost.

6.5.10. Benefits

A report on "Measuring the Value of Knowledge" by Business Intelligence Limited, [Skyme, 1998], recognizes the ambivalent problem of measuring the benefits of a KMS. "Many managers sense that knowledge management is important, but face the dilemma that they have difficulty in demonstrating the value of knowledge. Philip M'Pherson, emeritus professor of systems engineering and management at City University, London, wrote in 1994: "The status of information management is undermined in practice because it is difficult to ascribe value to information and knowledge in conventional accounting terms".

We can now list the experience from operating Faros, based on both feedback and actual observations. The experience has been organized into two groups - quantitative and qualitative advantages. Of course, in the end all advantages can to some extent be translated into a single, quantifiable number: profit. However, what is profit to one may be an expense to another. Thus, we have tried to separate what we consider "hard fact" elements from "soft fact" elements. Through our experience and observation of operators and process owners using Faros, we can list the following reflections on potential value creation for the company.

6.5.11. Qualitative advantages

Faros builds on what we call the "burden-of-proof". The company provides relevant references to a work process, saving the employees from guessing (often wrongly) which documents to relate to. This link will always go to the original document giving information about its owner, date of update, etc.

The interrelationship between documents can reveal inefficiencies, lost opportunities, or simply sub-optimal solutions on each of the parts, that are to be corrected by the process owner. The user's "home" at work is his or her work process, whether they are electricians, drilling engineers, scientists or service workers. That is, whether the job is functional or operational, every employee knows his or her own job. Thus, all navigation to and fro, structured or unstructured, has its base in the work process.

A company that clearly respects the time of its users, for value creating activities through installing a KMS, will obtain the employees' cooperation and admiration, as well as their innovative enthusiasm. This learning aspect is reflected

- By making the workers share their best practice with each other and comparing their work processes, new activities are triggered resulting in further learning.
- Through combining work processes with different types of relevant information, linked with instructional demonstrations in 3D and video pictures, the employees will experience the "job-reading-audio-visual" triangle as a powerful life-long learning support system.
- By using Faros to reduce the time-for-learning element, resulting in a steeper learning curve.

Through a knowledge system the employees feel closer to participating in the value creating processes, resulting in a competitive advantage in the market place. The *Faros Management Arena* can contain individual work processes for the management group. From a work process one can link to Key Performance Indicators, Tasks and Goals. The management arena will give an overview of human resources connected to their roles and responsibilities, and further down into the underlying processes, and the process owners, impacting on the bottom line. Furthermore, as the management may have difficulties from meeting in person, one can run *virtual meetings* connected to the actual meeting room.

6.5.12. Quantitative advantages

Time spent looking for information is money lost from not doing value creating work. JIT-JE information reduces the money lost. Example: 40-60 % of an engineer's time is used for searching, retrieving and storing information. Assuming the KM system can save each employee 20 minutes a day for looking for information, then, with an hourly wage pay of NOK 600, and a workforce of 1000, we are talking of a bottom-line saving of close to NOK 50 million.

A valuable consequence for the company is its ability to free bound time for the employees to create increased value for the firm. A properly developed knowledge system should aim at reducing searching, retrieving and storing time by a factor of 2.

Our experience with Faros is that the system is used to release entrepreneurial forces creating new/better operating processes and services. One Business Unit went from 120 operating processes to less than 100, and expects to simplify the operation to approximately 50 critical processes.

The system's ability to handle the quality and control aspect required in an operational or functional setting is vital to the success of an activity. One Business Unit connected its kitchen purification process to good practice, operating procedures and pictures illustrating how to purify the kitchen. The majority of employees regardless of their mother tongue will most likely understand such a concise method of illustration. Furthermore it will probably reduce the likelihood of a bacteria outbreak, and thus time off due to illness.

Electronic communications between offshore and land cost oil companies significant sums of money. The Faros system can aid in reducing this cost through easier access to information, and together with the onshore expert, navigate from the same processes into the relevant information. Here the discussion of correct measures can take place and be resolved. The use of Faros can reduce the amount of wrong diagnoses, wrong treatment and wrong implementation. A maintenance process for a gas valve linked up to a good practice document illustrating, with pictures, how to install an O-ring, will reduce the likelihood of a gas leakage and prevent the production unit from closing down.

Faros can be used as a work control system when the drilling engineer is to preparing for a new production well. He is on board a production platform, communicating with the onshore drilling manager. Together they go through the same virtual reality pictures of a drill's trajectory, making sure the safety zones of the other nearby production wells are not being violated.

As a distributor of computer-based learning, it can save a Business Unit travel costs for each employee participating in a course through Faros. In July 1999, the Faros project was completed on schedule. The operational responsibility has now been transferred to the Business Units. Compared to other projects, we believe Faros has had a favourable cost curve.

The project can be divided in four groups of activities:

1. Concept, methodology and navigating metaphor
2. Knowledge mapping and work process
3. Visualization
4. IT structure.

As the concept can now be copied by other Business Units within the company, and adjusted to their specifications, the unit cost of Faros will drop considerably.

6.6. Conclusions

6.6.1. Summary

"There is no limit to the supply of money. The bottleneck is in the supply of good ideas and sound projects. That is what we need in order to sustain the ability to create value in our society".

Percy Barnevik made this statement when he was CEO of the Swedish/Swiss ABB Corporation, during his keynote speech at the first Norwegian Entrepreneurship conference in Stavanger, in 1988.

Knowledge management is not about quick fixes or mathematics. Consequently, both the head and heart must be involved in the process of KM in order to succeed in building a KMS. It has become a hot issue over the last year or two. When we started out searching for clues in the autumn of 1995, we could find no Internet sites offering articles on the subject. Today, one University of Texas site alone has over one hundred articles on KM. The concept has many facets to it. However, unless your system is able to assist users in creating new knowledge, that is, the ability to transfer and combine, experience, draw out new knowledge, and disperse that new knowledge among the members of the Community of Practice, you do not have a KMS. We must avoid the pitfalls of TQM, BPR, Benchmarking and many other good concepts that came into the business arena, but were hyped up by the "fixers" as the "system to fix all systems". Do not destroy the potential of KM by using a quick fix from a group that is offering "the ultimate solution". Building a KMS takes time and effort from the people involved, just like the pig that got fully involved.

Knowledge management is not about Information Technology, although IT is a supportive tool. KM is something vastly more. If properly structured and used, KM has the potential of becoming a tool for unleashing the power of the brain upon the global business arena. KM may become to the business world what the Manhattan project was to the Second World War. Being able to harness the power of the organization's collective brain, and combining the results in neural networks among the COPs is simply mind-boggling.

KM thinking is in its embryonic stage, and the issue is how is the company going to benefit from such a creative avalanche, should it be able to build a system? In the words of the Austrian economist Joseph Schumpeter [1939]: Any organization should engage in creative destruction. If we do not improve ourselves, the competitors will beat us to it. The companies that are most likely to gain a competitive advantage from KM, are the ones capable of creating and experimenting with the concept before the "also ran" get to know what hit them.

Human beings operating in watertight compartments, not talking to each other, but minding their own business, have been the way of organizing intellectual capital. The controller at the top of the pyramid is the one who sets the conditions and secures the commanding height. Mistakes are made, and made over again, without anyone reacting to them. By not securing and converting tacit knowledge into explicit knowledge, we waste valuable assets in the form of human capital. Faros was borne as a result of many frustrating episodes taking place in Statoil back in the early 1990s. The company structure was in the melting pot, as were the policies and procedures. As a meta-system for KM, Faros has been able to answer some of the needs identified by the users at the time.

While the original idea was to match visualized instructions to the actual work processes and train people to do a job right before carrying it out, we realized that this was not enough to create a KMS. As we continued to develop the concept, new groups of employees saw the possibilities in using it and feeding us new impulses. This demanded more and more of us. Creating Faros has been a challenging process. We had to go up a trail nobody had been before. It was a steep learning curve, as the users always wanted the results yesterday. Then we had to establish the arena and the local Communities of Practice - inch by inch. Finally we had to ensure that the employees actually used the system, and then wait for their judgement. When it came, it was like an avalanche of happiness and pride.

Basing our navigation on the Intranet, that Statoil had no plans to introduce at the time, was one of the more difficult decisions. However, had we not decided on the use of the Web, we would not have been able to build the functionality we can offer today through IT. Likewise, we had to create the symbology for designing work processes, to be agreed to by other communities in Statoil. As we succeeded in one area, we moved on to the next challenge. We practised experience transfer as we were creating new solutions, through copying a solution made for one Business Unit over to the next. We also developed a feedback system for the communities to share experience and develop new and smarter ways of working.

We had to develop a new vocabulary, such as the Knowledge Room, Work Process Navigation and JIT-JE. This gave us a language of communication among ourselves while we were developing the concept. We learned to use many techniques for quick results. In the world of the Internet you do not have time for the "mountain pine" to grow. We had to move swiftly, doing rapid prototyping processes, mixing elements and run in front of the train. There were so many things to be done, and we were constantly fighting against the clock.

Focusing on the Faros Work Processes Navigation as the commonality, and main arena for finding relevant information for the users, we managed to create strong user participation. This was due to the following aspects:

- Policies and procedures became simpler, more accessible and easier to relate to,
- Swapping experience, using a process map indicating the process you are in, became meaningful, removed misunderstandings and the NIH attitude,
- Continuous improvement and learning became more relevant and understandable through having a job or process to relate to,
- The many databases, storing data relevant to their work, became a non-issue for the users, as they did not have to relate to them any longer.

We created knowledge rooms for both operational and functional Communities of Practice, creating a seamless and transparent way of navigating for information between them. The value to the organization, and the individual employee, has been confirmed by the feedback that we have received. Through this novel system of navigation we discovered how they could cooperate through a common concept, making it a fully integrated KMS. This has immense possibilities for a company with both functional and operational activities. That, of course, does not bar a company with only one community of practice from building Faros.

We wanted our colleagues to be the King of IT, and not IT's servants. Early experimenting with computer-based learning through the Internet, we linked the concept to the work process structure, and saw what creative powers developed in the intersection between the media and the work processes. This will lead to the creation of new knowledge and give unlimited opportunities for life-long learning. The result will permeate the organization for absorbing, sharing and utilizing new information in the creation of a more competitive organization.

While experimenting, we have also been building. As Faros has been tested and tried by the users, we have received positive feedback. This has encouraged us to persist. Faros has been shown to people of many categories, both inside and outside Statoil. When Faros is demonstrated to people outside our work environment, we encounter the following reactions:

- They immediately understand and easily follow the work process structure and how the concept can aid its users in their work.
- The observers obtain a good idea of how this can be applied within their own area of work.

This demonstrates a clear indication of a general, and generic, system that is not oil and gas industry specific. Statoil, as most other companies, has a jungle of net sites and thousands of web pages. Finding your way about is at times very difficult. Faros is the only system that has an embracing structure for easy retrieval of any information. Faros' novel method of knowledge mapping, capturing, creation, dissemination and sharing, has we believe enhanced the functionality of the virtual organization. Based on Faros' deployment and usage to date, it is possible to conclude that this has been achieved.

We have been fortunate enough to meet people of world class within the issue of knowledge, who know how to use their knowledge effectively. Yet, we are but at the very beginning of the journey into the matter of knowledge. Our economic system will continue to prosper through some degree of specialization. However, the companies must not place themselves in the position of the dinosaurs, specializing to extinction. Thus, mind over matter must be the way to the future. This is where the Knowledge Management System comes in. We have to stop talking and start acting.

6.6.2. Further work

If we were to start a new project, what would we want to improve upon? Improvements must always benefit the user. It is, and must always be, the user who is in the KM focus. Room for improvements can be found in the following elements:

- Technology
- Methodology
- Human relations

Technology concerns IT's technical elements related to the template and technological platform, while Methodology relates to building navigational structures, meta-systems and methods for implementation. But it is in the Human Relations element, how the idiosyncratic web of human links, behaviour, opportunities and threats for the individual employee and community are cared for towards the organization, that we find the key to real success in tapping the intellectual capital of the organization. Succeeding here will really mean prosperity.

If you cannot actively relate to a KMS, you are out of business!

6.7. Lessons learned

- The basis for the holistic Faros concept is the work process, and a navigator structuring relevant information around the work processes.
- Building redundancies into the holistic system to benefit the users' mental maps reduces the painstaking and time-consuming effort to find stored information.
- Creating a knowledge management system is a double whammer: it requires a bottom-up, as well as a top-down approach. Without the employees, you do not have anybody using the system, but without the full support of management, you do not have financial muscles, and connections to management processes, to complete the project.
- The purpose of Faros was to offer an empowering knowledge system enabling the employees to build a learning organization.
- The Faros vision, goal and product were based on the hypothesis that "learning takes place in the work process". This learning is best achieved with a combined multimedia effect.

- In order to build a people-friendly system you need to create an arena from where to navigate for relevant information. To achieve this we created a Knowledge Room.
- For a knowledge management system to succeed, you need it to be dynamic. That means, it is the responsibility of each employee to improve and reinvent the organization by sharing experience and developing new good practice.
- A KM system developed to serve both operational and professional communities of practice, secures the dialogue between the two groups of employees leading to new knowledge.
- A KM system has as its principal goal to put the burden of finding relevant information on the organization. That is, through the principle of JIT-JE, management must assign resources to the task of linking relevant information to the work processes developed by the users.
- Developing a feedback function, and coordinating the feedback of new ideas into the hands of the process coordinators, secures the creation of new good practice.

REFERENCES

1. Beck, J. C. and Daveport, T. H., (1999), *Attention!*, Andersen Consulting's Outlook, No. 2.
2. Chandler. A. D. Jr., (1962), *Strategy and Structure: Chapters in the History of the American Industrial Enterprise*, MIT Press, Cambridge, MA.
3. Foster, J., (1986), *Innovation*, MacMilland, London.
4. Jim, B. J., (1999), *Smart Business - How Knowledge Communities can Revolutionize Your Company*. The Free Press, New York.
5. Joseph, S. J., (1939), Business Cycles: *A Theoretical, Historical and Statistical Analysis of the Capitalist Process,* McGraw Hill, New York. See also James M. Utterback, J. M., (1996), *Mastering the Dynamics of Innovation,* Harvard Business School Press, Boston.
6. Nonaka, I. and Tekuchi, H., (1999), *The Knowledge-Creating Company*, Oxford University Press.
7. NRK, (1999), The BBC Television documentary "The Human Body" was shown during Autumn 1999 on the Norwegian Broadcasting Corporation (NRK). The episode on the Brain was sent 25.10.99.
8. Senge, P., (1999), *The Fifth Discipline*. MIT Press, London.
9. Skyme, D., (1998), *Measuring the value of knowledge*, Business Intelligence Limited, London.
10. Teknisk Ukeblad, (1999), no. 26, p. 5.
11. Williams, P., (1999), *The Antidote,* Sloan Management Review, no. 22, p. 22. CSBS Publication Inc.

CHAPTER 7

EXPERIENCE

> **Objectives**
> - Identifying the hindsight of developing a KM system.
> - Identifying the hindsight of implementing the system.
> - Identifying the hindsight of Good Practice of running the system.
> - Identifying the hindsight of improvement and innovation.
> - Understanding the role of the human factor in creating a KM concept.

7.1. Introduction

In "Hard Times", Charles Dickens started with the following: "Now, what I want is Facts. Teach these boys and girls nothing but Facts. Facts alone are wanted in life. Plant nothing else, and root out everything else. You can only form the minds of reasoning animals upon Facts: nothing else will be of any service to them. In this life, we want nothing but Facts, sir; nothing but Facts!"

In all endeavours, great or small, grand or insignificant, relevant or irrelevant, facts alone never make the mark. In facts, you find the rational, the exact, the dictatorial, the hard and the cold. However, in order to succeed in the field that has anything to do with human relations, this is the most important aspect of knowledge management (KM). However, you need something more. You need to include the quality of humanity; that is, you need to have empathy.

No experience is objective. Neither are the activities of human beings purely based on the rational, the factual. There is always some previous baggage to be carried around, which everyone refers to when passing judgement. You therefore need to understand the nature of man in order to understand the nature of knowledge sharing and creation. Thus, facts are good to have as long as they are blended with the human qualities of empathy and goodwill. Only then can creativity and innovation from experience transcend human boundaries and become great values for all stakeholders.

When starting out to identify ways and means to develop Good Practice based on shared experience, we searched high and low for the technology and mechanism of creating the Faros knowledge management system. We discovered that what we ended up spending most of our time on was the human aspect. People are needed in order to make something work. Unless you cater for, and focus on, the human dimension, systems per se will be cold, factual and inoperable. They will simply not be used.

Knowledge management is about contest, not merely technology. It must describe value creating processes, and activities within these processes. It should be releasing the power of innovation, changes in the way we do and organize work, and improved value creating activities. Above all, focusing on managing the organization's repository of knowledge requires a rethinking of the vision and objectives from its leaders with the purpose to do all stakeholders well.

In this chapter, we will share some of our experience learned while building the Faros system, and some facts for you to consider. This will include experience from both the development and the implementation phases.

7.2. The customer

Never underestimate the user of a system, or what we can refer to as "the customer". It is a misconception to believe that the customer is the manager with the biggest stick, or budget. If anything, the manager should be the champion, backing up his employees in their endeavour to apply or develop knowledge creating systems. The customer is the user of a system, regardless of what system we are talking about. The greatest advances we made were in close encounter with the demanding, and intelligent, customers. There is no better way to develop something than in cooperation with an intelligent customer.

secure that there was only one original document with the given information. We maintained that through the Knowledge Management System, each employee should be able to reach whichever document, or other type of information, he/she required regardless of his/her unit. The Just-in-time, Just-enough philosophy was a cornerstone in our KMS. Therefore, the employees had to learn not to store copies in various relationships, risking that the document in one data bucket had not been updated when the original document was getting reviewed.

7.3.4. *Intranet*

Another challenge was the Intranet. While Faros needed this technology in order to get the pilot to function according to agreed concept by the users, Statoil had not yet accepted it as a standard in the common computer system. We had to get permission to continue the development while utilizing a dedicated server, named the Lion. While the Faros project helped the introduction of the Intranet in Statoil, once the Web was introduced, everybody wanted to make his/her own home page. Now the argument became: we do not need Faros, we can develop our own home page. With more than 18 000 employees, one can imagine the chaos if every employee should have their own home page, linked to whatever information they thought was relevant, but with no way to share each other's experience, or develop Good Practice in a formal system. This shows how people conceive things in their minds. Not only did most employees and managers have a diffused understanding of KM, but they did not have a good idea of how the Intranet could be applied for their benefit.

In Statoil's Data Unit we found both "friends and foes" - whose job was to introduce the Intranet and the Web to Statoil. Some understood and supported the project. From these colleagues we also got both support and encouragement. However, from others who worked with introducing Lotus products for storing information, and those working with the introduction of the enterprise resource system, the opposition was monumental. One such IT person insisted that the only way to develop an information retrieval system, was through a logical hierarchy from a given data file down to the individual information document to be retrieved. In Statoil this could mean clicking one's way down five, six or maybe more levels before retrieving the document; that is, if it was stored in that file. If it was stored in one of the thousand or so data buckets, or under other rubrications, then you had to try another entrance. This way you still would be using 30-40 % of your time looking for relevant information, as was discovered in an analysis of time usage at Statoil's Gullfaks Business Unit.

7.3.5. Redundancy

What we found when interviewing the users was the need for redundancy in locating relevant information. In the information-seeking moment, an employee looking for information will be in a given frame of mind. His/her mode will reflect the type of information sought for. This was one of the important developmental challenges – making the same information available from several vantage points. In the implementation section below we will show how the users experienced the result.

We know that people who have to make quick decisions, need to check information in a hurry, but if they cannot find any, they may develop negative stress. Negative stress in a high-risk industry, such as oil and gas, or finance, for that matter, is a safety hazard for the employee, the organization and the environment. That is a further reason for implementing a holistic KM system in an organization.

7.3.6. Facilitation

The biggest challenge was the creative dialogue with the users. We were depending on the users making their tacit knowledge explicit and being able to identify how they worked. When facilitating matters for the users, both for how they work and what they do, the development team struggled on two fronts, getting the employees to dedicate time to engage themselves in this work, and finding facilitators capable of extracting the tacit values. Finding an expert who could both participate in mapping the processes and converting the mapping into live Web data was no easy job. In 1996/1997 there was simply not enough hands to be found who knew enough about the Intranet, the Web and Lotus/Domino.

Due to the shortness of time and resources, we tried to connect those who had something to tell with those who could facilitate. We needed to get words converted to action without any middle layers. Thus we had two types of gatherings: one-to-one activities and meetings. There were two types of meetings: workshops where major elements needed to be discussed in plenary sessions, and user meetings. In the latter type of meeting, where a user representative from each unit participated together with the project management team, we tried to achieve consensus on major development issues. The workshops were used for creative activities as well as for coordinating the many issues and activities making up the daily work. For facilitation we primarily used "one-to-one" type meetings, a preferred form by the users. We also held regular project management meetings.

7.3.7. Two clicks to the information

Identifying and making relevant information available to the users was a major point in developing the system. However, we had seen how the hierarchy of information could lead to five or more clicks before reaching the relevant data. This, we concluded, should not be the fate of Faros KMS. Thus, we established the vision - "two clicks to information".

In order to achieve the "two click" goal we had to design the navigator in a manner to compress the navigational steps. We developed the Knowledge Room, a metaphor giving several layers of information in one picture. We also experimented, and gradually introduced, the Java concept of field sensitive information boxes. However, the technology was very young, and we had great problems implementing it in Statoil's data technology system at the time. As visions grew, we had to suffer from inadequate technology. From a normal stating point in the Knowledge Room, we ended up with three clicks to the information.

7.3.8. The Knowledge Room

Once we hit upon the metaphor demonstrating the Knowledge Room, the users became very attracted to the Faros system. With the landscape in the background, the user feels in control when he or she is choosing the window to enter for information gathering. In order to develop a robust system, we decided to base it on the Lotus/Domino technology applied to the Intranet. We did not apply the Java technology for the main navigational sequences, but used it in certain non-sensitive areas. Each Unit would have its own Knowledge Room (KR), with the same service elements, but with each room dedicated to the individual unit. The most important "window" behind the KR is the Value Chain Arrow with the work processes. It is from this position one can reach all JIT-JE information. From the Value Chain Arrow one should be able to reach information in two clicks. Sometimes we ended up having to use four due to sub-processes, but that was not often.

The KR gives you access to any category of information you choose. Some of the information categories will be "hard wired", that is, they will be common for all units, while some will be dedicated to an individual unit's characteristic requirements. During the development we discovered that one division had a certain requirement that was not of interest to other groups. In order to secure the KR for this user group, we had to design a section of the KR for this type of information. But before we could do that, we had to have a consensus on what common information elements one could reach from the KR.

We applied search technology for the *unstructured information*. Today, this technology has been made more robust and stronger, capable of finding all subjects inside or outside the organization. Such a system is the intelligent search engine Corporum, developed by CognIT AS, and tested out in Faros.

7.3.9. *Improvement and innovation*

When a Statfjord process owner is going to give an opinion regarding a certain process to be developed in Faros, he will copy another Operating Unit, for example Åsgard. Then he will supply his comments on top of that process, circulating it among the team members, who will correct it if needed. In this way a process can be driven forward in a dynamic manner, and be completed in a matter of a fortnight. We are talking of a dynamic prototyping process, where the road is created as you go, identifying for each other how one understands the job ought to be done.

Utterback [1994] discusses the work process mapping in the innovation of process activities in a manufacturing operation. Such activities include finding new methods of glass production, oil refining and many more processes. His argument is that when innovation takes place in these processes (like reacting to a shallow gas pocket) it is also possible to map a work process, although it may be different from the routine type operation. In this chapter we have tried to identify the relationship between KMS, invention and innovation.

Management's responsibility is first and foremost to forge new paths in the jungle of the market place. Those who think themselves well planted with both feet on the ground are not really well planted - just planted, paralysed and unable to move. This permanent position results in an incapability to free them and move forward. Thus, the purpose of management is to innovate and market the organization and its products in the marketplace.

If management does not understand the innovative power of knowledge management this is blatant contempt for the organization's intellectual capital. It used to be so that management had the exclusive "right" to innovate and preclude all other employees from entertaining such thoughts. It was management who should bring to the organization the required vitality needed to stay in front of the competition. No longer so. Should management ignore the power of the organization's human capital, the results will turn up in the next year's annual report. The organization no longer has the luxury to find out five years from now if their strategic direction was a success or not.

The *Faros concept* has demonstrated its ability to be used as a rapid prototyping system for developing new concepts, products or services. By not applying knowledge sharing systems for innovation and improvement, this can cost management dearly. Not using all capable hands and heads for positioning the organization in the marketplace, may turn out to be catastrophic for the organization, and a good reason for firing the CEO – without a golden handshake.

In the application of Faros, we found that both operating and service units reinvented old practices, and created more efficient new processes. They did this together, and through such effort made the company more effective. Their belief in shared practice became stronger and more robust as they were themselves involved, together with the multidisciplinary Faros team, in developing their own work environment. In the interface between two operating units, both social and intellectual capital was created.

Figure 7.1 illustrates the resulting structure from employees' active search for improvements and innovation regarding their area of influence. The figure identifies how the *Faros Holistic Model* functions as an innovative tool. Bear in mind that you still need the organizational structure, and management's support, to release the power of the knowledge workers.

It has been demonstrated that *Entrepreneurship* [Hjelmervik, 1987] can take place in large organizations. We found that, given the freedom of employees to identify with new processes or products, either as a process owner, or a user, Faros became a pool of innovative opportunities. The feedback function we built into Faros made it possible for employees to send experience back to the process owner, further reiterated the fact that the Faros KMS was one of the best ways to improve the structure, or make innovative changes.

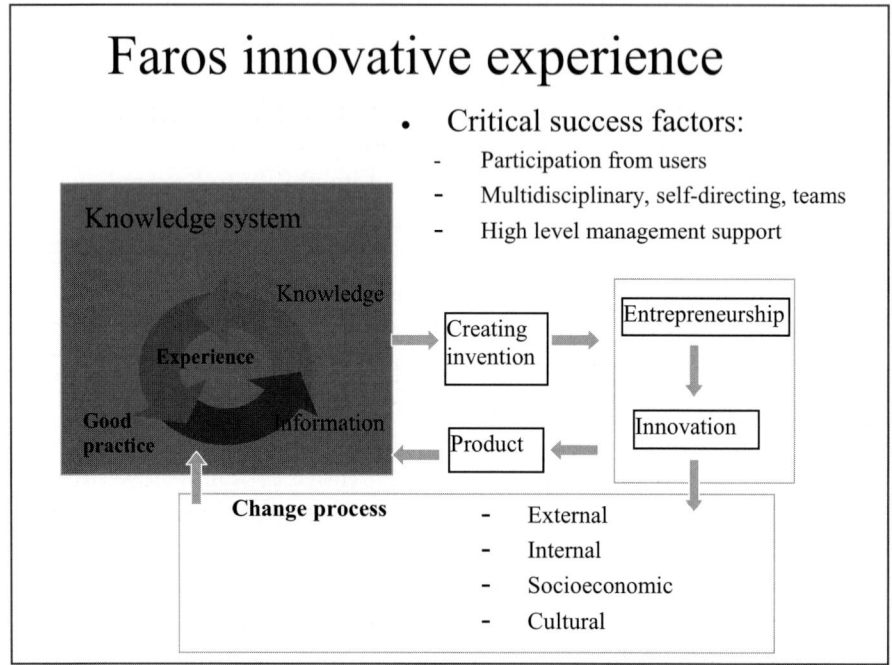

Figure 7.1: The Faros innovative experience

Making experience available to others (Figure 7.1) may trigger new associations concerning ways to operate facilities as it did for Statoil's employees who used the Faros system. It may also generate more effective operating processes. Furthermore, seeing applications in a new light may trigger inventive ideas resulting in innovative products or processes, as experienced in the case of Åsgard. Today, Åsgard is one of the most effective offshore hydrocarbon fields in the world.

7.4. Implementation

Moving from developing the basic concept to implementing it in the units was the next major task at hand. When talking of implementing, we describe both the Facilitation and the Usage of the Faros KMS in a unit. The word implementing can therefore be applied both to Facilitating and Usage. After some discussion with the users, this is what we could plan for in the winter of 1997. We decided to start facilitating for Faros in the D Service Unit (Pilot 1) in the winter 1997 and continue with the T Business Unit (Pilot 2). During the autumn 1997 the system was implemented in both units. In addition, we planned a start-up of facilitating the A Business Unit during the summer 1997, and the OM Service Unit in the winter 1998.

This section points out some of the things we experienced when facilitating and implementing the system for general use.

7.4.1. Service Unit

If we had to start anew, we probably would not have started with a Service Unit pilot. A Service Unit is a unit dedicated to providing service, such as construction, development, drilling, maintenance, catering, to the Business Units. A Business Unit, such as Heidrun, Statfjord, Troll, Trym or Åsgard, is responsible for operating the value chain. An organization's main value chain should always focus on what is the raw material on which the added value should be created, and forwarded to the customer. Thus, we have activities such as inbound logistics, production, and outbound logistics. By using a Business Unit as the model for the implementation process this will give the advantage of mapping the main value chain before mapping a more complex Service Unit's value chain. It is most likely the Business Unit's processes that dictate, and lead to, the need for the Service Unit's functions. Through such a process, one identifies what relationship the Service Unit has to the Business Unit. The "As is" mapping can now be expanded to "To be" mapping, securing the type of relevance the Service Unit plays in the greater scheme of things.

While the Business Unit plays centre stage for operating the organization, the Service Units are a must for the organization to function properly. There are several reasons for implementing a KM system in a service unit. First of all, it is the core unit for organizing all expertise within a functional activity in the organization. Secondly, some of its roles may be related to non-operational activities, such as R&D, or they are of a finite type activity, such as the analysis of an unscheduled event. Thirdly, with the many roles a Service Units has in the corporation, it may be difficult to synchronize them all through a process focus. Fourthly, we have the level of intellectual capital. As we sensed in another Service Unit, the average IQ was so high, and the individual employee so independently minded, that a consensus on what they wanted in a KM system was arduous to agree upon. Due to these factors one should always consider starting with facilitating the Business Units that are providing the cash flow within the organization.

In some organizations, however, such as those selling advice, a law office, a NGO or a government organization, "service" is the main business. It is thus paramount for the KM project owner to identify what is the core business within his/her organization,. Here it can be worthwhile to be reminded of Levitt [1963], who wrote a classic article about the American railroad demise. In this article he concluded that the American railroad was in trouble because they thought they were in the railroad business, while they in fact were in the transportation business.

Thus, in the D Service Unit it was difficult to implement the system. We started out by mapping two work processes. The mapping was primarily done by the Faros team, with the support of the process owners in the Service Unit. In addition, we had the support of a Service Unit facilitator. While the D-employees out in the operation found the system useful and functional, the employees within the core group at HQ, that is, people making up the D-staff, were less enthusiastic. As one service supervisor working in the staff unit said to me: "We (the service providers) are functional operators. We have to call it as we see it. There is no time to run to a computer to find out what is going on. Decisions have to be made on sight". What this supervisor did not understand was that it was exactly this attitude that resulted in unwanted occurrences in the operation, and which the Norwegian Oil Directorate made critical comments about. As the operating policies and procedures in the D-Unit were not followed, this was the cause of many unwanted events. That was a key driver for the D-Unit in requesting us to start developing the Faros KMS in the first place.

The people in the D-Unit, were substantial contributors to the design of the system. What we did not recognize as we started the implementation, however, was the importance of ensuring that the process mapping was done by the process owners, and supported by the Faros team facilitators. In order for a work process to be adapted for regular use, it is imperative that the process owner secures the process' authenticity by engaging the users in the act of mapping the activities relevant for bringing the value creation forward in the most effective manner. Due to unclear division of responsibility between the facilitating team and the process owners, it was difficult to get the processes mapped. Only by reaching a high level of authenticity can a Units "As is" processes be revised, evaluated and improved for a "To be" status.

In the operating units, the D-staff needed to communicate in a system that gave them access to information/Good Practice within their own function, as well as being able to connect into the Business Units' system. It was among these service workers that we found the greatest appreciation of the system. The main difference between service employees working in the staff units and the service employees seconded to the operating units lies in the attitude to searching for relevant information. Being away from the central group, one is rather "isolated" from the core, and subsequently has a greater need for relevant information.

At the head office, it is often argued that people can find all kinds of expertise across the hallway, or down the corridor. Unfortunately, this is great in theory, but in practice it does not function. As experts are moved more than 10 metres from one another, the daily visit is replaced by a weekly visit. Unless you have structured meetings with regular intervals, two experts within the same service unit, working on different floors, will only make unplanned calls to each other once a month. And, it is the unplanned calls that often are the start of a creative journey, leading to innovation and value creation for the stakeholders.

It turned out that the engineers, and other service workers seconded to the operating units, believed in, and became users of the system. However, the employees located in head office were much less enthusiastic about the system. It should be added that some of the head office employees were themselves trying to develop, and get approved, various types of software. There were, in other words, hidden agendas among these employees, which explain their lack of support for a general system.

7.4.2. Business Unit

The plan was to parallel the process in the T-Business Unit together with the D-Service Unit. In order to produce a quick result, we concentrated on the documentation part of the T-Unit's activities, and started the facilitation of the unit's HES (Health, Environment, and Safety) Section. The Section's function, among others, was to ensure the use of operating policies and procedures related to the operation of its hydrocarbon field. Finding the right type of document in relation to operating an offshore field was of great concern to T-Unit's management. By applying the Faros system structure, we started out converting Lotus/Word documents to Domino/Web documents, capable of being linked to a given work process. Then we systematized and linked the relevant documents to the appropriate window in the Knowledge Room.

The Unit wanted first and foremost to make the policy and procedures available electronically, and in a form that was easily accessible. Management's greatest concern was the security aspect of its operation. Should a task be performed without following the appropriate procedures, resulting in an unwanted event, management would have been criticized both within the company, but also in public. With Faros in place, no employee could say they proceeded with the job because they could not find the appropriate document – and there was no time for the long search. By entering Faros, you will find the appropriate document in seconds.

Facilitating the T-Unit meant restructuring and webifying the operating policies and practices, and linking them to the HES process. The facilitating team, supported by the HES Section in the T-Unit, did most of the process design. But again, the work was based on close cooperation with the users. The work went parallel with the discussion of the Knowledge Room design (see Section 7.5.3). We deliberately ran several development issues in parallel; one of them was the Knowledge Room. We did not have the luxury of running such a project analogously. Not only would it take much longer time for realization, and hence the start of the payback, but also the customers wanted to see results fast, and they got heavily involved in participating in the work. This was very good. With hindsight, however, one of the issues we spent too much time on was the initial design of the Knowledge Room. Due to this design dilemma, we lost some momentum.

On 1 January 1998, the T-Unit manager announced it was switching to the Faros KMS. An implementation guide was developed and added to the announcement. This became a milestone in the life of the Faros project. Prior to the announcement, we had information meetings with the operating staff and the HES employees. The facilitating team was also available as a light fire brigade, answering calls as problems occurred. However, there were not to be too many. There were still design issues to be developed further, but the system worked very well, according to the Unit's employees. As the Unit's operating employees only could access the HES process, the system was called Faros light. It was not until we started to facilitate the A-Business Unit that we got involved in phase 2 of T-Unit's total value chain.

We started facilitating the A-Unit's processes during the summer 1997. The advantage of starting at this point was twofold:

1. Experience from the Development phase and
2. Experience from the first Pilot phase.

We used the term *first Pilot*, because it turned out that all implementations had to be treated as *pilots* due to the underlying need for adjustments to the basic model. No two Businesses Units or Service Units were identical in all aspects of their functions. While the Business Unit has horizontal flow in its value chain, and thus can vary regarding the tools and equipment applied, a Service Unit crosses all Business Units, applying in principle the same work process to each and every Business Unit. However, due to its nature, each Service Unit has a unique role and task in the organization, and thus will apply its work processes in a different manner from the next Service Unit. The importance of these lessons was major, but at the same time we had to learn as we went along implementing Faros throughout the organization.

Our experience from the T-Unit was to get the users involved on a broad scale, not just two or three people to have as discussion partners, leaving most of the work to the facilitating team. Continuing with the A-Unit, we assigning process responsibility to 12 of the operating unit's most experienced employees. For the A-Unit we also designated "super-user" responsibility to some of users. Being responsible for a work process had additional consequences. As you described the "As is" work processes, you had the responsibility also to identify a possible improvement (a "To be") in the present practice. The payback was not simply to get a KMS up and running, but a revision of the work practice resulted in increased effectiveness of the Business Unit.

After nine months, we started to plan for completing the implementation process. This time we organized the users in groups and gave each group a "hands-on" training course of half a day. During two days around 100 employees were introduced to the use of Faros. This turned out to be a very popular way of introducing the system. By this time, the process owners, being part of the Business Unit's employee group, had been speaking to their colleagues about the system. The process owners were an enthusiastic bunch. Their enthusiasm spilled over on their colleagues and gave them a better understanding of how the system may help them in doing a better job. In July 1998, the A-Unit managers announce the implementation of Faros KMS as the Unit's knowledge system.

The learning aspect is important. When the operating employees become the process owners and super users, there is likely to be greater success than if the facilitators do most of the process development. The operator colleagues' standing with the rest of the employees in the A-Unit, ensured that most employees looked upon the system very favourable. Contrary to the experience in the T-Business Unit and the D-Service Unit, the A-Unit became our first holistic user of the KMS. The concept turned out to be so robust that also the T-Unit wanted a version as well.

7.4.3. The holistic model approach

Faros is developed along a holistic model approach. That is, we should be able to link all of an organization's activities for the purpose of collecting, creating, sharing and use new knowledge into the model.

Our experience from developing Faros is just that – a holistic concept. One of the key design hurdles was how to retrieve information. Furthermore, how could we ensure that all users would find the approach useful? Early on we started to experiment with a room concept. However the first design turned out to be confined and darkish. After having given the task to some professors, we ended up choosing a room where you could see out, opening various windows to obtain relevant information. The present Knowledge Room structure turned out to be suitable for both the Service Unit and the Business Unit. We let the user group participate in the final selection process. The content of the Knowledge Room, and the information bar at the top of the web page, was frozen during the spring 1998, two years after we first kicked the project off.

When implementing the system, the users, it turned out, did not find the original design appealing. Thus, while we strived to implement the system we also had to redesign some of the elements, namely what functions to offer and what the Knowledge Room should look like. One should remember that in 1996/1997 Intranet design had just arrived. No one knew how the users would react to design and availability of functions. From spring 1997 until summer 1998, we had to work in parallel with the implementation programme and redesigning part of the system. In June 1998, at a user meeting, we changed the Knowledge Room to today's visual standard and functions. It took 18 months from introducing the first graphical picture of the Knowledge Room until the users agreed with the concept. In order to get to that decision, we contacted expertise on the subject, and gave them the task of finding alternative graphical expression.

Creating knowledge requires that one is able to retrieve relevant information in order to put together new knowledge. All together we implemented various versions of Faros KMS in about ten Business Units or Service units. However, we know that some units poached on other units' systems. The reason for this was that the poaching unit found the availability of information organized in Faros "member" units quite adequate. Rather than investing in its own system (which would probably just require some adjustments to an already developed system) they used the other units' system.

The ability to retrieve the same information from various entrants was so good that Units that were not officially members of the Faros User Group, started using it. The reason why units without their own dedicated Knowledge Room could access the Faros web server, and use it for own requirements, was due to the holistic approach Faros Knowledge Management system is built upon. Through a navigational and structural methodology we succeeded in making information available, meaningful and shareable in one common standard.

7.4.4. Redundancy for JIT-JE information retrieval

Redundancy development is an important aspect of the knowledge retrieval system. The ability to retrieve information, regardless of what frame of mind, or work situation, someone is in, is important. But what is equally important is that you are shielded from information overload. That is, you should be able to determine what information you need when you need it. Thus, we developed information retrieval based on the philosophy of JIT-JE (Just-in-time, Just-enough).

From the analysis made after the implementation, that is, during the spring 1999, it became clear that the JIT-JE system was popular among the users. Faros simply appealed to both the high and low, blue and white-collar workers. An example is the crane operator having the responsibility for operating the crane (together with five others in the group), and making sure that health and safety regulations were followed (sole responsibility for cranes' Health, Environment and Safety).

Should our crane operator (John) require some information related to his functions in the crane, his mode of thinking would be the crane? If, on the other hand, he should be in the crane safety mode, he may not think in the "operational mode" at all. But here all the information on HES has been stored in a different database from the one the crane operator normally uses. But which one? If his problem was an emergency, how long time would it require to seek through the many databases it could have been filed under. And remember: no data should be filed in more than one original place.

We learned that due to the pressure the employee is under when taking decisions, knowing that a piece of information is available is great relief, regardless of vantage point.

7.4.5. Communities of Practice

There are many types of Communities of Practice (COP), both official (part of the commando structure) and unofficial (people with a common cause). We found many types, both official and unofficial communities in Statoil. The official COPs should function as they are part of the company's hierarchy, while the unofficial function due to personal interest. Yet, the commonality between them was that they did not function as well as they could have done.

It is safe to say that COP thinking is right when considering developing, and improving the organization's ability to create new values. As one Service Unit employee put it, through Faros I now understand better what service I should offer the Business Units. Thus, the Service Unit's COP should be better able to service the Business Unit's COP due to a clearer understanding of who to contact, what problems are they likely to encounter and how can we support their "agenda". But for a COP to function, one needs both engagement and purpose. In a knowledge sharing system, developed by the users, and with each work process dedicated to an "owner", we found the basis for functioning COPs. If you find types of recognition for employees when participating in the system, the combination of KMS and COP is valuable.

7.4.6. The practice of improvement, innovation and learning

There is no such thing as status quo in combination with prosperity. It becomes an oxymoron to strive for both tranquillity and innovative organizations in the market place. As long as someone is able to innovate and sell a better mousetrap than is available on today's market, he or she will accumulate value on account of others. Innovation forces change upon society and its institutions. In other words, you cannot have your cake and eat it.

Innovate or perish is the only way societies, and organizations, can prosper. If you do not nourish and seize, change, someone else will. A case in point: The global HUGO (Human Genome Organization) with participants from 22 countries had as its task to map the human genome. Completion was expected around 2002-2003. Craig Venter, chief scientist of HUGO, jumped ship and established a commercial business called Celera. In competition with HUGO, Celera was able to complete the mapping years before HUGO. Celera was able to make money out of their discoveries, even though they are similar to HUGO's. It may be unfair to compare the societal human genome project with the commercial project

Chapter 7 Experience 251

started by Celera. However, the fact that Craig Venter decided to jump the official project in order to make faster progress with the commercial project resulted in a quicker completion of unravelling the secrets of the human genome. In the process Genetech laid claim to several of the findings based on the results from the HUGO project.

Part of the Faros concept is an electronic learning space. We developed several learning elements that could be linked to various work processes. One such learning video was related to safe crane operation and maintenance.

In good time before the turn around for crane maintenance at A-Unit, the process owner gathered the crane group for a dry run. They linked up to the work process in Faros, went through the process relevant for the job at hand and clicked into the video as needed. As they went through the procedures, and video shots, displayed on the wall from a video cannon, they discovered a mismatch between the work process and their own experience from last turnaround. At the last turnaround the maintenance team had to wait for a week, with the equipment out of function, before they were supplied with a missing piece of equipment. That piece should have arrived together with the other equipment and maintenance gear, but took one week longer out to the platform. The order took just so long to be processed. By starting the order processing for that piece one week earlier, the team reduced the inactivity of the crane by one full week. Should the platform be depending on a fully operational crane for its production of hydrocarbons, one week could have been costly for the organization. This way Faros helped improve the work process for crane maintenance. With one hundred smaller or larger processes to one operation, think what potential a knowledge creating and sharing system can offer an organization.

Thus, if you want to succeed in the marketplace, it requires an organization with the ability to apply its human capital to improve products and innovate for commercial exploitation. Unless the organization has the ways and the means to support such behaviour, it will not be able to renew itself as a progressive and prosperous unit. At a given point in time market demands will change, and the actors in the market place change with them. The experience from implementing and running the Faros KMS has demonstrated the system's ability to support improvement and innovation in companies.

The S-Business Unit asked to have the Faros system implemented. It took us no more than three months to copy the A-Unit system, make the necessary changes to fit the S-Unit operation, and start implementation. Within another month, three major work processes were introduced - the three containing several sub-processes. The project resulted in reducing the time from start to implementation by nine months, or reducing the process to one third of the A Pilot. Although the structure was the same, the elements were different. Thus, just like HUGO project, Faros could be exploited by new Business Units and Service Units faster than the prototype "unit due to the project's ability to assimilate into new" units. That means that Statoil, as an organization, can exploit new knowledge faster than its competitors.

This ability to combine experience in the circle of knowledge with innovative opportunities leads to a change process in organizations. Such change processes will always be risk related. However, unless one is willing to change, you will be stuck in the quagmire, resulting in a slow death. Only by improving or innovating the value change, is it possible to end up with the opportunity to serve the market needs in the future. This is what we were able to identify in the Faros project.

The process of experience transfer is also part of the improvement, innovation and learning circle. We discovered that through the feedback function, the basis for the transfer circle, new ideas were developed and new insight was gained. An oil company operates in many fields around the world. The philosophy of life-long learning can be very costly in traditional methods of operating a learning system. We wanted to change that through the video courses linked to the work process. But, through such a system we discovered the strong learning effect it had on the employees.

Due to the distance between HQ and the location of the Business Units, Faros gave good support to distance collaboration, as was pointed out by an operator in the A-Business Unit.

We were sitting in our office offshore, while a service provider was sitting in Stavanger. Through the same system (Faros), we were able to identify the problem and develop a new solution regarding the work process. The improvement, innovation and learning circle found in a holistic knowledge management system is valuable, even explosive, for the organizations that are capable of harnessing its power. An interesting aside is that it attracts both young and old employees in their quest for learning.

7.4.7. *Developing Good Practice*

In order to develop *Good Practice* you need employees to agree to share experience. Thus, experience sharing and transfer are the key ingredients to building a case for Good Practice. Some people also call it the "latest practice". But how do we know it is the latest. Maybe, what we consider the latest is in fact outdated in other organizations and non-functional.

How did we develop Good Practice in the Faros KMS? The feedback loop was actively used to suggest ideas about other ways to carry out a given task. The person offering an alternative to present practice sent the proposal to both the process owners located in the Service Unit, and to the person responsible for the process in the Business Unit. Should the person making the suggestion belong to the Service Unit in question, he or she should send a copy to the manager. The reason is that a suggestion should never be sent to just own mailbox. After many discussions we came to realize that if this has gone unchallenged, a suggestion box or a suggestion dropped into just one person's mailbox, often results in non-committal action. Towards the end of the Faros project, we started developments towards creating an automatic addressing of experience. That is, the system should be able to identify who you are, who is responsible for the process you are working on, and who is responsible in the Business Unit representing the process. This work is now being continued in CognIT A.S, which we hope will be able to serve employees with genuine solutions to the challenge.

Once the process owner has received feedback to his process, he will evaluate the feedback for originality and improvement content. Should he find the submitted proposals valuable, he will call a meeting with the representatives from the Business Units to discuss the possibility of changing the current Good Practice? Through a given process, the result will be encoded in the relevant work process, and appropriate links will be made to where one can read about the new Good Practice.

7.5. Industrializing Faros

We found it useful to develop roles for the participants to fill when entering the realm of a knowledge management system, as well as standardizing products, applications, and business modules.

7.5.1. Roles

A KMS requires different roles and functions by the actors. Exploiting the organization's intellectual capital requires a different organizational structure than that found in the hierarchical organizations. For the system to function, that is, for a knowledge system to result in capturing, creating, delivering and using information-to-knowledge creation, you need to assign roles enhancing the relevant behaviour, resulting in the desired effect – improved bottom-line results.

7.5.1.1. Process Owner

The purpose of the Process Owner role is to make sure that there is a person responsible for all aspects of keeping the process operational. That means, all activities within the process, all changes to the process, all new Good Practice and innovations resulting from the process and possible removal of the process, should be the responsibility of the Process Owner. The Process Owner may, or may not, have line functions. However, it must be a senior person, being in a position to influence the organization's decision-making processes.

Furthermore, the Process Owner should be responsible for identifying all process-elements and sub-processes within the main work process, and assign responsibility for mapping all elements of the process. Such responsibility can be assigned to Super Users as well as other users. The Process Owner is also responsible for securing appropriate evaluation of the individual process elements, or sub-processes, and assigns critical values to the activities. These values relate to the effect the activity has on the main process. Criticality is assigned to three elements: Health, Environment and Safety; Costs; and Operation. In order for an activity to be very critical, you assign a value at the high end of the scale, with a low criticality on the lower end of the measurement scale.

The task of identifying the values of a process must be a joint effort between the owner and the user. However, it will always be the user who knows the function of an activity best, and whether or not the intended activity has a critical impact on the process. One example can be the use of an electric truck on board an offshore oilrig. While the truck is part of the maintenance process, it is not deemed a critical part. Thus, the activity can be described verbally and linked to the point in the process where such a tool is required used. The function does not, however, require its own sub-process description.

While the owner is formally responsible, and must approve the final criticality evaluation, it can be left to the users to identify the critical values for the work process.

7.5.1.2. Super users

Mapping of the many functional activities within a work process is a role left to the Super users. They know, and can define, describe and connect each of the sub-processes and activities within the process. It is the Super users who can support the Process Owner in updating or changing the process. Super users are needed to support the other users within the process domain. This group of users may be part of the Process Owner's panel for recommending changes to the process. While the Process Owner comes from a Service Unit, the Super users may be in charge of the process within their operating domain.

7.5.1.3. Users

These are all employees working within a given process area. They are the ones who give life to the process, and who are the closest to suggest changes in the process when required. They will send these change suggestions to the Process Owner as well as the Super user in his or her operating domain.

7.5.1.4. Champions

All organizations, and parts of organizations, require leaders. Flat structures require fewer leaders. But with each leader having more people reporting to one person, he or she needs a different function in order to be effective. One such function is the champion's role. We have realized that if a KMS is to function according to its intentions, someone needs to support the use of the system. The champion is the leader of a Business Unit or Service Unit. He or she must support, and cherish, the use of the system. The champion must find methods to encourage use through various forms for remuneration, not necessarily economic compensation and annual employee goals.

7.5.1.5. Facilitator

As the name indicates, the Facilitator's task is to support the process of creating a Knowledge Management System. In order for the organization to identify potential changes to the work process, you need to develop an "As is" situation description. Through facilitation, the Facilitator's job is to help in the Process Owners, and users, describing the work processes, sub-processes, activities and tasks that take place in the operation on an "As is" basis.

Furthermore, he or she will support the linking up of all process descriptions, and all relevant information, against all identified processes. Relevant information being for example Good Practice examples, regulatory or organizational procedures, tables for calculating a physical phenomenon, technical specifications, learning or demonstration video and other documents of interest.

The Facilitator will also support the users in identifying the difference between critical and non-critical work activities, and help choose the ones that will support an effective work process. The non-critical activities, or processes, should be linked to the main work process as a description of activities that may support the critical process. However, it should be the task of the Process Owner to ensure that his or her process is functioning optimally, resulting in a more effective operation.

7.5.2. Organizational structures

All research on innovation suggests that hierarchies reduce improvements and innovation. Thus, in order to succeed as a learning organization, new ways to structure the organization may be beneficial. New formal and informal functions will force themselves upon the organization once you allow people to connect with free will. In the USA, the saying goes: whenever a new campus is being built there is a question of where to put the walk paths. The answer is: leave it alone for a while and create the walk paths where the students have blazed the trails.

The same is true for your organization. There will be organized Communities of Practice, both formal and informal, as the knowledge system is being implemented and used in the organization.

7.5.3. Standard products, applications and business modules

In previous chapters, it has been pointed out that knowledge management is not an IT system. However, without the IT element, there would not be an effective KMS. Thus, we needed to develop some IT related elements, along with the non-IT-related products.

The IT related elements are the Navigator template, Work Process Navigator, Feedback Function and technical details such as Internet, Java and object oriented drawing tools.

Applications are, among others, the Knowledge Room, Work Process methodology, Good Practice methodology, Redundancy methodology and the Electronic Learning System.

The Business modules are such functions as Project Directive, Process Mapping Structure, Symbol Structure and Implementing Guide.

All these elements are proprietary applications for the Faros system. However, one can see clearly that such applications are required to develop should one decide to go for a KMS.

7.5.4. The business case

According to a user analysis in Gullfaks, the operators are using 30-40 % of their time searching for, retrieving and storing documents. Another analysis found that 63 % of all IT-users could not find a letter written by a colleague and saved to a data filing archive. According to the Dutch-British Unilever, 80 % of the employees repeat mistakes made by themselves and other employees.

If, by implementing a KMS, one is able to reduce the employee's time for document handling (find, process, store and deliver) by 10 % of his or her total disposal time (conservative estimation), you may reduce costs by close to USD 0.75 million per 100 employees/year. In addition you have all improvements made to the business processes, and innovations in the organization, resulting in both improved effectiveness and new business opportunities.

7.6. The engaged user - key to success

We found that making things complex and difficult to grasp will result in a lost cause. To succeed with developing and implementing a system for knowledge sharing, you need to apply the old principle – KISS, *keep it simple stupid*. Create simple solutions based on the process the users and process owners know. Leave the data technology for later.

Enable the users to fully understand the process thinking and demonstrate how to develop the "As is" processes. Visualize how the process thinking may result in a "To be" process development, resulting in new and improved value flow. This will result in transferring "ownership" for the operation of the organization from a few managers to the total employee population. Such ownership will engage participation from the many.

In order for the employees to appreciate the "ownership" role in full, also visualize how the organization's vision and goals are tied into the "To be" process. The best visualization of how to reach the future is by demonstrating the management's engagement and the win-win possibility for the employees. Compensating employees for an extraordinary engagement does not necessarily require a monetary reward. Recognition, or what the artist Andy Warhol called the "15 minutes of world fame", may be an equally valuable compensation.

Make sure the employees get immediate feedback whenever they are going that extra "mile" to support the KMS. Also make sure that the feedback is being distributed to the Community of Practice. And, furthermore, let the COP become engaged in a positive competition of value creation.

7.7. Verification of Faros

On 4 April 1999, a team of internal auditors delivered their findings regarding the Faros project's implementation in the relevant Business and Service Units in Statoil. The mandate was to evaluate, on a independent basis, the need for a KMS in Statoil, its relation to the various data systems, profitability/effectiveness potentials, and customer satisfaction.

The audit report made the following conclusion:
- *Cost:* Acceptable
- *Quality*: Customers (users) found it to be of high quality
- *Service*: Good service from the Faros team.
- *Facilitation*: Customers experience the Faros team as very good in supporting the work process development.
- *Statoil system structure*: Need for an organizer such as Faros, a seamless navigator being able to link to all different systems.
- *Experience transfer*: Important support for co-ordinating and use of experience traverse Business and Service units in Statoil.
- *Work process development system*: an important contributor to mapping of work processes in the organization.
- *Corporate competency*: Important contributor to raising the company's knowledge base, and development of new Good Practice.
- *IT solutions*: Experienced as good.
- *System quality*: Faros has been internationally in the forefront, and is as good as can be expected given the technology.

7.8. Conclusions

In this chapter, we have attempted to share with you some of our experience learned while building the Faros system, and some facts have been highlighted. Among other things, our experience from both the development and the implementation phase has been included in their summarized form. We have stressed that knowledge management is about content, not merely technology. It describes value creating processes, and activities within these processes. It is a means to release the power of innovation, changes in the way we do our work, and organize it, as well as improved value creating activities. Above all, focusing on managing the organization's repository of knowledge requires from its leaders a rethinking of vision and objectives with the purpose to do all stakeholders well.

Most of all, the focus of the chapter had been on identifying the hindsight of developing a KM system, implementing the system and Good Practice of running the system.

7.9. Lessons learned

- In a knowledge management initiative, the human factor is centre-stage. If left out, one has a cold and inoperable system that is destined to fail. The reason is that KM is about content, not merely technology. To create content, you need people both to fill in and to use it.
- The KM system must be user friendly. Missing out on the understanding of users' needs and you have a system only for the few, which is the technologists.
- The creating of a KM is done to make your colleagues operate better. That is, regardless how the technology develops, each and every employee should be able to contribute to the value creating effort at full capacity.
- Never start developing a KM system for the whole of the organization at the same time. It will drown the project group within a very short time. Secure a good pilot, a reference case to demonstrate how it should be done.
- While it is difficult, strive to limit the number of clicks from a work process to the relevant information no more than three.
- For a KM system to function, you need a holistic system encompassing both operating and service organizations. Where the operating employees feel they "own" the local processes, and become Super users, this will ensure great success.
- There should be only a single original storage of a document, but many avenues to that information. It is important for the users to have many avenues to find same information. That means: redundancy.

- The process of experience transfer is part of the improvement, innovation and learning circle leading to new Good Practice, resulting in improvements in the company's performance.
- When creating a KMS, make sure to apply the right roles to the right people. A Super user is not a Facilitator, nor a Champion. It pays to have the roles cleared up before starting.
- Use as many of the standard IT solutions as possible when building the knowledge concept. Untested IT products have a tendency to create turbulence, resulting in the users dropping out.
- A knowledge system without a *learning capacity* is useless. They are the four elements: finding, creating, sharing/using and re-using/learning that make up the KM concept.

REFERENCES

1. Dickinson, D., (1992), *Lifelong Learning for Business: A Global Perspective,* Conference paper, Oxford University.
2. Levitt, T. (1963), *Why the American Railroad was in trouble.* Harvard Business Review: Market Myopia.
3. New Horizons for Learning: http://www.newhorizons.org.
4. Utterback, J., (1994), *Mastering the Dynamics of Innovation.* pp. 107-195, Harvard Business School Press, Boston.
5. Hjelmervik, O. R., (1987), *Turning on the Intrapreneurs.* Scandinavian Oil & Gas Magazine, 11/12, Oslo.

CHAPTER 8

MONITORING AND MEASUREMENT IN KNOWLEDGE MANAGEMENT

> **Objectives**
>
> - Understand the importance of the measurement of intellectual capital in knowledge-based economy.
> - What is the difference between scientific management and knowledge management?
> - Understand the need to measure results.
> - What do today's measurement systems measure?
> - Understand criteria for a KM monitoring and measurement system.
> - Know how to measure intellectual capital in your organization or company.

8.1. Introduction

Measuring assets has been an occupation developed over the last century or so, and has primarily been the subject of measuring fixed, or tangible assets. Intangibles, such as goodwill and *intellectual property* (patents, patterns, drawings, etc.) have been more controversial. The reason is, just like much else in real life, some men like the mother, others the daughter, just as some women prefer older men, younger men and others. To put a value on feelings, hunches, colours or words is difficult. Especially before the market has been asked to judge. It is therefore we are addressing the issue of measuring knowledge, or *intellectual capital* with great humility.

In this chapter, we will introduce some thoughts about how to measure the value of knowledge. It will not be an exhaustive search for the truth (as we do not believe in absolute truth), but rather an attempt to touch the mountain tops. It will be just like standing on top of a peak on a mountain, above the fog. You can see many peaks around you, but not the valleys, with their magnificent and varied fauna, below. So, it is with knowledge. You cannot evaluate, in a reasonable manner, the knowledge embedded in the mind of a person. (The knowledge embedded in artefacts is called information, while the knowledge embedded in your mind is true knowledge. In the discipline of *knowledge management*, we are, unfortunately, often mixing the two).

Existing measurement models are almost exclusively derived from the analysis of systems. We argue that this makes them suitable for measuring knowledge embedded in artefacts and activities already converted to facts and figures. Our approach makes a clear distinction between a value-derived knowledge creating model and those derived from systems. We will describe how our value-based KM *Monitoring Model* (KM3) (see Figure 8.4) can achieve definite benefits within the knowledge management discipline.

8.2. Scientific management vs. knowledge management

The field of *knowledge management* is not new. History is littered with cases illustrating how entrepreneurial people have created imperfect competition by applying new knowledge or old knowledge in new ways, to a market situation. Measures have been developed for identifying indicators that determine an economic situation or a quality assurance programme. Often, a financial test can give indications as to whether or not a given organization has appropriate on cash, earnings, capital base or debt level.

Academics have often helped management to create systemic indicators, or measurement methods in order to identify what is going on in an enterprise. The purpose of these is to map the past, and give an acronymic description of the status quo. Management's intention is both to establish past achievements and apply these rear-view images onto the future, by planning future activities based on past performance. In theory it is possible, but in practice impossible. As long as you are operating with financial measures resulting from tangible production, it is possible to apply quantitative measures to determine the present situation, just like F. W. Taylor. Taylor formalized the principles of scientific management, and put forward the fact-finding approach. His methods were largely adopted, and were a replacement of the old rule of thumb.

In 1909, he published the book for which he is best known: *Principles of Scientific Management.* (Taylor, 1909) A feature of Taylor's work was stopwatch timing as the basis of observations. He started to break the timing down into elements and it was he who coined the term 'time study'. Taylor's uncompromising attitude in developing and installing his ideas caused much criticism. Scientific method, he advocated, could be applied to all problems and applied just as much to managers as workers. In his own words he explained:

> *The old fashioned dictator does not exist under Scientific Management. The man at the head of the business under Scientific Management is governed by rules and laws that has been developed through hundreds of experiments just as much as the workman is, and the standards developed are equitable.*

Taylor had the following four objectives for *scientific management*:
- The development of a science for each element of a man's work to replace the old rule-of-thumb methods.
- The scientific selection, training and development of workers instead of allowing them to choose their own tasks and train themselves as best they could.
- The development of a spirit of hearty cooperation between workers and management to ensure that work would be carried out in accordance with scientifically devised procedures.
- The division of work between workers and the management in almost equal shares, each group taking over the work for which it is best fitted instead of the former condition in which responsibility largely rested with the workers. Self-evident in this philosophy are organizations arranged in a hierarchy, systems of abstract rules and impersonal relationships between staff.

Before scientific management, such departments as work-study, personnel, maintenance and quality control did not exist. What was more, his methods proved to be very successful at the time. People such as Henry Ford, Pier DuPont and Alfred Sloan were all disciples of Taylor and his methodology. By applying such measurements to planning, one is in fact extrapolating the past into the future. Such was the application of strategic methods through most of the second half of the last century.

In the 21st century, however, Taylor's scientific methods do not suffice. In today's knowledge-based economy, other measures are required for the organization to monitor its progress. Unfortunately, the world still uses financial statements and units produced and sold as measures of progress and profitability, so called "bean counting". Why is that? One reason is the long history of using scientific measures (accounting and counting methods) in describing an organization's situation. Another is the length it takes for standard accounting measures to be acknowledged as universal, so those stakeholders in another country can study an organization in one country. A third reason is lack of a general agreement on "soft" measures. But it is exactly the "soft" issues which are the dynamos driving the world, and prosperity, forward. This dynamo is the human brain.

Taylor's hard line and mechanistic optimization focused on scientific management and came under fire when the words soft elements appeared on the scene. Herbert Simon came forward in 1944 as one of the first to significantly challenge Taylor's thinking for this reason. In "Administrative Behaviour" Simon [1972] points to the fact that managers must try to satisfy requirements rather than optimize when they only have incomplete knowledge and information. Decisions have to be made in spite of *soft constraints*, *fuzzy constraints* and elements that are non-cognizant to the manager. Simon was the first to print the figure concerning the cognitive aspects of management, which in turn leads to the issue of how to measure its value.

Today we know the value of being able to count the time a machine takes to produce a nail. But we know very little of the process taking place in the head of the machine builder, the very instrument management is depending on to achieve profit at the end of the day. Knowledge management is the discipline underpinning the value of soft issues. KM is a managerial approach focusing on an organization's ability to utilize its intellectual capital for knowledge creation, value building and profitability, all part of building a learning organization.

Today, most people agree that KM is concerned with effectively connecting those who know with those who need to know, and, furthermore, being able to convert personal knowledge into organizational knowledge. There also seems to be an agreement that managing knowledge requires collaborative understanding. Managing collaboration require special skills, less emphasis on individual achievement, more on teamwork, as well as effective connectivity.

KM, therefore, is the discipline required to achieve organizational learning, that is, an organization's ability to share and utilize its intellectual capital (Edvinsson and Malone, 1997) *for capture, create, deliver and use knowledge.*

In order to succeed with turning personal knowledge into organizational knowledge, one needs a repository, and navigational, system for structured and unstructured information, and a philosophy of *redundancy*. A *knowledge management system* (KMS), therefore, is the structure required for creating dynamic organizations for learning, resulting in:

- Rapid response to changing business environment
- Continuous improvement and innovation
- Improved bottom-line results.

The information and communication technology (ICT) is just a technical enabler for the organization to create a more effective KMS. It is the issues of measuring soft capital we must develop, if we are to succeed in building the competitive organization for 21st century.

8.3. The need to measure results

As part of its responsibility, management has a need to understand the progress of various parts of the organization and aggregate these parts to a corporate level. We call such a measurement system a Management Information System. It is based on the principle of Taylor in as much as bits of information from the lower echelons flow upward in the hierarchy, being aggregated in business unit elements until they are packaged into a corporate setting for the senior management to act on. At this level the owners can trust that such information will not be "misused". That it is not bestowed upon the employees at large to be privy to such information is understandable in lieu of Taylor's Scientific Management approach. This is exactly the mentality required to kill the "bird that laid the golden egg".

On the other hand, regardless of how much you are working with aggregated numbers they are still historic data. They do not tell you what is going to happen in the future. For that you need other measures. This is the conflict - what measures to use for determining future success:

scientifically derived accounting data projected forward in time, or some other measures, based on "employees are the most important assets", combined with systems supporting improvement and innovation? The paradox is, should you go for what will create a winning organization, and then you need to trust your organization. That means, you need to share with the employees information required to create a holistic action pattern within the organization. Only then do you have a true value creating organization, consisting of employees with only one agenda – the agenda of the organization.

This conflict between established standards and new ways to measure value creating assets and balances (status quo) is also one of responsible reporting. Disclosing immaterial values has its price: how reliable, who to believe, what about stock market, creditors, public at large, ability to sustain bad times, how relevant are these? You have probably more questions than answers. Using a consistent set of standards across industries gives a better basis of judging past performance, and you can compare apples with apples. But it does not give answers about who will perform better in the future. Also, present scientific measurement systems are good for control and compliance, but do not function as a management tool for future growth. Finally, while KM is concerned with sharing knowledge (controlled by the employees), that is capturing, creating, delivering and using knowledge (see Figure 8.1), structural capital (controlled by the management) is concerned with retaining knowledge.

In terms of the stock market, there are two basic ways of assessing value. One assesses the future potential and the other past and present earnings. The two approaches can yield extreme differences in value assessments, something that has been explored extremely well during the peak of the "dot.com" era and after. Companies were valued according to their innovative capabilities and colonizing potential (material share again). The stock of e-business companies, supplies of search engines and telecom equipment companies were valued according to a future market and their future market share. The latter reflects the value of their technology and their marketing and management competence.

Chapter 8 Monitoring and Measuring in KM

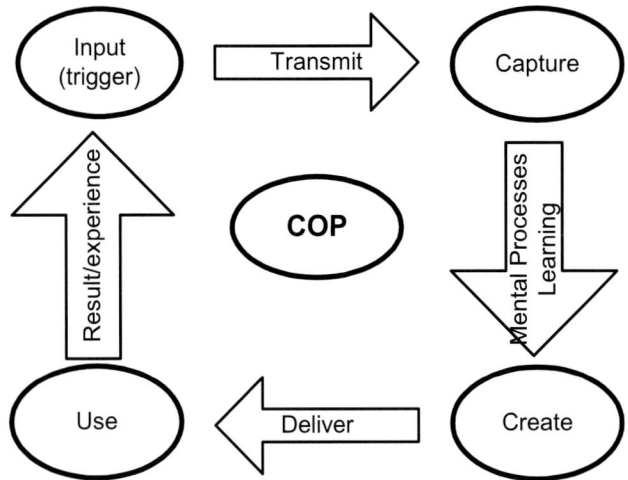

Figure 8.1: The structure of knowledge management

Today, we see financial analysts using a standard *P/E-indicator* (price versus earnings) to assess the value of companies. The P/E indicator is basically a book value indicator that reflects past performance rather than future potential. The real value is probably somewhere in between. The real value will also be very fluid depending on how well the competence and the total ability of the company comply with the market arena in which it operates. The lack of more accurate means of measurement puts analysts, investors and existing owners in a difficult position and stock values tend to fluctuate with current understanding about the state of the company, which can lead to devastating results.

When measuring an organization's capital and operation, it all boils down to a perspective on what to measure - past or future? It is our belief that while you need the financial and scientific measurement systems to measure past performance, you need other measurement systems to reflect the value of an organization's intellectual capital for future earnings. What to measure will depend on what you are focusing on. In the following sections we will outline the different types of measurement systems applied today, and give an outline of what we consider to will be a better way of monitoring knowledge in action.

8.4. What today's measurement systems measure

Reading an annual report today, you will find that the basic ingredients, such as Profit and Loss, Balance Sheet, Cash Flow, Economic, Financial and Accounting indicators are the same the world over. This is due to international standard agreements. Then we have different additions to standard reports, such as the American K40, regulating certain aspects of any business listed on an American stock exchange. When the international standard organization receives proposals from members, or other sources, to add, or change, measures of evaluating enterprises, it will take years before changes are implemented. However, by applying standard units of measurements such as Cash Flow, Return On Investment/Equity and Asset Test, you may apply such standards to your own measurement model for measuring for example the use of Intellectual Capital in your organization.

Table 8.1 shows you a Measurement Matrix (Skyme, 1998). The purpose of this table is to give a taste of two sets of measurement systems: *Macro-economic* systems and *Micro-economic* systems.

While the Macro system develops global indicators of what is going on around the world, the Micro system tries to monitor the pulse of the individual organization. However, it seems to us that most still do not address the central issues of how to anticipate future earnings based on a finite stock of knowledge capital, and knowledge embedded either in artefacts or the human brain.

The right-hand column is our attempt to develop a system that is capable of monitoring the value creating processes of *intellectual capital*. This will be further explored in Section 8.5 below.

While there is a growing appreciation for valuing intangible assets, the issue of impact and use is unclear. The above matrix tells us what types of data are used to arrive at the results. As it is only established accounting methods that are allowed to be applied for reporting financial statements, identifying which of the many unauthorized methods of evaluating human resources, is a challenge too great for this chapter. Still, the report by Business Intelligence can be worth reading due to its details about the many suggestions of unauthorized methods of measuring intangible values.

Chapter 8 Monitoring and Measuring in KM

Table 8.1: Measurement matrix

	MACRO		MICRO				
Type of measure	National Competitive Indicators	OECD	Value-based Cash flow	Intangible -Brand -Patents - Knowledge	Performance Example: Balanced Scorecard	Intellectual Capital	Knowledge Management Monitor (KM3)
Results The index is about…	Mix of hard (GDP, inflation etc,) & soft educ, people) factors	Establishing an understanding of the nation's level of knowledge	Value-based mgt approach for company "drivers"	Estimates the value of intangible assets.	Balancing financial against non-financial indictors	System of modelling different types of intellectual capital	Evaluation the results of KMS
I will try to measure…	Competitiveness and wealth creation in order to compare nations	Macro economic factors needed for creating knowledge	Cash flow generation: Cash flow return on investment	Matrix combining market assets vs. market value	Performance along several dimensions	Three categories of capital: - Human - Structure - Customer	Input-Process-Output
It can best be applied to…	National economic system and structures	Macro indicators e.g. Intellectual capital, knowledge networks and learning	For-profit organizations	For-profit Organizations	For-profit Organizations	For-Profit Organizations	Both For-and non-profit Organizations
It will give the following type of results…	Ranking countries for investment purposes	Knowledge creation in a nation	High correlation between indicators & company valuation	Puts value on the business knowledge	Profitability, customer satisfaction, skill level, productivity	Brings out the hidden values in an organization	- Rapid response time. - Continuous improv. and innovation - Improved results
Its importance is in the following …	Evaluate your next investment or establishing a business,	Innovation survey and maps of external sources of knowledge	Evaluate opportunities of tomorrow.	Focus on business outcome.	It helps to move from financial driven to mission-driven	Visualize and develop measures that reflect the intangible	Creation of new knowledge for value driven KM strategy

The purpose of measuring economic quantities for *enterprise performance* has been to identify the husbandry of the shareholders assets, given the finite supply of Land, Capital and Labour. While the emphasis was on the two first, today's emphasis is on the latter category, and due to technology, the world's enterprises are becoming less dependent on unskilled labour and more on skilled employees of all categories. Furthermore, today's picture is different on two other accounts. First of all, the single focus on shareholders has been shifted out with stakeholders. That includes the interest of such elements as the employees, customers and society. Secondly, a singular focus on return to shareholders no longer identifies required value creating activities within the enterprise. Let us look at some of the issues determining the development of measuring knowledge assets' impact on future earnings:

1. What is important for future growth?
2. How well is intellectual capital paired with structured capital?
3. How well are skills and experience taken care of and applied?
4. What is done to develop Good Practice based on skills and experience?
5. What is the organization's ability to innovate?
6. Is the organization structured to attract, and retain, talented employees?
7. Is the organization's remuneration system structured to honour value creating employees of all levels?
8. Is the organization's vision and goals designed to secure leadership within its chosen area of endeavour?
9. What is the optimal return to all stakeholders?

The question is if the owners will allow the Board to establish measures for identifying what activities to promote in order to optimize the return to stakeholders? For that to happen, the owners must understand the issue of human capital and how it influences the bottom line.

8.5. Criteria for a KM monitoring and measurement system

In this section, we will discuss the issue of developing a model for monitoring the application of intellectual capital for the purpose of optimizing value creation.

8.5.1. The aim and objective of monitoring KM

Knowledge management is the discipline of managing both tacit and explicit knowledge. As this also means knowledge residing in people's minds, KM must therefore have a vision to be an instrument for employees. Thus, by doing something good for the employees, management gets better through optimizing value creation for the stakeholders

---

Vision
- Make our colleagues' workday simpler and with a better overview.
- Make work processes more secure and qualitatively better.

…. and

Purpose

- Effective work processes through JIT-JE information.
- Secure experience transfer.

Given that intellectual assets are a finite resource at management's disposition in an organization, the objective of such system is to secure:

- Rapid response to a changing business environment
- Continuous improvement and innovation
- Improved bottom-line results

Securing these objectives, results in increased value creation for all stakeholders, and longevity for the organization.

8.5.2. What to measure

In the *Measurement Matrix* above, we have seen examples of measurements based on both hard and soft data. In the case of "Value-based Cash flow" we see that you need to level cash flow (hard) against investment (hard). In the case of *Balanced Score Card*, the inventors of that system try to balance financial indicators (hard) with non-financials such as internal processes (soft), customer portfolio (soft) and rate of innovation (hard/soft).

Establishing a monitoring system for KM is not without problems, as the authors of other measurement systems have seen before.

8.5. Criteria for a KM monitoring and measurement system

Nevertheless, due to the importance of identifying monitoring principles for the benefit of the employees, we attempted to establish the process for such a monitoring system. The process is shown in Figure 8.2.

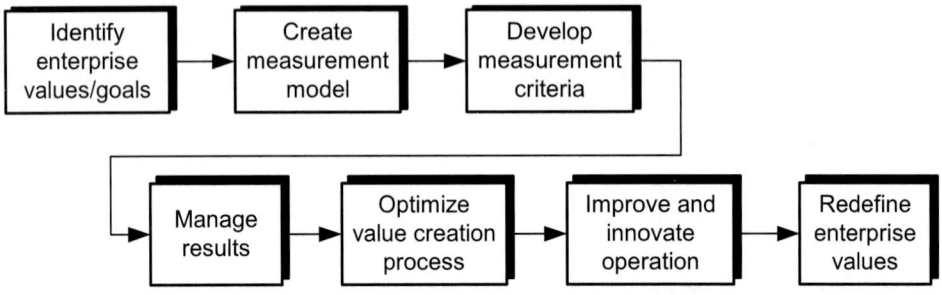

Figure 8.2: The process of a monitoring system

In Section 8.5.1, we identified vision and purpose, what management is concerned with on behalf of the employees. We also considered objectives, what management hopes to achieve through making their employees good. From this framework, and linked to the organization's value/goal statement, we should be able to identify elements going into the creation of the measurement model (see Figure 8.2).

In order to develop a monitoring model, you need to know the following:

- Values and goals of the enterprise (Section 8.5.1)
- Objective(s) for implementing the system (Section 8.5.1)
- Process for developing and using such monitoring system (Figure 8.2)
- Anatomy around which KM will be created (Figure 8.3)
- Holistic process model relevant to the KM system (Section 8.4)

A measurement system, such as the Balanced Score Card, is created for the purpose of observing the results of actions that management has taken related to the organization's vision, purpose and strategic intent.

Chapter 8 Monitoring and Measuring in KM

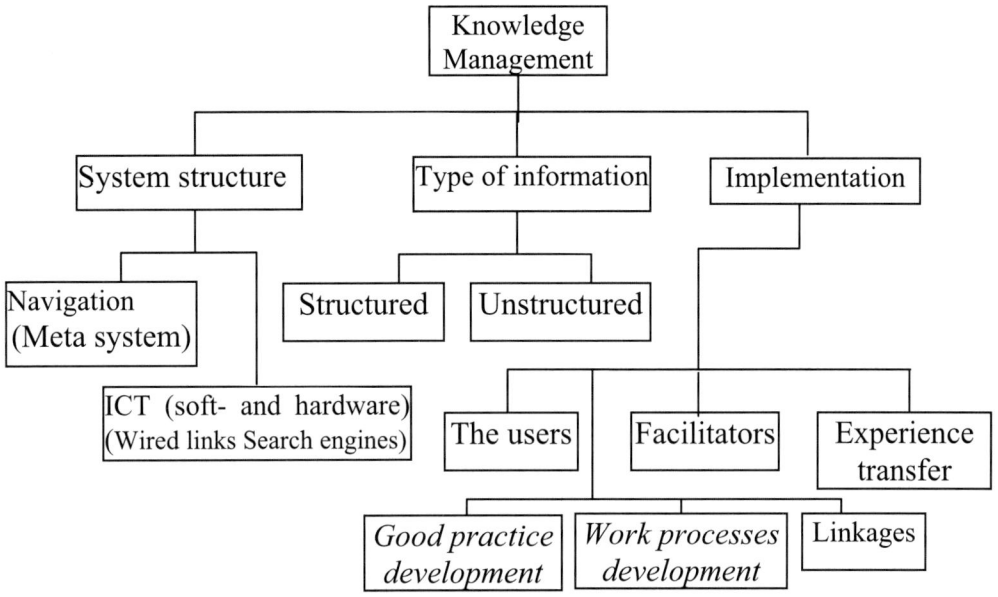

Figure 8.3: The general anatomy of a KM system

Measuring and monitoring systems are complementary to knowledge management since KM activities, that is, current work processes, can be measured and monitored relative to the company's strategic intent. Thus, while a measuring system is a static point in time observation, KM is dynamic, securing continuing improvement and innovations in the company's value chain. The dynamism comes from the process orientation found in the holistic KM model. It supports current work processes, and creates the arena for supporting and implementing, improvements and innovations created by the employees of the organization resulting in improvements in the company's performance. The result of KM will be displayed in the monitoring model as can be seen in Figure 8.4.

The model starts with the company's value statement that then is being translated into a set of objectives and strategic intentions. In order to achieve the strategic intent, management is required to establish its own work process in the form of activities elements. These elements will be connected to the operative and functional work processes developed by the users, and based on the issues raised (see left-hand column in Figure 8.4) as a result of the management work process. By monitoring the many products coming out of the work processes, management can measure the results in form of issues converted to factual information. The products coming out from the work processes will be cumulated and aggregated into management issues (see right-hand column in Figure 8.4). The results of the work processes (some of them hard facts and others soft results) may be converted into quantitative numbers to be measured against the management's strategic intentions.

8.5.3. *How to apply the result*

A KM monitoring system is different from the measurement methods listed above. The purpose of monitoring a KMS is to identify the development of people issues in relation to improving the output of the organization. Improved output can be a result of for example increasing value creation or reduced costs. Figure 8.4 indicates a knowledge management-monitoring model, which is called KM3.

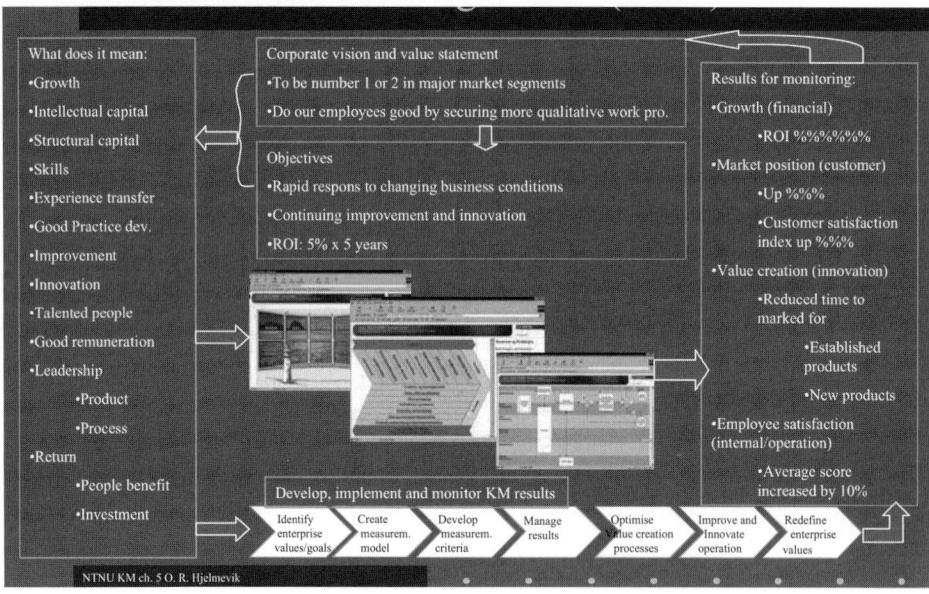

Figure 8.4: KM monitoring model (KM3)

8.6. Case study

We have now given a framework for how to monitor the KM model implemented in your organization. Based on this chapter, your task is to develop a monitoring system capable of meeting the objectives for implementing the system.

Chapter 8 Monitoring and Measuring in KM

Examples

1. Value and goals for the organization
   - To be the number one or two within its market segments by being best on customer and employee relation. The vision is to make the employees' workday simpler and with a better overview, and work processes more secure and qualitatively better.

2. Objectives of a KMS
   - Rapid response to changing business situation
   - Be able to respond to the business situation through continuous, and rapid, improvement and innovation
   - Increase return on interest (ROI) by 5 % annually for next 5 years.

3. Develop the process for creating a monitoring system
   - Identify information that goes into the process.

4. The anatomy of KMS
   - When creating the process, make sure to monitor the relevant elements.

5. The holistic process model
   - This model is supposed to yield the results you now have decided to achieve. The task is to be able to develop a measurement system capable of achieving the objectives.

Questions you should try to find answers to related to the points in examples above are:

1. What makes customers satisfied? What makes employees satisfied? How can we make the workday simpler for the employees, and qualitatively better for the products and processes we deliver? What does it mean to have more secured work processes?
2. How can we ensure that the organization can react appropriately to changing conditions; to organize processes for improvements and innovation; and to secure better profitability through better ROI?
3. How will you describe what type of information that goes into the process of creating a monitoring system?
4. How will you make certain that you are monitoring the system in the right way, using the correct indicators for such monitoring?

5. Having designed a method for monitoring the output from a holistic KM system, how will you secure that the results are in fact being implemented in the KM model, for better competitiveness?

8.7. Conclusions

The field of management models and measurements is not new. There are many financial, quality and production measurement systems that have been developed. However, in the knowledge-based economy, we need monitoring systems that measure the outcome of intellectual capital. This chapter has attempted to outline some of the challenges encountered when attempting to measure knowledge creation as basis for value added activities.

Monitoring a knowledge management system entails the issue of measuring "soft" assets. Such assets are human capital, intellectual properties, customer relations and value creating processes. No present bookkeeping systems are able to report true values regarding these elements. Therefore, one needs other measurement systems to link up to the task of managing knowledge within an organization. Such a monitoring system must have the capacity to become standard, have the flexibility to meet individual requirements in an organization, and be robust enough to be tested.

8.8. Lessons learned

There are no perfect metrics for knowledge work, but this chapter provides you with a good starting point. We have introduced some well considered thoughts and approaches to help you measure the value of knowledge. Existing measurement models and matrices are almost exclusively derived from the analysis of systems. Our approach makes a clear distinction between a value-derived knowledge creating model and those derived from systems.

Keep the following tips in mind while devising knowledge management metrics for your company:

- Measurement of intellectual capital is important in knowledge management and metrics define knowledge management success.
- Intellectual capital is an important asset for a company in knowledge-based economy. Robust metrics help measure the business impact of

knowledge management. Well-chosen matrices serve as the indicators, tools, and guidelines that can help shape both your company's knowledge management system design and its knowledge management strategy. Knowledge work and knowledge management system performance must be one of your core metrics if any knowledge management initiative is to succeed.

REFERENCES

1. Taylor, F. W. (1909), *Principles of Scientific Management*. Harper, New York.

2. Edvinsson, L. and Malone, M. S., (1997), *Intellectual Capita*: *the proven way to establish your company's real value by measuring its hidden brainpower,* Piatkus, London.

3. Skyme, D, (1998), *Measuring the Value of Knowledge,* Business Intelligence Limited, London. (www.business-intellingence.co.uk).

4. Simon, H. A., (1972), *Administrative Behaviour*, 2nd edition, McMillan, New York.

CHAPTER 9

STRATEGY AND STRUCTURE: *SCENARIO 2010*

> **Objectives**
>
> - Understanding why exploiting resources for value creation has been man's secret for success.
> - Identifying structural developments throughout the history of mankind.
> - Trying to project some trends within the way people structure their productive resources.
> - Understanding why knowledge management will become the most important discipline for competition in the future.

9.1. Introduction

In order to maintain or strengthen their raw material and market position, international organizations need to rethink their strategy of resource exploitation. This chapter identifies a possible management structure for future international business organizations.

While history has told us not to believe in absolute physical laws, the laws of economics are even less absolute. Just like physical paradigms, both macro- and micro economic theories, from time to time have been forced to yield to newer theories, thoughts and ideas. This chapter provides a basis for discussing the challenge of managing resources in the 21st century and identifies a possible management structure capable of leading the challenge of harnessing intellectual capital for improved value creation.

We will discuss the following topics:

- Historical structures
- Moving from our heritage to modern market economics
- Change agents that will challenge us in the 21st century
- Structure follows strategy
- The knowledge society
- The new order of things

With reference to history, we start with Gutenberg and move to the year *2010*, where we have described a few possible scenarios. We have also identified some of the change agents that brought us to the year *2010*. Back to our time, we must evaluate which strategy to follow, and what structure to design to match the strategy.

Information and communication technology is the basis for the "world's" move into the knowledge-based economy. Of course, we are talking about roughly 1/3 of the world that is the Western world. There is a long way to go before the other 2/3 of the world will get up to our standard of living, if ever. Why are we moving into a knowledge-based economy, and why the name "knowledge-based"? Over the last 25 years or so, we have had researchers and futurists following the shift in the application of human resources from labour intensive to capital/machine intensive production of goods and service.

From the younger Stone Age, around 10 000 years ago, Man moved from a nomadic culture to an agricultural society which included planting the fields with wild wheat and taming animals. Down through history, we have developed ways to survive and prosper, constantly experimenting with new ways to make life bearable. Some of these shifts are based on economic changes, while others are based on technological methods. We call these major breaks with the past a paradigm shift. For example, the move from a *nomadic culture* to an *agricultural culture* was an economic paradigm. On the other hand, the transport of produce from the farm to the market by cart and oxen, rather than by people's feet, will be called a technological paradigm.

The reason for moving from an *agriculture society* into the *industrial society* was due to a technological paradigm. Up to the age of enlightenment, most of society was occupied with working the fields for harvesting staple foods. In the industrial revolution, the factors of computer to the world, and created the basis for the information economy. But for a knowledge society to develop, you need to put information in the hands, and minds, of the people who will be using it to create new knowledge. For this, you have to turn to the Personal Computer. The PC is the second leg to bring us to the knowledge-based economy. It is also developed and commercialized by the Big Blue (BS).

But it was Netscape, with its practical approach to the Internet and the World Wide Web, which changed the future of distribution of both information and commercial products overnight. Netscape's business idea turned traditional industrial logic on its head, with its supply and demand paradigm, finely tuned since the time of *Adam Smith*. Rather than producing goods, developing channels of distribution, and through the channels, offer both goods and services in the market place, Netscape wanted something different. They created a new economic paradigm by producing one original unit and then offering it as copies on the WWW. This is the paradigm that will cement the foundation for the knowledge economy.

You delivered your own production and distribution services to the Netscape business by bringing down the product in electronic format and converting it to value on your own PC, through the screen, printer, fax, in form of an article, drawing, engineering specification, book, and so on. Or you could redistribute the product via your Internet or Intranet connection to new potential customers of the one original product offered by Netscape. Netscape was pioneering a new world and was successful in doing so. It prospered from its innovative means of communication. When Microsoft introduced its Explorer with what can be described as brute, economic muscle, Netscape failed to reinvent itself. It became a Microsoft copy dot without the same muscle and started its fall into oblivion. This way Netscape saved both production and distribution cost, while you became its marketing and distribution channel – without any cost to Netscape. No other company had such growth in value during such short period of time, as Netscape. During a few years in the 1990s Netscape went from a turnover of 0 to several billion dollars, based on the philosophy of developing, and distributing, only one original product.

Netscape understood its mission, and took advantage of its timing. In the process they made knowledge creation through electronic learning possible by making information readily accessible. Peter Drucker [1995] maintains that the foundation for a business activity is "Environment, Mission and Core Competency". For a business to be able to meet new challenges as technology develops, the technological basis must "be known and understood throughout the organization", according to

Drucker. Thus, for the employees in an organization to understand the basis for its own raison d'être, developing a system for experience sharing, learning and knowledge creation is required.

In the new *knowledge economy organizations* will be made to take the major responsibility for learning, according to Davis and Botkin [1994]. Companies will have to bear most of the responsibility for teaching their employees competitive focused education, based on the philosophy of "life-long learning". While companies will concentrate on fewer suppliers in a supplier-network, new technology (multi-media, interactivity, etc.) that will revolutionize learning, leading to new need-focused knowledge by the organization.

The technology driven change leads to knowledge-driven change. In the knowledge-creating scenario, learning is being redefined, moving its modus operandi from the classroom to the business premises, where technology and *Community of Practice* (COP) bring the learning aspect into the knowledge-based economic paradigm. This new paradigm results in a demand for new structures, reducing the tall hierarchies to near-networks, with focus on customers' needs. While the 20th century businesses found the military hierarchy of the 19th century useful, partly due to the principle of Taylor's Scientific Management, 21st century business needs to sport a different game. That is the game of core competency [Hamel and Prahlahad, 1994], knowledge sharing and change, all in a value chain network structure.

9.3.2. *Dateline 2010 – New societal demands*

Assuming that the consequences of the terrorist attacks on New York (World Trade Center) and Washington (Pentagon) in September 2001 have not resulted in serious financial and social consequences for the Western world, let us now identify three possible scenarios for the early part of the 21st century. We will focus on three headlines in the year 2010: *health*, *knowledge* and *life style*. We choose these key words rather than focusing on technology, such as information and communication, transport, medicine, food, and energy. With the knowledge-based economy being based on man's needs, both as individual and as groups, we felt it more relevant to focus on life rather then on technology. After having identified the three scenarios outlined below, we will take a look back from the vantage point of 2010.

9.3.3. *Scenario: Health*

The economy of health is of great importance in our daily chores. Due to great advances within the biotechnology, Western societies stand at the brink of deep-rooted changes both as individuals and society. The individual's health situation, both physiological and mental, is being challenged. Poor sperm quality resulted in low birth rates within the white population, while it grew in the Third World. However, according to the WHO, third world countries have not stopped the population growth. At pregnancy, the women can check unborn babies for severe damage in order to reduce defective births. New gene-manipulating technology will remove defects from the DNA in the fetus.

The medical profession moved from treatment to prevention as its main criteria for keeping a healthy population in the society. Due to genetic advances and biotechnology, Parkinson's disease, cancer, physiological and mental old age illnesses are now within reach of curing and prevention. Chemical, physiological and generic based human behaviour are now in the process of being understood. Biotechnology will be part of crime prevention, treating potential villains at an early stage with new test methods in primary schools.

Genetically developed farm produce will lead to a reduction in the intake of animal fat by the consumer. The technology will be used for "tailor made" vegetable food. Epidemics, starvation and water shortages continue to deprive parts of the Third World from having a decent life. However, new energy technology is available to supply Third World countries with energy and water, should the West be willing to finance such a project. This issue is a question of politics and business.

9.3.4. *Scenario: Knowledge*

Micro-technology has moved from futuristic research into the development and near-production stage. This technology is now capable of building its own production system for goods such as micro-fans for use in super fast computing systems, giving the possibility for each heat producing element having its own cooling system. Likewise, within gene-technology, micro-organisms will be able to remove defaults in the basic chromosomes, as well as "build" their own lungs, artery, chemical, medical and food production. Due to advancements in computers and knowledge creation, the advanced nations with the top 3rd of the world population have just agreed to cut pollution by 50 % within 2010. New-car production has replaced more than 50 % of its engine systems with hybrid engines, consisting of a fuel cell and electric/solar motor system. Cold fusion seems to be on the brink of success, and solar energy systems may be competitive within a short period of time.

Sensor- and fibre-optic technology for mobile phone/satellite and multi-media transmission use the Blue Tooth technology is now offering great potential as these technologies are merged with audio/visual/data technology. Due to the merged electronic technology systems we now have products on demand throughout the world. We can anticipate the weather for farming, flooding, earthquakes and tropical storms with greater accuracy weeks in advance. This gives society the lead-time for preventive action.

Robot and micro technology, for the fully automated production of durable and non-durable goods such as buildings, cars, kitchen equipment and furniture, and automated service on the Internet (search engines and intelligent agents) are common in the Western world, reducing its dependency on the import of goods based on cheap labour. New houses are so called "intelligent houses" run on sensors for heat, cooling, garbage disposal, lighting, etc. Windows regulate both light and heat/chill transmission.

For the computer literate learning is life long. One result of the global web is a common approach to education by Western nations. In primary and secondary schooling we now see great commonality, while at the post-secondary level we see a breaking up of traditional college and university education. Some of the leading schools and universities are able to attract students via the Internet from around the world, while the local educational institutions that are less well known outside national borders, have difficulty competing. This is partly due to a superior programme structure and popularity, but also partly due to one common language: English. With English as either first or second choice for the pupils in all primary and secondary schools globally, getting into post-secondary education gives the students possibilities of choosing from among the best around the world.

The greatest challenge to traditional learning institutions is corporate universities and schools. Motorola, Matsushita, and GE have their own educational systems with university-level courses. Some of them, such as Arthur D. Little at Cambridge, Massachusetts, the world oldest registered engineering consultancy organization, have even allowed external students into their programmes. The reason why this may be posing a threat to the established, century old postgraduate liberal and college educational organizations is not as much the competition in numbers as competition in real-live case studies. By using its own business as a laboratory, with the "hands on" managers and experts as teaching material, the students get the latest in the knowledge creating game. The business, on the other hand, gets to pick the best brains who cross over to their programmes.

The business universities also have money. Through applying money to learning, biotechnology has reached the threshold for supporting a higher degree of absorption, digesting and converting information to knowledge. Furthermore, the global business network is able to channel new information to their learning centres, making the students better prepared for graduation, with a higher level of competency.

In the world of artificial intelligence, machines can now do simple household work, maintenance of factory halls, schools, etc. We are seeing a horizon where manual labour may not have to be carried out. With the multinational organizations controlling more than 60 % of world trade, and the universal use of computer technology in the Western world, there will be a global force fighting many issues with the United Nations.

Smart identification cards and biometrics are in the process of removing money as a trading commodity. Furthermore, the card will get you in and around everywhere you wish to go, provided you have enough credit to your name, or card. The universality of a common card protocol means the sale of medical services the world over, holiday rentals, and living systems, can be set up without any difficulty.

The world consists of three regions: European Union, the Americas and the Asian regions. A formal meeting protocol is being established to deal with issues between the three blocks. The most important criteria are Quality of Living, Service and Trust. These criteria will be the basis for all interregional relations. Sustainable development is the foundation for all economic activities in the three blocks. Ecology is becoming the biggest growth industry, with new scientific discoveries as its basis.

9.3.5. *Scenario: Life style*

Democracy is the basis for all societies included in Western world. We can e@vote, e@mail, e@cyber.walk, e@love, e@learn, e@work and so on. What about e@sleep? That is humanity's next project. Yes, we are all working in projects. No "lifetime employment". We are all part of the nomadic culture. Teams and projects are moving around the world, using the home as one's base, when one is at home, that is. Sleep is becoming a commodity that you can trade, just like your holidays. Thanks to biotechnology.

Today you can get everything tailor-made. The turn around processes of production systems are measured in fractions of minutes. Due to, among others, new materials, a car can be produced in less than a day, compared to close to two weeks in 2001. This has had its cost on the working population. We are only served by a few global organizations within each of the major industry segments. All other companies are regional, competing on criteria not available to the global organizations.

Sensor technology communicating with your brain makes sure to flash your mood colour of the day on all from kitchen to car. And in communication with the house, the sensor secures a comfort the world never has experienced before. The car, primarily in plastic and aluminium, has its sensors aimed at other objects coming in its way, stopping the car if that is the smartest thing to do. The yellow stripe in the road allows the car to communicate with whoever the driver chooses, give you the speed you are allowed to drive, and gets you to your destination in the quickest possible way. Of course, the brake may be used, but the autopilot will take care of critical elements.

During this year, the earth's population will be roughly 7 billion. We are living primarily in large cities, and urban areas. Our life style is dependent on clean air, clean water, clean streets and clean houses. "Our back yard shall not be polluted, others may be". Criminality is low, and we are primarily occupied with creative work. Our holidays are being spent in quality resorts, or on quality travel, where learning through fun and sport is the main activities. Mental training is part of our daily exercise. Clothing can be purchased designer-ready by having an external scanner take our body measurements, and a mental scanner does our mood.

Creative work means few household duties. Robots will primarily do these. Although the workweek is 30 hours, our creative mind is constantly "working" on new challenges. An active recreational life has great advantages for the companies we are working for. Due to new production and distribution methods, the employees or rather, the "employees-for-rent", have creativity that is rented for the benefit of solving a given employer's problem. These nomads, moving from employer to employer, prefer the life on the move. The reason why the nomads can be satisfied with moving about is because the challenges of 2010 are of a nature where you need highly educated generalists with a special competency, working in holistic teams. That is the way brainpower has decided to organize themselves. No one wants to take permanent employment; this becomes the code of the nomads.

The Middle East's oil control on the world's energy price continues to be a bone of contention between Asia, Europe and America on the one hand, and militant Muslims on the other. After the fall of the Ibn Saud-family in Saudi Arabia, instigated by the fundamentalists, there is a drive by the West to become hydrocarbon independent. Food production is now controlled by 80 % of the large global conglomerates. Due to micro-technology, we can produce most of our daily needs locally. This reduces the need for transportation 50 % worldwide.

9.4. The change agents that brought us to 2010

9.4.1. Leading technology

The future, as described above, is based on leading technology for competitive advantage. Within the three scenarios we can identify the following technologies that made it possible for us to enter the competitive arena of 2010.

Health
- Biotechnology
- Brain technology
- Micro-technology
- Ecology

Knowledge
- Micro-technology
- ICT: Data/multimedia/communication/virtual reality/fibre, etc.
- Energy conversion technology
- Ecology/recycling
- Agent technology for ICT
- Sensor technology

Life style
- Political consumers (voting by their wallets)
- Intelligent consumers
- Lifelong learning
- Networking
- Creativity
- Infotainment

- Knowledge farm/Nomadic workers

9.4.2. Other change agents

Demography

The population growth in the Third World has been significant during the last few decades. However, we are now seeing signs of a slow down.

Water & food

Also in the Third World there is an increasing tendency to demand clean water and healthy food. The anticipated grand migration of people from South and East to the West in the last decade of the 20th century did not take place. That does not mean it will not take place at a future date, but if it happens, it will be on a smaller scale than the world had guessed. Regardless, it is clear that we must prevent the Third World from hunger and water shortages. That is the challenge for Western societies.

9.5. Structure follows strategy

Now we are in the *new millennium*, what do we see ahead of us?

9.5.1. The company's social profile

Management's most important task is to exploit the creative resolve of the employment force. The political consumer is the company's most important customer. Remember the New England Volvo customers of the 1960s and 1970s. They bought Volvo cars due to their image as safe and clean, with a social employee policy. This way Volvo entered the US market without having to compete on price alone.

The West's growing awareness of environmental issues, the emerging power of the political consumer, demand for a shorter work week, more empowerment to the employees, growth in the average level of knowledge among the employees, and the fashion industry is fighting for survival in a market where "everything goes". Branding also becomes a paramount issue when everything else in the competitive area is equal. A company's brand reflects its quality, its innovativeness, its social and environmental conscience. In short, the brand reflects the perceived value regardless of the type of stakeholder who views it.

In 1984 Peter Drucker [1984] forecasted that the forthcoming industrial paradigm was not electronic- or biotechnology; the new technology was going to be "Entrepreneurship". Why? Because for an organization to survive, you needed to understand the complete market mechanism, you need employees that are able to form a holistic mental model of the market in their head, and help position the company relative to that model. That is the task of the entrepreneur: to look for opportunities, assemble resources to deal with the possibilities and apply those resources in a manner the old generals positioned their troops, but without the hierarchical structures that most certainly will delay action. These are the skills required by the future organizations, ability to convert information to knowledge, to action and innovation.

9.5.2. IT/IS industry

With the explosion in Information and Communication Technology (ICT), it is natural for it to participate in forming the way we do things in the future. Tomorrow's management structure will not avoid the sophisticated solutions of the coming generations of ICT. Thus, the nomadic culture, with relative flat structures, few managers, with a span of control unthinkable for the old school of no more than half a dozen people reporting to one manager, will mean important changes. These are changes that will impact both the organizations offering products and services and the supply and demand side of the market equation.

In a special report, "warfare 2000" [1996], the U.S. News & World Report maintains that the "ones and zeros, not bombs and bullets, may win tomorrow's battles". The magazine has made the following observation:

Table 9.1: Data transfer rates and soldiers required to cover area

Type of war	U.S. civil war 1865	WWI 1915	WWII 1945	Gulf War 1991	Future war 2021
Data transfer rates (words/minute)	30	30	66	192 000	1.5 trillion
Soldiers needed to cover 10 square km.	38 830	4 040	360	23.4	2.4

As the reader can see, there is a huge change in the numbers between World War II (WW II) and the Gulf War, a time where the computer and communication technology became widespread in the west. From the table we can guess that we will see further changes in the way data is transferred and wars are fought in the future.

9.5.3. The petroleum industry

Looking at the petroleum industry, one can anticipate great changes to the way the industry will conduct its business. Before the 1973 Yom Kippur War between Israel and the Arabs, it was primarily the oil industry's "Seven sisters" [6] who dominated the world's oil trade. The later takeover of Aramco [7] by Saudi Arabia and the "re-birth" of OPEC (Organization, for Petroleum Exporting Countries), effectively stopped the flow of cheap oil. The industrialized countries, headed by the Netherlands, started the energy-savings drive, developing new technology and methods of saving energy. Since that time, the oil industry has never been the same.

With a peak of more than USD 40 per barrel of oil back in 1984, the price explosion led to a drive to develop new technology for hydrocarbon exploration in hostile regions such as the North Sea. In such regions a barrel of oil may cost four times, or more, to produce compared to the sandy dunes of Saudi Arabia. But it is not the threat of scarce resources that drives up the price of oil, but the threat of war. When experts are saying that the world is running out of oil, the price falls [Combell, 1996], but if America starts bombing Iraq, the world's 3rd largest holder of oil, the price of oil starts rising due to a fear of a short-term oil shortage.

The drive to secure new sources of energy, such as hydrogen through cold fusion, or energy technology such as atomic, wind, solar or fuel cells, is still not a commercial success, although there are many prototypes around. Some of these prototypes will succeed and become commercially viable technology, while others, such as wind and cold fusion, may not be commercial propositions for decades. For anyone who is interested in environmental issues, surely it is better to build effective fuel cell systems, with CO_2 slug catchers, than windmills which are eyesores and cause noise pollution and still need the grid. None of these issues were been resolved as the world moved into the 21st century.

In which way will society advance on the issue of energy? Reducing demand, finding more energy, or developing technology that is more energy effective or all of the above? We believe that for the goal of

---

[6] Standard Oil Company, founded by J.D. Rockefeller in 1870, was in 1911 split up by the U.S. Supreme Court into many companies. The most important original Standard Oil companies became before recent mergers: Esso (later Exxon), Mobil, Chevron, Amoco, Arco, Conoco and Standard Oil of Ohio.

[7] Saudi Aramco was founded by several of the "seven sisters" together with Saudi Arabia. After the Yom Kippur war, the Saudies forced the foreign interests out of the company. Aramco is the world's largest oil company measured by oil-in-place.

the West to be energy independent, you need a new paradigm, not in technology, but in organizing resources. We need a learning paradigm.

9.5.4. Network

We have already seen how networks and teams have developed as part of a management system. A network system is particularly effective for experience transfer, as they are "colleague" based. "He who is not in, is out" can stand as a peer-scrutiny metaphor. That is, a knowledge system not in use by its communities will die. Should there be an undermining of the use, no manager will be able to force its acceptance, baring two conditions: Peer pressure and the employee review programme. In the latter, management can use a stick and reward practice, where monetary reward or punishment can be applied. The first, peer pressure, however, is more to the point. Here you have the self-justice system, making sure that anyone depending on another colleague for information, gets it, and if not, can move together with colleagues, to pressure the "unwilling" to share and participate. You do not need management to follow this up.

A recent study by Patrick Lambe [Lambe, 2001] indicates a digital divide between generations. Pre-Internet workers do not readily initiate a social relationship through their computers. Their attitude towards limitless collaboration is somewhat reserved and their tolerance to endless updates via e-mails, SMSs or other channels is quickly saturated. However, the younger Internet-oriented generation typically responds to receiving 100 e-mails a day as being in the loop. This means that they feel included and the net is not unusual for this new group of workers. Consequently peer-oriented, rather than manager-based stimuli drive the collaborative and creative work for these people.

Professor Jeffrey Pfeiffer [1994] has observed that "Because most people are inherently social creatures, deriving pleasure from social interaction, groups exert a powerful influence on individuals. ... Teams work because of the peer monitoring and expectations of co-workers that are brought to bear to both co-ordinate and monitor work". Also he argues that: "If competitive success is achieved through people, then the skills of those people are critical.... It seems clear that learning ... on the job is by far the most important factor (that) will determine the nation's economic prospect in the next (century). – Then it is important to build a (multi-skilling) work force that has the ability to achieve competitive success and that cannot be readily duplicated by others".

The rapid shift in the technological development combined with the *knowledge revolution* (example: Moor's Law or the anticipated cancelling of Moor's Law due to an even faster change of paradigms), will demand a corporate strategy of constant change. Such changes will mean rapid movement of the company's troops (its intellectual capital) from one value process to another. Rapid shifting of company's resources and continuing process review for more effective value creation will be the order of the day. "Multi-skilling" is the team's ability to learn, securing a colleague's ability to move from one process to another or one project to another. This is the central issue of life-long learning in the neural organization: the ability of the employees to do rapid turnarounds for new tasks, and together with the new team, learn the required skills to do the new job. All this is based on the organization's core competency and business strategy.

Unfortunately, unless the corporate strategy has a focus on future earnings, and thus has a knowledge management system capable of supporting the corporate resolve, corporations will specialize themselves into oblivion, as they are moving down the wrong strategic track. This is what happens to Kent Olsen's Digital Equipment Corp., which he started fifty years ago. In 1975, DEC had a market value of about USD 75 billion. In 1995 it was sold under Chapter 11, having close to nil market value. They chose to be better and better in the wrong technology.

9.6. The knowledge-based society

Is man just a fraction, or a complex being? According to the German poet Fredrick von Schiller [8], man is a complex creature, consisting of several parts. Man's freedom does not lie in the physically freedom, but in the freedom of morality. One can be physical free without the freedom to choose according to one's moral conviction. If that is the case, man is not free unless he is free to choose from conviction. Freedom to choose is therefore a fundamental need embedded in the human being.

With an escalating level of competency, combined with data cum information technology, society stands on the threshold of the *knowledge-based society* (some will maintain we are already there). For the corporation to deprive employees from getting all relevant information relevant to decisions will in the end result in havoc for the organization. The *knowledge-based economy* will require management to create a holistic system in which employees can enter for retrieving, developing, sharing and use new information for knowledge-creating purposes.

---

[8] Schiller, F. von, (1759-1805), German poet, philosopher and scientist.

9.6.1. The organization of resources for economic gain

"If the rate of organizational change has to keep up with the rate of business change, and this, in turn, with the rate of technological change, then the organization is going to be in such constant turmoil that the old models will not work", according to Davis and Botkin [1994]. If a company is to survive such a constant change, it will require a very flexible structure, filled with very flexible employees. Some of these employees will not even be truly employees, but only a distant relative of them.

Earlier we have concluded that in the year 2010 novel technology as we know it today, will be in daily use, either in the area of multi-media technology, biotechnology or materials technology. However, on the frontier of social technology, the way people work and interact, will still be at the embryonic stage compared to what the technology can offer of opportunities. This rapid implementation, and assimilation, of technology is due to the information flow-taking place along the corporations' main artery (the value chain), where it is soaked up by the work teams and converted to new nourishment for the corporation - value-creating opportunities.

In an article in the *Economist* [1996] it says in regard to a discussion on lean manufacturing principles, where outsourcing is the subject, "... One must have sympathy with the fact that lean production is a superior way for humans to make things". But anyone thinking "lean" ought to be forewarned, for it is not simple. Beside, it has no impact on what is a corporation greatest challenge today: coming up with new products. Lean may be a superior way to make things, but not to invent them. Unless you have a method, system, or other means of soaking up the nourishing information into the organization's arteries and converting the information to knowledge, the organization will eventually grind to a halt, just like Woolworth, after more than one hundred years of operation [Hjelmervik, 2000].

Thus, the process is more important than the product. Yesterday it was the horsewhip, today it is the gas-pedal and tomorrow it will be the electromagnetic stripes. Regardless of current products, being able to develop and process new opportunities is the greater challenge. Thus, as Theodore Levit [1963] said: The railroad companies almost went out of business because they failed to understand they were not in a product type of business, rather a process type of business transportation.

In the oil industry, the production of oil is today a commodity. The more important, and profitable, part of the industry lays in the end where technological and the human intelligence meets in a symbioses of new inventions and better understanding of the environment – the finding, developing and recovering of hydrocarbons in the most economical manner. The process of finding, treating, and marketing the hydrocarbons requires human insight, and a holistic understanding of the value chain. In this aspect the human quality outsmarts any technology. Thus, it is the social technology, the collaborative aspect and not the ICT that is crucial to secure knowledge creation.

It is through the flow of data that information is converted to knowledge in the mind of the employees, and then into action. But it is also through human actions that eighty per cent of accidents are caused. The flow of information is therefore the basis of economic activities, but for man to act according to economic intentions he must be proficient, he must be knowledgeable. Profitability is dependent on the organization's ability to apply resources in a knowledgeable manner. Through applying the right set of resources, together with the right structure of the value process (the holistic model), one can create the optimal economic output. Information without intellectual capital to convert to knowledge is useless; knowledge combined with the wrong type of information can be catastrophical.

As we mentioned before, the right information matched with intellectual capital can make money. Remember the story about Rothschild who entered the London Stock Exchange one morning, when he had the information about the outcome of the Battle of Waterloo. Then with his usual customary grave face, he proceeded to sell shares in the Bank of England and other core stocks in every sector of the English economy. The tactic resulted in making the other investors believe that Napoleon had won, and a general panic reached the trading floor. As the sell-off forced prices to rock-bottom levels, Rothschild's agents started to buy up the stocks at a fraction of their real value. The Rothschild's with its empire stretching around the globe is still one of the richest families in the world.

Putting it the other way around, knowledge can be combined with the wrong information. We can simply refer to the use of the comma. As the Governor was going to pardon a prisoner standing in front of the hangman's rope, the messenger misplaced the comma in the Governor's letter. He wrote: "Hang him, not wait for me", with a catastrophic outcome for the free, but lifeless prisoner. Knowledgeable people with the capacity to act will do so when they believe they have enough information to make a positive decision. Should available information be incorrect or factually wrong but believable, the outcome may be lethal.

Knowledge management is about combining Just in time – Just enough information with knowledgeable employees. Acknowledging the need for matching correct information with intellectual capital at the intersection of application, what are the elements that will form the industrial structures of 2010, and beyond? The most important growth engines today are information and communication technology, biotechnology and globalization, although the latter may run into conflict with part of the global population.

But the growth engines are generic types that will influence industrial structures throughout the world. To put it into an industrial context let us identify criteria that will be influenced by these motors:

The technological paradigm shift
- New understanding of physical laws and human behaviour
- New materials
- New processes

New opportunities
- Health: escalated possibilities for body treatment, and mental treatment; enlarged quality of life; extended life expectancy
- Communications: faster speed, reliable performance and higher quality
- Physical transport: faster, higher, more comfort, increased quality
- Electronic transport: faster (Moor's Law outdated), smaller, cheaper
- Learning: data – information – knowledge – wisdom
- Nutrition: more food – cheaper, more on offer, improved quality, faster growth
- Shelter: better, cheaper, more on offer, larger area per person
- Energy: improvement of access, cheaper (in a historical perspective), enlarged volume per person

Information flow in the corporation
- Direction: from vertical to horizontal
- Improvement: from "top-to-bottom" to "bottom – up"
- Span of control: From 7 to 70
- Demography: growth rate slowing, new type of food products. Changing needs – women in work, knowledge farms/nomad workers, increased standard of living throughout the world and increased demand for effectiveness.

Structuring of resources

- Military development: All structures of human resources stem from how societies have organized their survival. From the City states in Mesopotamia 5000 years ago, where societies organized the work forces for harvesting and defence, till the present organization based on Bismarck's hierarchical structure of the army. The sketch below [9] indicates part of the development of military structures.

  It was the development of the "pinching manoeuvre", using flanges and dividing the enemy's army in two, which led Alexander the Great to conquer the known world around BC 330. The Flange strategy, developed by Alexander the Great, was based on his belief in the use of flat, flexible, structures, not only the deep colons (the Palanx) of soldiers pushing each other forward into the enemy's territory. Only a few layers separated Alexander from his men. But when he was developing his many military concepts, such as using light infantry together with the cavalry, he wanted direct reports from the men themselves to hear the "war stories" directly, not being distorted by the middle management (officers) layers. This way, together with the experienced soldiers, he could adjust and find the optimal relationship in the application of resources directly on the target.

  This organizational structure of using flanges was adopted by Napoleon, and used successfully in many battles. However, due to haste, he became an offer of his own success as he stretched his forces in the attack on Wellington in 1815. The Prussian leader, Field Marshal Blücher, was waiting in the eastern wing, to serve the same blow to Napoleon as he himself had served to others.

- Economic development:
  Alfred Chandler [1962] demonstrates the take-over of power from the founder/entrepreneur to the hired manager (see Table 9.3). As Sloan's generation of managers took over in the period of 1911 – 1925, the hierarchical structure found under Bismarck's military organization received a dominating position in Western countries' business structures.

---

[9] Von Clauswitz, Karl, (1780-1831). "On War", A Prussian general and strategist. On War is an account of military strategy. He considered Alexander the Great to be one of world history's greatest military strategists. Von Clauswitz served under Field Marshal Blücher as he aided Wellington with his pinching manoeuvre in defeating Napoleon at Waterloo.

Table 9.2: Military strategies

	Military Strategies
Direct Method	Persian (500BC): Man against man
	Athens (490 BC): Use of Phalanx method at/Marathon
Indirect Method	Alexander the Great (331 BC): Use of flange attack at/Abela
	Napoleon (1803): Use of flange attack at/Austerliz **Napoleon** (1815): Use of direct attack at/Waterloo
	Bismarck (1815-1897): Continuous development of the hierarchical model

One who played a significant role in supporting the hierarchical model was Fredrick Taylor and his theory of *scientific management*. Breaking down the production of a thing into individual job-pieces, timing the execution, and devise methods of assembling the pieces, was the success of Henry Ford. He applied *Taylor's theory* with great success. Adam Smith's division of labour had found true disciples in Taylor and Ford. In this context the hierarchical model was well suited. But it was not until the manager-for-hire, today called CEO, Chief Executive Officer, that we got the corporations with their many ways to divide up the work, bureaucratize the organization, fragmentize responsibility and centralize the decision-making.

In order to anticipate the future, you need to understand the past. In a scenario development one needs to look at the internal workings of how things have developed, as Table 9.3 above identifies. Table 9.4 below draws the line of development from around 1900 along four drivers: management regime, value creation, core competencies and oil prices, ending up in 2010. While you may have some thoughts about these developments, try to create images of what the future may be like.

Table 9.3: The emergence of the corporations

Strategy and structure for the emerging corporations			
The companies	Standard Oil, N.J.	General Motors	E.I. du Pont de Nemours & Co.
The founders	J.D. Rockefeller		Eugene du Pont
Period of empire building	1880 - 1925	1903 - 1920	1902 - 1920
Leading the charge organizational structures, such as multi-division and decentralized	Teagle/Sadler	Alfred Sloan	Pierre du Pont
Implementation year	1925	1920 - 25	1920 - 25
Purpose Responsibility to the operating manager for each division. The President is strategically responsible.	Divided into the "seven sisters" by the US Supreme court in 1911. Challenge: New paradigm Mechanical eng'g <ul><li>Electric power generator</li><li>Petrol engine</li></ul>	Operated a string of carriage plants using the network principle up to 1905. Bought Buick in 1903. Produced a few hundred cars, while establishing new brands such as Cadillac.	Eugene duPont established the company E.I.duPont as a gunpowder factory around 1800. As the founder died in 1902, his three sons, Alfred, Coleman and Pierre were chosen to continue.

Management regime

One of the business drivers during the 20th century was the change in the way resources were managed. As the population, and the consequential demand for goods and services, grew, so did the task of managing the resources of value creation. The two most trend-setting cases were the breaking up of Standard Oil, where the dominating owner, J.D. Rockefeller, had to leave its owner/management to a hired/management corps. The other case was the handing over of the close to bankrupt group of automobile factories, named General Motors by its founder, W. Durant, to a management group headed by Alfred Sloan. The transfer from Owner/Entrepreneur to Administrator/Manager, which is from the innovator to hired hands, removed the decision-making function away from the immediate owner of the resources. One reason for this, as in the case of Durant of GM, was the lack of ability on part of the owner to handle the complexity of the decision-making processes, resulting in potential loss of resources. The process of moving the decision-making to where information gave an optimal point of vantage had begun.

An entrepreneur sees the opportunity, organizes the resources for seizing the possibility, and executes the plan with the vigour and force necessary to succeed. Making money is only a measure of the entrepreneur's success. As Roger Babson, the founder of Babson College, Wellesley, Massachusetts said: "Gold is good only for filling teeth and gilding picture frames. The fun is in the striving and not in the arriving. Money earned is of no use until it is usefully invested or given away". For further readings on entrepreneurship refer to Drucker [1985] and Hjelmervik [1987].

As the 20th century progressed, a need for new structures appeared. Neither Rockefeller, DuPond Sr., Ford (who almost ruined his company by offering "any colour to the buyer as long as it was black"), nor Durant was able to structure the productive resources to supply the growing markets for goods and services. In two of the technologies shaping the 20th century, Walter C. Teagle in the petroleum business and Alfred Sloan in the automobile industry were among the pioneers in the development of structures securing consumers the supply of comfort for modern living.

Table 9.4: Economic development 1900 - 2010 and the business drivers

Years	1900	1950	1970	2000	2010
Management	Owner/ Manager	Hired/ Manager	President/CEO Administrator/ Owner	Facilitator/ Manager	?
Value Creation	Increase owners worth	Increase worth of owner/mgt.	Increase worth of stakeholders	'Empowerment'	?
Core Competencies	- Steel - Car/Aeroplane - El-power - Petrochemical - Telephone	- Methodology (Taylor/Ford) - Structure (Sloan)	- Stock options - Market computers	- Intelligence - Knowledge - Globalization	?
Oil Price (USD)	1.5	2.5	22	30	?

During the 1950s, the matrix organization was introduced into the market, focusing on two-dimensional responsibility, such as geography and functions, as the axis for operations and service within the organization. While the decision-making sits in the operation division, service supplies it with expert help. After 1960 a new trend was taking hold in how to organize intellectual capital: the Conglomerates. Here the idea was to structure business that gave synergy together in an umbrella company. This way one could own a production company, a transport company, and a travel company, because transport could give synergy to both travel and the distribution of goods.

But this way of running a "general store" did not seem to give the owners value, and so we got corporations, with their core business structure, in the 1970s. The core business structure was based on the idea of organizing resources in Central Business Units (CBUs). Their purpose was to identify which businesses the organization was in. Those businesses the organization did not want to participate in (that which they did not make money on) were spun off. With the core business concept, the hired managers took the decisive step of moving from company to corporation, replacing the term "General Manager" with "President and Chief Executive Officer" (CEO). After all they were the leaders of corporations, leaving the day-to-day operation to "Chief Operating Officer" (COO), who coordinated the decision-making functions with the Business Unit Managers.

At the dawn of the 21st century we see a move from tall hierarchies to flat, network-like organizations. The reason is that the owners lost control. Decision-making in tall hierarchies is slow, burdensome and ineffective. This was fully demonstrated by Rosabeth Moss Cantor [1983] who wrote the barrier breaking book on the failure of tall hierarchies as a structure for organizing intellectual capital in value creating processes.

In the knowledge-based economy we need new types of structures, pushing the responsibility and decision-making processes to where the knowledge resides: the knowledge workers. They have the point of vantage for combining intellectual information to a symbiosis for decision-making. Due to the fast phase of industry, neither the CEO, COO nor the local business president is capable of making a better decision than their employees sitting close to where the decision is made. The most important role of these managers' in the knowledge-based marketplace is the role of facilitator and champion. The CEO becomes the Chief Facilitator. The Chief Facilitator's primary role will be to create a knowledge management system, giving the decision-makers the tools required in order to making the right decisions.

Value creation
Another driver was of course the raison d'être of business: value creation. For the beneficiaries of value creation, the owners, the purpose was to create wealth for themselves. As the owners started to hire in

management, it became clear that the managers needed to have wages to match the responsibility. With WWII approaching, the world was getting out of the long depression started with the crash on the New York Stock exchange in 1929. Stock holdings started to become common again. The hired managers also became interested in holding shares in the company they were running. They got opportunities to receive shares as a form of compensation.

With the long period of prosperity in the twenty-five or so years after WWII, businesses grew, as did management compensation. Due to the size of the corporations, no individual entrepreneur or group of entrepreneurs could be a dominant owner of one of the stocks traded on the Big Boards (particularly in New York and London). Soon management took over the owner's responsibility, Management started to dominate the organizations, and the big businesses became administrator/owner run and chaired, by combining the role of the President with the Chairman of the Board. We got the company man, company store and company style (Thomas Watson Sr. wanted all IBMers to use dark blue suit and white shirt with tie. This way he created the "Big Blue" style).

Senior management, the top layer, became confident about its own worth. At the same time they wanted to make a stronger bond between middle management and the corporation. Taylor's methodology did not just apply to the production of goods, it was also used by management to build bureaucratic hierarchies, with many layers of middle and lower management/supervisory functions. The bigger the hierarchy a manager could build, and hold on to, the better standing, the more money, and the greater the macho effect in the organization. Senior management needed to secure middle management's adherents and loyalty. Subsequently they introduced a compensation package including things like stocks and bonuses. This compensation package tied the middle manger to the company's flag-post. But did they add much to the creation of value. Some did, but probably less than what we could expect.

Thus, how long was Adam in Paradise? Lo and behold a new paradigm arose. The industrial growth period after WWII started to slow down. In 1972 we saw signs of harvesting in the Western economies [Porter, 1990 & Drucker, 1985]. Here, Porter discusses the drivers of value creation: Factory driven, investment driven, innovation driven and wealth driven. While the largest Western economies were in the innovation-driven stage both before and after WWII, they seemed to be moving into the wealth-driven phase as we moved into the last quarter of the 20th century. It is in the wealth-driven stage that harvesting and a downward turn of prosperity sets in. This is where Drucker comes in. He argued in 1985 that the new economy belongs to the entrepreneurs. Only through a rejuvenation of innovative forces will the economy prosper. Thus, moving back to Porter's innovation-driven stage in the economy, you will require widespread entrepreneurship.

We move now to a new phase in the evolution of the global economy: Information. This makes knowledge into new type of smart product, as well as intelligent consumers. Management suddenly discovered that it is the workers, both white and blue collar, which possesses the difference in the value creating competitive market place. Thus, companies start to train employees in core skills. This intrinsic value creation made by stakeholders led to a growing awareness of the right to know, and participate in the decision-making process. Not least this was a result of many failed investments, mergers that went bust and other acts of mismanagement, resulting in the loss of jobs and stock values.

In the final leg of the 20th century, executives finding the knowledge workers to be greater value creators than the control-seeking and turf-protecting middle management, transferred empowerment to the regular employees. Employees became a knowledge-worker, and were invited to participate in the decision-making process, sit on the Board of Directors and be part of communities of practice. However, company leaders complained that the investment in new technology did not pan out in value creation. Employees lacked a lever to make the company, and themselves, good. They had to be furnished with a tool, a stick, like the one Archmedis was looking for when he wanted to move the world.

The development of core competency and technology in the 19th century such as steel, steam, electricity, cars and telephone, was the basis for the growth in the 20th century. Only through lasting innovation will society prosper. Stop innovation, and you will see the start on a downward spiral into the abyss. As we turned into the 20th century people started looking into the air and onto the ground for the inventions emerging in front of their eyes, and saw an explosion of new opportunities. The Wright brothers and Ford were some of the opportunities that almost finished the railroad [Levitt, 1963]. As the population grew after the Dark Ages, and technology became available, people wanted to take part in the prosperity. It was Henry Ford who, aided by Frederick Taylor, supplied the goods needed to get consumerism underway.

The automobile gave consumers the basic freedom to move around at will for shopping and other activities, and thus gave rise to consumerism. But there was more to modern living than the automobile. When the Second World War was over, and the most critical components in the civil society's production system were re-installed, a new phenomenon emerged: how to get rid of the products produced in these very efficient factories created through the scientific management?

Theodore Levitt gave us the Marketing Myopia, or marketing short-sightedness. He wanted us to see the broader picture, reflecting the type of business a company was in, not a generic description of what it was called or produced. Thus, the railroad was not in the railroad business but in the transport business. Marketing became the focus. You had to go out and tell the customers that need and want your product what it could fulfil. Thus, the railroad companies could fill the need of transportation. Before the era of marketing it was the era of engineering (late 19th and early 20th century). Two of the best marketers of concepts were Procter & Gamble in soap and IBM in computers.

In 1948, the first commercial computer was ready for the market. At the time it was anticipated that in the USA there would be a market need for these computers of no more than a dozen units. However, computers became the most "God given product" this earth had developed. Not only did IBM become the king of the bits and bytes, but also they developed a culture as strong as any Marine Corps. And all of that on a simple word "Think". That was Thomas Watson Sr.'s mission statement. In 1975, "Big Blue", which is the nickname of IBM (International Business Machine), tried to develop a Personal Computer (PC) (so-called 5100 series). But due to the raw power of IBM's mainframe computing machines, such as the 360 series and its successors, and their macho standing in the company, the little PC project got squashed before it even took off.

It was not until the IBM chairman; John Opel took over that the leading computer manufacturer, and one of the world's most profitable organizations, started to make headway. In July 1980, the project initiator for "Project Chess", William C. Lowe, presented the project proposal to IBM's Corporate Management Committee, chaired by John Opel. "You have to have people free to act, or they become dependent. They don't have to be told; they have to be allowed". [Chopsky &Leonsis, 1988] The Project Manager, Don P. Estridge was told to report directly to Opel. Nobody in the mainframe division was to get near the project while under development. Within one year IBM had its PC out on the market at a unit cost of USD 2.880, featuring Intel 8088 microprocessor, 64K memory and one 160K floppy disk drive. Now there were two serious (and many other) contenders on the desktop market: Apple and IBM.

Core competency
But as the level of education started to raise among the employees, and a demand for insight started to spread out to all regions of a corporation, management had to supply extra training for the employees to keep up with the flow of information, technology and new practice. Thus, the third business driver was the ability to compete through identifying and developing employees with core competencies needed to stay ahead in the game. As the level of skills and other insights rose, the recipients wanted more knowledge. They wanted to participate in decision-making and other company activities. The new turn of the screw came when decisions got lost between the execution level (point of delivering a product or service) and the operator. Particularly this is the case when accidents happen as a result of incompetent management. In one offshore installation, operated by oil major, with four hundred employees on three shifts, there were 10 layers of management/supervisors. Responsibility was pulverized, and when the blame should be handed out, fingers started to point in convenient directions.

At the very end of the 20th century we focus on knowledge. That means, the world (at least the richest 1/3) started to ask the question about the effect computers have had on profitability. What about the human capital working in factories, offices and service institutions? They were, after all, the focus of IT. But did IT serve its purpose? Of course not. The market got some intelligent products, such as robots that have the capability of vacuuming your floor without breaking your china, or washing machines for washing your silk underwear without tearing it. You got the mobile phone system where you can see multimedia being used in constantly smaller phones. But have we become more effective?

This type of rhetoric should be removed. Certainly, there are plenty of examples of becoming more effective due to computers. But how can you explain the absence of tellers and clerks in banks and post offices? They have all become "computers". How would you otherwise be able to reserve a seat by air from Oslo to Manaus in the Amazon and have your luggage checked through all the way? And what about JIT supply and payment of modern retailers?

Have we, the members of the information society, become more informed and smarter as a result of this fantastic story of how IBM finally helped put the PC on the market, and in the process made Bill Gates one of the world's richest men? The answer to the first question is probably no. The reason for Bill Gates' fortune is that IBM chose to go for an open operative standard, and Microsoft's Windows operative system. Paul Strassmann, an IT iconoclast according to Alan Cane [2001], maintains that "...no relationship can be demonstrated between the amount a company spends on computer systems and its profitability. And none ever will be" strong words, considering that the statement was made in 2001. His argument is based on the fact that operating effectiveness only contributes 15 per cent to the companies' profitability. This is where the application of IT by human capital comes in. We need to increase productivity, improvement and innovation in organizations. We need stronger focus on team collaboration, life-long learning, and the process of value creation.

With the world getting constantly more intelligent, both from an employee's and a consumer's standpoint, the leaders of business, including the global business actors, should be interested in making the world a better place to live. It all comes down to this: Will the 21st century be able to turn the IT "failure" into success by applying it to the benefit of the human capital? That is the question we need to ask, and which the world is waiting anxiously for an answer.

Oil

The last of the business drivers to be applied in the scenario evaluation is oil prices, one of the most important input factors for the production of goods. As can be seen, its major revolution came as the Yom Kippur War took place. The Organization for Petroleum Exporting Countries (OPEC) having been inactive as a political body up to 1973 became a force of political force as the Israeli-Arab war broke out. Within a few years the price of oil had increased manifold. Since that time, it has been very cyclical, but never back to the low of the 1960s. OPEC has been able to structure its interests so as to maintain a stable price over the last few decades.

Whether OPEC will be able to maintain such stability in the future is a recurring question. With stable prices in the middle layer, around USD 22-27, everyone is happy. Over USD 30, and you are getting threats of inflation and hardship in the importing countries. Too low and you are getting an unstable economic and political development in the powder-cage of the Middle East.

The global warming issue is another aspect of oil prices. Should they stay high, new technology will be developed making the end product, the energy, cheaper. We already have seen bursts of project when prices escalate, and with falling prices the energy effective projects are dropped. But the global warming issue does not go away as long as we are emitting huge quantities of CO_2. However, we do have relative benign technologies, capable of reducing both the output of CO_2 and catching the

CO_2 in re-circulation bins. This capability is in material technology and biotechnology. These two technologies will be some of the key technologies focusing on supporting the world of tomorrow, and will be part of the knowledge-based economy that is now emerging.

9.6.1.1. The knowledge-based economy

Looking at these four drivers, they are all moving in the direction of facilitating the knowledge economy. The new paradigm, the knowledge-based economy [Thurow, 2000], can be compared with the grand paradigms of the past, such as moving from nomad and hunting societies to agriculture, industrial and now knowledge. For each shift, man's needs for staple goods, shelter and energy relative to his capacity to produce, were reduced. Today, food represents a small fraction of a human being's income potential in Western societies. As we moved from the industrial economy to the knowledge economy, we moved from labour intensive to capital-intensive factors of production.

In the knowledge economy:

- The individual will create new knowledge based on accessible information
- The individual will be a flexible resource, moving around from project to project
- The corporation's operative focus: automated production
- The employees will be organized in temporary work process teams, picked from functional teams and Knowledge Farms
- The value creation process will require: work process focus - project orientation – team manning – core functional teams

The most important aspect of the knowledge economy will be access to information capable of forming the basis for the creation of new knowledge. For this to happen, companies must shift focus from IT to knowledge management.

9.6.1.2. Life-long learning

From a historic perspective, learning has always been continuing. If we look at the Macedonian society, one will find a willingness to continually improve the ways and means of developing the society. Knowledge creation, sharing, applying and innovation are a hallmark of such society. You find the same traits in the first part of the Roman Empire, and a thousand years after the fall of Alexander the Great's Empire in 330 BC, you find the emergence of another great builder of society – the Vikings. The common denominator of these three societies is their global influence. All three societies ruled the known world at the time for a short period. Through development of learning methods, they were able to prosper and expand their respective territories.

In the 20th century, management felt that their task was to exploit resources, natural or human, until there was nothing left, leaving giant craters in both nature and mind. This exploitation has not gone without problems, as can be seen from the age of the companies listed on the New York Stock Exchange. Here we only find a few percentage of the total number that is older than 10 years. In other words, through mining a company's human resources, without putting new knowledge back, will result in hardship for the company. It will come to a grinding hold. For the corporations to survive in the knowledge-based economy, creation of new knowledge will be the sine qua non of core competency.

Continuing learning through sharing, developing and creating new knowledge requires an atmosphere developed by management and employees in a trustful relationship. The strategic intent of the corporation, therefore, must be to install a knowledge-creating capability that will support life-long learning for its employees. Such a system will create employees who are:

- Knowledge workers
- Holistic in thought and action
- Knowledgeable decision-makers (empowered)
- Sharing, learners and users (transfer and use experience).

9.6.2. *Strategy followed by structure*

Starting in 2010, let us sum up what we have experienced in the period 1900 to 2010, and try to build it into the model as can be seen in Figure 9.1.

While we previously tried to identify four drivers that are important for the development of business, in Figure 9.1 we have tried to identify five elements in the development of the *industrialized society* during the 20th century. The five axes are: market characteristics, organizational structures, value growth, learning and the oil prices.

9.6. The knowledge-based society

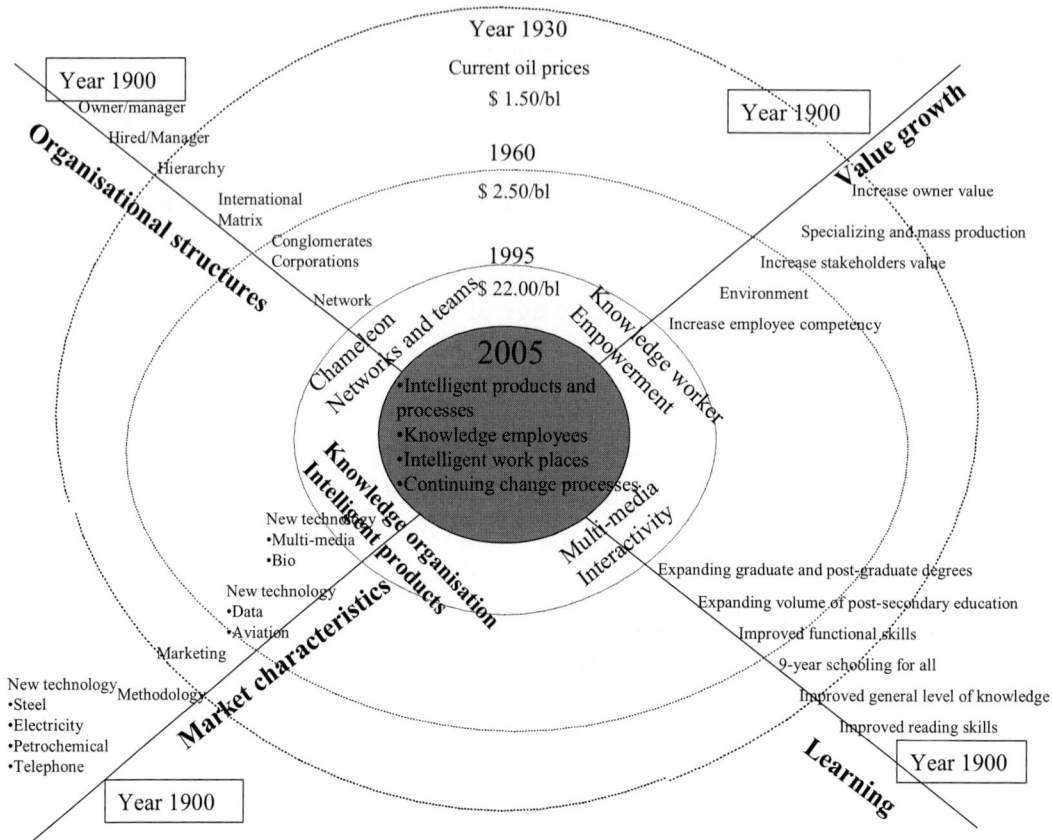

Figure 9.1: Some elements in the development of the industrial society during the 20th century

We also saw a tendency towards the knowledge society. It is more than likely that a reduction in tall hierarchies, empowerment and learning will result in the corporation's conversion to knowledge-based organizations. Those who do will be the leaders within their sector of the economy.

When you create your own scenario of what the world will be like in the years ahead, put it into the framework seen above, and try to identify core competencies and structures that will influence your own company strategy in the area of knowledge management.

If the strategy is the *learning organization*, the structure will be the *knowledge farms* and *nomadic workers*. We will see different layers of connectivity and employment. We will also see a turn to learning vacations, intelligent products, dynamic work processes making the organizations fluid and with a Chameleon's ability to change. Empowerment will be applied throughout the organization, and communication will be a full multimedia interactivity. The value creating processes will consist of knowledge production, as the production of goods will be a replication of the agricultural-cum-industrial development. Products, like cars, washing machines and computers will be staple goods. What will be important is the company's capacity to put intelligence into its products.

9.6.2.1. Strategy

A strategy for the knowledge-based economy, in the first decade of the new millennium, will require a leading edge company to focus its core competency on knowledge. That means a strategy to develop a learning organization. The set of core competencies required to stay ahead in the market place includes the following:

- Holistic knowledge initiative based on work processes
- Continual, agile, restructuring of value creating processes
- Life-long learning to benefit the value creating employees
- Knowledge teams moving along the value creating axis
- Empowerment for just-in-time decision-making

These capabilities can lead to the following:
- Employees closer to the point of decision-making most capable of taking decisions (Think global, act local)
- Reduce middle layers between decision point and top management to a minimum
- No manager without a value creating function
- Core team follows the value creating process through the organization, for maximum experience transfer
- Span of control enlarged. No turf building
- New ways of parallel processing tasks for reduction of the throughput time
- Intelligent products. More knowledge into the products
- Production systems that repair themselves

Knowledge employees are demanding to get increased participation in the decision-making processes. Faster throughput time from idea to market may lead to increased volume and quicker market saturation. *Intelligent products* whether capital or consumer goods result in a gap between the advanced and the less advanced companies. The competitive advantages go to the companies with knowledge as there core competency, and secure its employees life-long learning opportunities. Global reach may not necessarily mean greater profits, as knowledge companies are surviving on a regional basis.

9.6.2.2. Structure

In order to execute the above strategy, one needs the following structure: The leading edge companies (there will be no room for the "also rans") will establish themselves within the area of competence they see as their competitive stronghold. The basic structure will be a so-called virtual organization: a core strategic group with few employees, but with strategic alliance partners and Knowledge Farm satellites, with nomadic workers belonging to various constellations going in and out of the organization on various types of contracts. The core group will be in control of, and do in-house development of core knowledge work. All other activities will be outsourced.

- Capable entrepreneurs will manage core value creating units. In the near network structure, managerial capabilities resemble that of the entrepreneur's.
- Cross-border functional communities and networks with budgetary, personal and quality and safety responsibilities are doing the structuring of companies' value creating processes. For each major process, a process owner is being assigned.
- The knowledge-focused organization will be a hybrid of the old hierarchical structure and the neural network structure found in a human brain. The reason one cannot exclude the one for the other is the need for structures. While the tall hierarchies demand too much rigidity, the neural networks demand too much detachedness, with no limits and control. In any value-producing organization certain checks and balances are required. We therefore have ended up with a loose structure with some hierarchical elements to it, taking care of certain formal requirements and needs put in place by the stakeholders. The network structure element offers a flexible, knowledge creating and rapid marked adjustment mechanism to meet the changing technological developments.

9.7. A new order of things

One must have an eye open for the fact that there is nothing that is more difficult to start, more questionable in its outcome, or more dangerous to execute then to introduce a new order of things.

Remember that the renewer has strong enemies in those benefiting from the old system, while he has only lukewarm supporters in all those that stand to benefit from the new. This lukewarmness is a result of human beings' lack of belief, because they do not believe in the new, unless they have sure experience from it.

9.7.1. The networks and the virtual organization

The network structure is not anything new in the 20th century, or in the enterprise of man. The thing that divides today's network structure from that of Alexander the Great, the Macedonian king of the Byzantine era (BC 330), is the electronic technology developed during the last half century. Ever since Man organized himself for the harvest of food and finding shelter, he has been occupied with the issue of communicating with other individuals in order to be understood.

What is new since Gutenberg is that the technique of communicating, the method and application of sending messages has changed rapidly from duplicating by paper to duplicating by electrons. In addition to old-age direct communications, today we also communicate indirectly using methods such as writing, film, sound, Internet and application such as telecommunications, film and computers. Today's means of indirect communication is faster. While the hierarchical structure requires that each lower level breaks down the message into constantly smaller instructions to be fed to the "foot soldiers" as the "gospel truth", the network model is designed to offer optimal flexibility for decision-making and learning.

In the virtual organization, argued Grenier *et al.* [1995], the leaders are the evangelists and the cheerleaders. The hierarchical management's only purpose, in the virtual organization, is for counting heads and paying out wages. The most important employees in the virtual organizations are the knowledge workers capable of mastering multi-capabilities, digesting new information quickly, participating in the production of new knowledge and being able to share that knowledge with the team. According to Ray Grenier and George Metes, there is no point to fixing information on paper: not for sharing, not for distribution, not for management, until the information and knowledge takes its final form imbedded in a product or service.

Furthermore, the engine of virtual operations is clearly information and communication technology, and the fuel is that wonderful blend of information and knowledge, the soul of this machine is the concierges of key individual and team competencies, supported by a set or few organizational roles. The organization really is not the point any more. What counts is collaborative operations across all sorts of boundaries.

9.7.2. What implications will these future perspectives have on organizations?

For the employees:
- More empowerment
- Life-long learning systems using multi-media technology
- Being knowledge farmers/knowledge nomads
- Greater self-realization
- Greater freedom
- Team work
- Creative work.

For the organization:
- Process oriented value creation
- Focus on intellectual capital
- Intelligent products (less service; more customer support)
- Escalated knowledge creation, sharing and application
- Shorter time from idea to market
- Quicker turn-around for new products
- Increased profitability.

For the societies participating in the technological development:
- Growth in global communication
- Increased use of multi-media communication and high speed transfer of sound, picture and data
- Global/local market opportunities.

The knowledge-based economy will have the resemblance of a turbo economy. But while the turbo economy is in our definition, a bubble economy, the foundation of the knowledge economy is based on what is in people's minds, and that they are able to learn, and apply knowledge, faster. We know that in a fast changing world, commercial activities have a tendency to lose sight of the market mechanisms. Understanding the market dynamics, timing and customer requirements in the knowledge economy will be the mark of good leadership. The best to identify these changes are the employees sitting at the interface with the user/customer. It is the holistic, experience transfer system that will secure transfer of knowledge along the neural structures to the corporate leadership. This, in turn, will secure competitive organizations.

The survivors will have to adapt to a seamless value creating process, building cross-divisional and cross-functional teams following the value process from idea to market. This way the leading companies will maintain their leadership in the market. The company only executes those tasks along its value process that require special knowledge. All other activities, such as bookkeeping, will have to be outsourced.

The company will be organized in functional units as its core capabilities. This will influence the way the organization is structuring its resources. Within the hydrocarbon industry, for example, you will find the core competency to be finding and exploring for oil and gas. Once a field has been discovered, plans for its depletion are developed, required oil/gas producing equipment is being built and installed, and the running of the production systems can be assigned to a contractor. Operating this way will require fewer management levels, and a larger span of control. A knowledge management system is capable of supporting all stakeholders in a network structure.

9.8. Conclusions

Before the organization of the value creating resources around work processes was understood, it was required that management identified and organized activities into distinct production elements, with each element reporting to a manager. This required tall hierarchies, with a senior manager responsible for a given activity. The individual department underneath the senior manager concentrated its attention on one element of the product, reducing their scope to a few steps of the value chain. This compartmentalization reduced the overall view of the value process, with its sub-optimization as the obvious, and only, consequence.

Once the integrated, seamless, value creating processes were understood, the need for artificially divided units of production, with their watertight compartments, was completely useless.

Based on the scenarios described above, some possible consequences can be seen from the process-based production of goods and services:

- During the next few years, organizations will reduce their hierarchies for the production of goods and services. Each leader will receive a wider span of control, making him or her coach and champion, rather than a provider of insight and knowledge.
- In a large corporation you will find that the tall hierarchies have been shrunk to 5-6 levels of management.
- Each major value creating process will have a process owner with the responsibility for supervising the value process across corporate boundaries. Each process owner will be responsible for securing the value creating processes, and sub-processes, going through the corporation until the product/service is leaving the organization. That includes upgrading the processes and replacing it with new Good Practice, and securing appropriate benchmarking activities. The process owner will normally be located in a Service Unit within the organization.

9.9. Lessons learned

- Never has access to raw material played a smaller roll as an economic lever then today. In order to maintain or strengthen their market position, traditional companies supplying goods and service need to rethinking their strategy of resource exploitation.
- Both macro- and micro-economic theories have been forced to yield to new thoughts ideas and theories from time to time, just like physical paradigms.
- We are today witnessing the dawn of new structures, materials, and methods of distribution, rendering the old laws of logistics void. A virtual world, where things can be produced on time, and distributed throughout the world using the Internet technology, is only the beginning of new economic realities.
- In the centre of the new economic realities stands Man. The most important resource to fuel the economics of the 21st century is intellectual capital.
- The 21st century modern human being focuses on the individual, but not as a progressive and caring virtue, but as exemplified in the growth of egocentricity and selfish attitude.

- The ability of the employees to act according to their own interests, and achieve their own ambitions, must be part of the organization's scenario of the factors in future production. This requires that organizations provide the right types of opportunities for its human capital.
- The management challenge of the 21st century will be to conceive a strategy of how to harness and harvest the resources of human capital. This requires a restructuring, and simplification, of the organization. Part of this organizational strategy is about empowerment. That is, securing decision-making powers to those closes to where the decision must be made.
- One of the best ways for an experience transfer system will function, is if it is organized as a peer system. That is if you do not participate with your experience, you are out of the network. No management threats, barring firing and demotion, are more effective than peer pressure.
- The knowledge-based economy will require of management its ability to create a holistic system in which employees can enter for retrieving, developing, sharing and using new information for knowledge creating purposes.
- The frontier of social technology - the way people work and interact, will still be at the embryonic stage compared to what the ICT can offer of opportunities.
- Regardless of current products offered in the market place, being able to develop and process new opportunities, is the greater challenge. For that you need human capital and knowledge systems.
- In the period of tall hierarchies, the larger the bureaucracy and the taller the hierarchy, the better standing and more macho image the senior executive had in the organization. And, most important, the more would the manager be able to demand in salary and other fringe benefits.
- The ability to compete through identifying and developing employees with core competencies needed to stay ahead of the game of business is an important business driver of the 21st century.
- For the corporation to survive in the knowledge-based economy, creation of new knowledge will be the sin qua none of the core competency.
- If the strategy is to create a learning organization, the structure will be the Knowledge Farms and Nomad Workers. What will be important is the company's capacity to put intelligence into the products.

- The Learning organization secures for its employees' life long learning opportunities. This is in accordance with one of the most important manifestations of the 21st century: the individualization of man.

REFERENCES

1. Cane, A., (2001), *Guru who sees no profit in computers*, Financial Times, 28. June, p. 9, London.
2. Chandler, A. C., (1962), *Strategy and Structure*, MIT Press, Boston.
3. Chandler, A.D. jr., (1961), *Strategy and Structure*, Chapters in the history of American Industrial Enterprise. MIT Press, Cambridge, MA.
4. Chopsky, J. and Leonsis, T., (1988), *Blue Magic: The people, power and politics behind the IBM Personal Computer*. Facts on File Publications, New York.
5. Colin Campbell, (1996), Aftenbladet, p.13, 16. Aug.,
6. Davis, S. and Botkin, J., (1994), *The Monster Under the Bed*. Simon & Schuster, New York.
7. Drucker, P., (1954), *Innovation and Entrepreneurship*, Harper & Row, New York.
8. Drucker, P., (1985), *Innovation and Entrepreneurship*. Harper and Row, New York.
9. Drucker, P., (1985), *The Practice of Management*, Harper & Row, New York.
10. Drucker, P., (1995), *Managing in time of great change*. Butterworth-Heinemann Ltd, Oxford.
11. Grenier, R. and Metes, G., (1995), *Going Virtual*, Prentice Hall, New Jersey.
12. Hamel, G. and Prahalad, C. K., (1994), *Competing for the Future*. Harvard Business School Press, Boston, MA.

13. Hjelmervik, O. R., (1987), *Entrepreneuring*, Scandinavian Oil –Gas Magazine, 1&2, Oslo.

14. Hjelmervik, O. R., (1987), *Turning on the Entrepreneurs*, Scandinavian Oil-Gas Magazine, 11&12, Oslo.

15. Hjelmervik, O. R., (2000), *Faros, A light in the darkness*, Knowledge Management Magazine, Vol. 3, Issue 5, London.

16. Jean-Jacque Servan-Schreiber, (1958), Le Défi Americain.

17. Kanter, R. M., (1983), *The Change Masters, Corporate Entrepreneurs at Work.* Counterpoint, London.

18. Lambe, P. (2001), *Wiltgenslein's ladder*, *Knowledge Management*.

19. Levitt, T. (1964), *Modern Marketing Strategy*, edited by Bursk, E. C. and Chapman, J. F., Harvard University Press.

20. Levitt, T., (1963), *Market Myopia*, Harvard Business Review.

21. Peter, T. J., Waterman jr. and Robert, H., (1982), *In search of Excellence.* Warner Books, New York.

22. Pfeiffer, J., (1994), *Competitive advantage through people*, Harvard Business School Press, Boston.

23. Porter, M. E., (1985), *Competitive Advantage*, The Free Press, New York.

24. Porter, M. E., (1990), *The Competitive Advantage of Nations*, The Free Press, New York.

25. Ries, Al and Jack T., (1986), *Marketing Warfare*, McGraw-Hill Book Company, New York.

26. Schumpeter, J., (1911), *The Theory of Economic Dynamics*, University of Vienna.

27. Taylor, Alfred, Scientific Management.

28. The Economist, (1996), *Commenting on a book called "Lean thinking"*, 14.09.96, s. 71. Publisher: The Economist Newspaper Ltd,, London.

29. Thurow, L. (2000), *The Knowledge Based Economy*.

30. Warfare 2020. (1996), The U.S. News & World Report Magazine, August 5, New York.

INDEX

A

Access layer · 84
Adam Smith · 285, 301
Administrative document
    Navigation · *202*
Administrative documents · 202
Agent technology · 291
Agricultural culture · 280
Agriculture society · 280
Alexander the Great · 315
Analytic philosophy · 130
Applications layer · 118
Artificial Intelligence · 71
Artificial Neural Network
    Introduction to · 91
    Radial based function · 95
    Self-organization Map · 95
    Standard backpropagation · 95
Artificial Neural Networks
    Classifications · 95
    Learning rules · 93
    Supervised learning · 93
    Unsupervised learning · 93
Åsgard Navigator · 196
Attribute searching · 112
Attribute types · *See* Knowledge elements

B

Balanced Score Card · 177, 271, 283
Benchmarking · 177, 283
Best practice · 3
Best Practice · *See* Operating Practice
Big Blue style · 305
Big Boards · 305
Bill Gates · 308
Biotechnology · 291, 299
Boltzmann learning · 94
Brain technology · 291
Business intelligence · 63
Business System · 147
Business Unit · 154, 155, 202, *245*
Business universities · 289
Byzantine era · 315

C

Capital-intensive · 310
Case-based reasoning · 106
    Characteristics · 108
CCDU
    Sequence of · 153
Central Business Units · 284
Change fatigue · 4
Chief Knowledge Officer, CKO · 28
Cognitive capacity of organization · 5
Cognitive process · 88
Cola-and-hamburger culture · 284
Collaboration · 17
Collaboration and innovation · 31
Collaborative
    Intelligence layer · 88

Platform selection · 83
Collaborative system · *216*
Communities of expertise · 32
Communities of Practice · 164, *250*
Communities of Practice matrix · 192
Community of Practice · 286
   Concept of · 152
   Matrix · 174
Competitive advantages · 314
Competitive focused education · 286
Computer network · 73
Conglomerates · 284, 304
Consumerism · 306
Content management · 50, 71
Content Management · 17
Content searching · 112
COP · *See* work process
Core business · 304
Core competence · 30
Core competencies · 3
Core competency · 296, 306, 308
Corporate · 284
Corporate memory · 3
Corporate strategy · 7, 296
CORPORUM · 17, 51
   Applications · 60
CORPORUM Technology
   Shortcomings of · 64
Customer · 232
Customer value · 11

D

Data extraction · 89
Data layer · 21
Data vs. information · 38
Data warehouse · 19, 89
Data-driven decision support · 89

Decentralized hierarchies · 284
Decision-making · 4
Defuzzification · 99
Demographic change · 282
Demography · 292, 299
Digital Equipment Corp · 296
Document management · 26

E

e@technologies · 289
E-business · 72
Ecology · 291
E-commerce · 14
Economic development · 300
Economic paradigms · 283
Economic processes
   Macro · 283
   Micro · 283
Economist · 297
Educational organizations · 288
Enterprise performance · 269
Entities · 139
Entrepreneurs · 306, 314
Entrepreneurship · 241
Expert systems · 3

F

Faros · 234
   Concept of · 158
   Implementation of · *208*
   In Statoil · *190*
   Knowledge management system · 148
   Navigator structure · 166
   The innovative process · 242
   The model · 147
   Work Process Navigator · 188
   Work processes · 170
Faros concept · 241
Faros Holistic Model · 241

Faros Management Arena · 222
Faros vision · 146
Feedback
   In knowledge management · 159
Feedback function · 172
Fibre-optic technology · 288
Financial measures · 262
Firewalls · 84
First Pilot · 246
Futuristic research · 287
Fuzzy constraints · 264
Fuzzy inference mechanism · 98
Fuzzy Logic
   Logical operations · 98
Fuzzy Logic System
   Introduction to · 96
Fuzzy set · 96
   Membership function · 96

G

Gateway · 81
General Motors · 302
Genetic Algorithms
   Introduction to · 100
Genetic operations
   Chromosome · 100
   Crossover · 100
   Generation · 100
   Mutation · 100
Globalization · 299
Globalization, · 284
Good Practice · 195, 252, 318
GroupWare vs. Web-client interface · 81
Gutenberg · 282, 284

H

Health · 286
Heuristic knowledge · 48

Hierarchical search strategy · 112
Hierarchies · 284
Holistic · 146, 152
   Faros Model · 178
Holistic model
   Approach of · *248*
Human capital · 309
Human cognitive · 7
Hydrocarbon industry · 317

I

Industrial economy · 310
Industrial society · 280
Industrialized society
   Five elements of · 311
Infobanks · 26
Information · 299
   Extraction technology · 50
Information and communication technology · 10
Information extraction · 51
Information management · 38
Information theory
   Traditional · 127
Information vs. knowledge management system · *213*
Innovation · *182*, 212, 306
Intellectual capital · 1, 7, 11, 147, 148, 262, 264, 268
Intellectual property · 261
Intellectual resources · 4
Intelligent enterprise · 44
Intelligent products · 314
Intelligent search · 193
Internationalization · 284
Internet · 18
   Front end search engines · 60
Internet technology
   Emergency of · 70

Internet-oriented
 generation · 295
Intranet · *237*
Intranet, smart · 26
Intrapreneurship · 212

J

J.D. Rockefeller · 302
JIT · 283
JIT-JE
 Concept of · 10
Just in time – Just enough · 299
Just-in-time just-enough
 Holistic knowledge creation · 160
Just-in-time/just-enough · 25

K

Knowledg
 Tacit type · 73
Knowledg*e*
 Acquisition · 49
 Categories of · 45
 Competitive advantage of · 41
 Definition of · 5
 Dimensions of · 44
 Explicit type · 6, 45, 73
 Ground truth · 47
 Intuition form · 47
 Judgement · 47
 Key komponents · 47
 Logical layer · 21
 Management · 38
 Presentation layer · 22
 Sharing · 23, 49
 Tacit type · 6, 45
 Types of · 46
 Webster definition of · 5
 What is it_ · 40
Knowledge and information · 41
Knowledge and innovation · 42
Knowledge asset · 32
Knowledge Base · 51

Knowledge creation · 147
Knowledge Desktop · 16
Knowledge economy · 4
Knowledge economy
 organizations · 286
Knowledge elements
 Attributes · 114
Knowledge employees · 313
Knowledge engineering · 25
Knowledge extraction · 51
Knowledge farms · 312
Knowledge granularity · 109
Knowledge management · 2, 7, 23, 262
 Basic elements of · 14
 Faros system · 187
 Frameworks · 34
 Life cycle of · 15
 Monitoring model (KM3) · 262
 Organizational · 7
 Personal knowledge · 7
 Structure of · 267
 Ten strategies · 26
 Who is it for? · 14
Knowledge management
 system · 10, 265
 Holistic type · 147
 Technical infrastructure of · 145
Knowledge mapping · 202
Knowledge movement · 147
Knowledge Navigator · 180
Knowledge officers · 6
Knowledge propagation · 147
Knowledge revolution · 295
Knowledge Room · 149, 159, 164, *196*, 239
Knowledge services · 17
Knowledge sharing · 127, 286
Knowledge sourcing · 31
Knowledge utilization · 49
Knowledge village · 202
Knowledge workers · 28
Knowledgeable employee · 7

Knowledge-based economy · 8, 176, 280, 296, 310
Knowledge-based society · 296
Knowledge-focused organization · 314

L

Labour intensive · 310
Leading technology · 291
Lean production · 297
Learning · 202
Learning capacity · 260
Learning effect · *211*
Learning organization · 312
Learning organizations · 3, 182, 189
Life style · 286
Life-cycle of knowledge · 75
Local Process Owner · *See* work process

M

Macro-economic · 268
Management
    Components of · 6
    Financial management · 6
Management arena · 199
Management Information System · 213
Management objectives
    Diversity of · 14
Management process
    Hierarchical structure · 151
Management regime · 301
Market characteristics · 311
Market economy
    Darwinist · 9
Marketing Myopia · 307
Marketing warfare · 283

Matrices · 284
Matrix organization · 303
MBO · 283
Measurement matrix · 269, 271
Measuring assets · 261
Meta searching · 111
Meta-system · 163
Micro technology · 291
Micro-economic · 268
Microsoft Windows · 308
Middle East · 291, 309
Military development · 300
Military intelligence · 63
Military strategies · 301
MIMIR
    Approach of · 55
    Technology of · 51
Monitoring system · 272
Multidivisional · 284
Multimedia technology · 19
Multinational organizations · 289
Multinationals · 284
Multi-skilling · 296

N

Napoleon · 300
Natural language processing · 128
Navigational aids
    of Faros Knowledge Room · 195
Navigator · 159
Netscape · 285
Network system · 295
Networks · *See* Faros Knowledge Room
New millennium · 292
Nomadic culture · 280
Nomadic workers · 312

O

Oil Exporting countries (OPEC) · 309
Oil prices · 301, 311
One minute management · 283
Online analytical processing, OLAP · 89
Ontologies · 131
Ontology · 54
Operating Practice · 165
Operating Units · 157
Organization
    Learning organization · 6
Organizational structures · 311
Outsourcing · 297

P

P/E-indicator · 267
Pilots · *See* First Pilots
Pinnacle of power · 282
Porter
    Drivers of value creation · 305
Process elements · 91
Process Manager · *See* work process
Process networks · 164
Process orientation · 159
Process Owner · *254*, *See* work process
Professional and operational COPs · 191
Profitability · 298
Project management · 7

Q

Quality management · 284

R

Redundancy · *238*
    In knowledge management · 159
    Philosophy of · 265
Relativism · 136
Repository layer · 120
Return on investment · 268
Robot · 288
Rothschild · 298

S

Scientific management · 301, 307
    Objectives of · 263
    of Taylor · 150, 263
Scientific measures · 264
Search engines · 72, 112
Sensor technology · 290
Service Unit · 155, *243*
Service Units · 153
Soft constraints · 264
Soft measures · 264
Stakeholders · 153, 264, 314
Statfjord · 240
Statfjord field · 209
Statoil
    Faros KMS · 148
Strategic planning · 283
Strategy · 282
Strategy and structure · 282
Structure · *314*
Structured information · 161, *193*
Subjectivity of understanding · 139
Supplier-network · 286
Survival of the fittest · 183
Syntax vs. semantics · 140
System thinking · *219*

T

Taylor's theory
  Division of labor · 301
Technical documentation · 202
Technical support · *207*
Technological paradigm
  shift · 299
Technology management · 8
Third World countries · 287
Throughput time · 313
Total Quality Management,
  TQM · 15, 205
Transport layer · 119

U

United Nations · 289
Unstructured information · 161,
  194, 240

V

Value chain · 166, *198*
  Elements of · 165
Value Chain · 152
Value creation · 304
Value creation process · 310
Value growth · 311
Value of knowledge · 262
Video conferencing · 108
Virtual meetings · 222
Virtual organization · *315*
Virtual reality world · 281
Vision · 234

W

Web navigator · 197
Web technology · 18, *206*
Western cultures · 282
Wisdom · 43
Woolworth · 297
Work process
  Management of · 162
  Navigator · 160
Work process navigator · *196*
World Wide Web · 79
Worst Practice · 165